D1736172

One Nation...

Indivisible?

One Nation...

Indivisible?

Sara S. Chapman
and
Ursula S. Colby

State University of New York Press

Published by
State University of New York Press, Albany

For information, address State University of New York Press,
90 State Street, Suite 700, Albany, N.Y., 12207

Production by Michael Haggett
Marketing by Dana E. Yanulavich

Library of Congress Cataloging-in-Publication Data

Chapman, Sara S., 1940-
    One nation, indivisible? / Sara S. Chapman and Ursula S. Colby.
        p. cm.
    Includes index.
    ISBN 0-7914-4837-1 (alk. paper) — ISBN 0-7914-4838-X (pbk. :
    alk. paper)
        1. Political participation—United States.   2. Democracy—
    United States.   3. Political parties—United States.   I. Colby,
    Ursula S., 1929-   II. Title.

    JK1764 .C448 2001
    320.973—dc21   00-035779

10 9 8 7 6 5 4 3 2 1

Contents

Preface

Until late on December 12, 2000, when the U.S. Supreme Court, in an unprecedented action, in effect chose the nation's president by a 5–4 conservative Republican majority, Americans had remained remarkably calm amidst the post-Election 2000 tumult. The often incomprehensible twistings and turnings of the vote-counting saga produced neither pervasive public hysteria nor constitutional crisis. Party-based bitterness in the fight over the presidency seemed largely confined to extremists on both sides: the partisans hungry for the spoils and power of victory. To be sure, there was unprecedented partisan nastiness and manipulation, particularly as waged on behalf of the avowedly moderate Republican candidate whose campaign theme, ironically, was the nation's need for bi-partisan unity. ("I can lead. I will end bi-partisan warfare and unite the nation," he had asserted throughout.) But partisan wrangling was not characteristic of the electorate, nor of the growing number of political moderates who came to office both in the states and in Congress.

Most Americans came to accept the election result as a tie. Never before had margins in both houses of Congress and in the race for the presidency been so narrow. Not for a century or more had the U.S. Senate been precisely balanced between the two major parties. Voters believed that errors in Florida's tabulation of votes were probably not worse than in many other states. They concluded, sensibly, that we can and must improve our systems by the 2002 midterm election, toward which many soon turned their attention.

In the constitutional process that moved the nation toward resolution of Election 2000, many could see how constitutional strategies are designed to protect the nation, enabling decisions, even in so close a race. They saw which aspects of the process were voter-driven, which were legislatively determined—and why—and which depended upon judicial interpretation. They recognized the potential destructiveness of partisan overreaching in any of these interdependent elements of our government.

Throughout, the process provided dramatic illustrations of the flexibilities, but also the frustrations, of federalist democracy.

One Nation . . . Indivisible? describes the effects of corrosive partisan extremism in our government since the rise to power in 1994 of the intransigent, ideology-driven Republican Right Wing. The election provides an especially vivid instance of the problems we examine and, like the book, dramatizes the responsibilities and powers of the people to confront and correct these.

Indeed, the issues of Election 2000—threats to the very character and perpetuation of American democracy—made this perhaps the most important election of the last half century. They include: virulent anti-governmentalism; uncompromising single-issue politics based in narrow political, religious, and social ideologies; and, perhaps most important, significant deterioration of federalist principles in the organization and relationships of state and federal government.

Even before Supreme Court actions in the disputed election so powerfully reinforced them, vital, unresolved questions about federalism—about the relative powers of state and federal government in the nation—gave special importance to voters' consideration of the responsibilities of a new president and Congress in appointing members of the Court. Widespread awareness of the persistent ideological conflict among conservative Republican and more liberal Justices had alerted Americans to the relevance of the Bench in matters directly affecting their lives. The extraordinary political partisanship the Court demonstrated in December revealed clearly how dangerous to American democracy partisan ideology has become. As everyone knew all too well, these events followed on the harsh reality that, since 1992, the Republican Right Wing had waged a persistent, ideology-based effort to destabilize the presidency, including their enactment of only the second presidential impeachment in American history.

Tests to Americans' democratic systems in the years 1996–2000 were substantial. Election 2000 tested us yet again. It would be disingenuous in the extreme to declare, as some do, that the centrist campaign Republicans waged was the death knell of the party's conservative leadership and power. In early December, Tom DeLay, conservative Republican Whip in the House of Representatives, stated confidently, "We have the House. We have the Senate. We have the White House. We have the agenda." Confronted with such intransigence, Americans are asking whether the nation is doomed to continuing extreme partisanship or has reason to hope for relief from the political warfare of the 90s.

Election 2000 will occupy an important place in the history of American politics:

- Questions about federalist government reappeared in new guises and freshly sharpened rhetoric. Americans uneasily confronted ambiguity where certainty had seemed assured. Who would and should control the resolution of the disputes engendered by vote-counting issues? Whose interpretation of contradictory laws should prevail? Would the people's trust in government survive? Would those who had supported the losing candidate accept the winner as the legitimate president?

- The prospect of a candidate's winning the popular vote but not the required Electoral College votes provoked new debate about this aspect of the national election process that could well result in a Constitutional amendment. Designed to assure both broad representation and a certain distance from public passion in choosing a president and vice president, the College is often accused of giving individual votes for electors in small states a disproportionate impact. Others favor direct popular election of the president to eliminate perceived redundancy and achieve a more "democratic" outcome.

- Given the Supreme Court's decision to end the Florida recount, Election 2000 will bring changes in the state and federal statutes defining responsibilities in elections.

- By highlighting the importance of every vote, Election 2000 is likely to lead to national legislation boldly affirming citizens' right to vote. Over time, constitutional amendments and state laws gradually broadened voting eligibility in the United States from the Framers' first definitions. However, this expansion was achieved by a process largely based upon "shall nots," rather than "shalls," identifying groups whose rights to vote were or were not denied for a variety of stated reasons.

- Legal action seems likely to prohibit a super-charged press from announcing the winners of elections in states or the nation before polls close nationally and reasonable certainty about the results has been established.

In the five weeks preceding December 12, many factors gave rise to a tenuous optimism about the possibility of a voter-led movement toward greater conciliation in Washington and the states. The *New York Times*, for example, reported on November 20, 2000 a finding by analysts at the Pew Center for the Study of the People and the Press that "fewer people than in previous elections said their votes were *against* one candidate rather than for the other." Other preliminary studies emphasized that the closely balanced outcome of the election—in 46 states, a change in five or fewer races would have changed party control—came in response to campaigns based in the political center of each party, not the intensely partisan fringes.

New alignments among the voters supporting each party in the election also seemed promising. Democratic strength lay in heavily populated states, large cities on both coasts, and across the northern tier; Republican votes came from more rural areas in the Sun Belt, the plains, and the Rocky Mountain region. Yet in the big, so-called "battleground states" of the midwest, the contests were all very closely decided. To some, the midwest appeared a welcome balance point, where voters would continue to seek deliberative government on behalf of a broad middle ground.

Further, the presence of political moderates newly elected in both the states and Congress, encouraged guarded optimism. Emerging bi-partisan coalitions pledged to avoid reducing legislation to the lowest levels of possibility—those usually most susceptible to compromise. They proposed casting the net of ideas more broadly, to "compromise upward," as some have said, working to avoid gridlock and create opportunities to respond to the peoples' priorities. In this context, senior members of both parties, people such as former senators Warren Rudman, Sam Nunn, George Mitchell, and Howard Baker—all of whom had left the conflicted government of recent years—urged collaboration and cooperation upon Republican and Democratic leaders and party members.

Both candidates claimed to recognize that partisan extremism and ideology-based politics do not work and do not represent the wishes of the American people. Although George W. Busy repeatedly declared his distrust of the federal government he aspired to lead and pledged its further weakening in favor of the states and the private sector, the Republican Party Platform was based in federalist traditions recognizing the necessity of collaboration between state and federal government for effective *national* government.

Thus, despite massive frustrations, Election 2000 yielded reasons for hope. Yet signs of impending troubles for the nation were never distant. Immediately after the election, Democrats promised "chaos" in the Senate if Republican leadership did not award them an unprecedented, equal share of committee leadership roles, to which Republican Conservative Leader Trent Lott's first response was, "Never." His stalwart colleagues Tom DeLay and Dick Armey are still in place in the House of Representatives. The 5–4 decision by the U.S. Supreme Court on December 9 halting the recounting of votes in Florida struck many Americans as dangerously divisive and almost un-American in spirit. "Preventing the recount from being completed will inevitably cast a cloud on the legitimacy of the election," grieved *The Boston Globe* on December 10. There were even warnings that the legitimacy of American government as a whole might have been undermined.

When the Court, divided behind a facade of agreement, announced its decision in *Bush v. Gore* late in the evening of December 12, the reverberations were immediate and profound. The conservative Republican majority's reasoning in declaring Florida's recounts unconstitutional seemed suspect to many in its reliance on time constraints Republicans and the Court itself had created. As of this writing, a long shadow over the people and the government for years to come seems inevitable.

Looking ahead, wisdom and vigilance on behalf of American democracy will be more than ever essential. Just days before the election, Stanford historian David Kennedy argued in the *New York Times* for "new institutions of government that will be commensurate" to the challenges the nation faces. When a recount of votes in Washington finally confirmed the election to the Senate of Democrat Maria Cantwell, she said, "I will not participate in partisan politics . . . We run as Democrats or Republicans, but we must govern as Americans." In *One Nation . . . Indivisible?* we show why we agree with David Kennedy and Maria Cantwell—and with all other Americans who will not surrender their views of possibility.

Cape Cod, Massachusetts
December 13, 2000

Acknowledgments

_____

We wish to thank many advisors, colleagues, and friends who have provided support to this project: Patricia Albjerg Graham and Linda S. Wilson extended invitations to work at the Harvard Graduate School of Education and at Radcliffe College, respectively. Paula Rayman and Sue Schefte of the Radcliffe Public Policy Center extended many kindnesses, as did several Fellows of the center: Lisa Dodson, Florence Graves, Wendy Kaminer, Gail Leftwich, and the late Sharland Trotter. All offered discerning advice about matters more fully in their fields of expertise than in ours and helped us gain confidence in our own explorations. To Mona Harrington, who generously read the entire manuscript-in-progress, we are especially grateful. We are also quick to add that errors and omissions are ours alone.

We also want to thank the excellent reference staffs at the Widener and Kennedy School libraries at Harvard University, as well as at the Eldredge Public Library, Chatham, MA., where Irene Gillies and Amy Lux were unfailingly patient and resourceful. Alan Chartock lent special encouragement, as in the past.

Family and friends have borne with us and continued the conversations of a lifetime, an important source of convictions that this book contains.

Introduction

Democracy American-Style

There is nothing I dread so much as a division of the Republic into two great parties, each arranged under its leader and converting measures in opposition to each other. This, in my humble apprehension, is to be dreaded as the greatest political evil under our Constitution.

—John Adams

We have had founded for us the most positive of lands. The founders have pass'd to other spheres—but what are these terrible duties they have left us?

—Walt Whitman

A partisan bent . . . has led to mean-spiritedness and total loss of collegiality. There is rarely a consensus, even on the most practical and ideologically neutral matters. Issues that go to the heart of the values we hold as a nation have become so partisan that the imperative to win subsumes the necessity of governing.

—Former U.S. senator Dale Bumpers (D-Ark)

As Americans approached Election 2000, despite a booming economy, greater financial security, and better prospects than we've seen for more than thirty years, many of us believed that ours is a deeply troubled period in the nation's history. We are alienated from our national government and we've increasingly dissociated ourselves from participation in national, or even local civic life.

1

Realizing that the political party controlling Congress is always likely to be accused of partisan extremism by the opposition, we must ask today whether events since the Republican Conservative ascendancy in 1994 have not demonstrated virtually unprecedented ideological partisanship. As a period that has yielded vicious politicization of vital issues, the '90s rank with the years preceding the rancorous election of Thomas Jefferson in 1800 (which almost split the nation) or those that led us into Civil War sixty years later. The alienation most Americans now feel from their national government is largely a result of ideology-based partisan politics in the extreme.

Built upon the concept that extensive separation of powers in government would be essential for the survival of our democratic, Federalist Republic, the Constitution envisioned a national government divided, yes, but divided structurally, to assure broad representation of the people's interests at state and national levels and to protect us against the domination of political factions or individuals likely to enact extreme, ideology-based legislation infringing upon the private freedoms of Americans or otherwise subverting the law. The wisdom of the Framers has proven more important than even they might have imagined.

Under the Constitution, the federalist organization of government complements and reinforces its purposes. The two come together; they are recognizably congruent.

Since the Conservative regime of Ronald Reagan, but especially after the congressional ascendancy of his followers under former house speaker Newt Gingrich in 1994, both the balance and the commitments of our national government have been seriously weakened. In shifting policy development responsibility and authority increasingly away from federal government toward the states and private agencies, Republican Conservatives have brought to bear a dangerous antigovernmentalism that has both created imbalance in the distribution of powers and prerogatives so carefully established by the Constitution, and denied long-standing federal support to the social welfare of the people. National government as dominated by Conservative Republicans today has abandoned many Americans' beliefs about its responsibilities to citizens and to opportunity in our democracy.

Of late, Americans have voted, if we voted at all, to keep separate the political powers of the president and of Congress. Some of us, Conservatives and moderates of both parties, have also supported moving the locus of policy-making largely away from central government to states and localities, believing that less damage (not more good) may be done closer to home. But Americans have not yet contained or deflected the kinds of division that Conservative Republican ideology, publicly committed to no compromise, built into government throughout the '90s.

But let us drop back a bit. After the presidential election in 1996, thousands of Americans were asked to assess the state of the nation and their relationships to government. In response, we described a nation drifting away from its ideals, lacking direction for the future, and mistrustful of its institutions, both public and private. While most appeared hopeful about individual progress and prospects, overall we revealed deep mistrust of the federal government and of its institutions. The Republican Conservative-led investigation, impeachment, and trial of a twice-elected president and the peoples' near loss of a presidential term of office to deeply seated partisan conflict, have only increased Americans' unprecedented alienation from their government.[1] But we had reported feeling powerless and suspicious long before Conservative Republicans sought to remove the president.

Dismissive and cynical in 1996, before and after the election, we blamed elected officials and bureaucrats for the many problems that remained unresolved: the quality and future of public education; an endangered environment; the distribution of income; the future of Social Security and Medicare; campaign financing abuses; and the power of "big money" to decide the course of national affairs. "It's all just politics," many said later, in 1997: their way of explaining, and dismissing, distant political processes they believed were unrelated to the problems citizens care about. In March 1999 the Schorenstein Center for the Study of Politics at Harvard University announced that 71% of Americans believe politics in the United States is "disgusting."

To many, politicial activity had become irrelevant at best; at worst it was perceived as a threat to national and personal economic and social well-being. And even now, most Americans continue to express little interest in relationships the United States should pursue with other countries of the world. In October 1999, National Public Radio reported that 82 percent of us believed Congress should support the failed international treaty banning further testing of nuclear weapons. Nevertheless, when the Republican Conservative-led Congress rejected the treaty, analysts predicted that proponents would be unable to make it an important issue in Election 2000.

Since 1994, the nation has been under unrelenting assault by uncompromising Conservative Republicans, both in and out of government.

Their divisive, paralyzing partisanship and its effects upon American civic life emerged at their most forceful and malignant in the politically driven investigations of President and Mrs. Clinton, both preceding and following the Clinton/Lewinsky scandal. In the Lewinsky matter, of course, the president was ultimately forced to admit to family, friends, colleagues, and finally to the American people both an illicit relationship and a pattern of outright lies about it. For Clinton's Conservative political opponents, the Lewinski episode was simply the best-known and most fully documented instance in a pattern of dishonesty and reprehensible behavior. For most other Americans, presidential infidelity, coarseness, and betrayal exacerbated a disillusionment with government that runs broad and deep.

Nevertheless, Republican Conservative-instigated investigations of the Clintons' public and private lives, begun before the election of 1992 and continuing to the present, have uncovered no illegalities. They include but are by no means limited to the years of Independent Counsel Kenneth Starr's Conservative Republican-backed pursuit of the president: the tragedies of lives ruined and opportunities lost by many who had been allies to the Clintons before and after their arrival in Washington; a brutally partisan presidential impeachment in the House of Representatives, where Conservatives brought moderate Republican colleagues into the partisan fold; the continuation of partisan politics in the Senate trial that followed; and the virtual paralysis of the national government in Clinton's second term, years of opportunity lost to the nation and to all Americans. The expense to the public of Mr. Starr's investigation had come to more than $47 million by the time he left the case in October 1999.

In mid-1998, as the Starr investigation and prosecution of the president dogged forward, Americans received a midterm report card on the quality of our civic life in the form of a detailed, bipartisan *Report of the National Commission on Civic Renewal*, led by former education secretary, Republican William Bennett and former senator Sam Nunn (D-GA). Mary Leonard wrote that according to the *Report:* "Public trust in politicians and government is about as low as it can go, and neither good economic times nor some encouraging social trends are getting Americans off the sidelines and into the action of creating a more civil society" (Leonard, "US Suffering from Civic Blues," *Boston Globe*, 25 June 1998). The study was sponsored by the Pew Charitable Trusts whose president, Rebecca Rimel, stated: "Corrosive cynicism has crippled our civic spirit, and a sense of helplessness has zapped our civic strength." The *Report* asserted that, compared to earlier generations, Americans today place less value on what they owe society and whether they need to play by the rules or to fulfill obligations as citizens.

A dramatic indication of Americans' rejection of politics, if not of government itself, is the percentage of those eligible to vote who actually came to the polls in the '90s. In 1996, the percentage of eligible voter turnout was a widely reported seventy-two-year low for presidential elections: ninety million Americans chose not to cast their votes. The most popular reason given for not voting was "Too busy." The second most popular reason: "Not interested." Many who voted reported that negative campaign ads failed to correspond to their concerns but contributed significantly to their generally negative impressions of the candidates and the government.

In the 1998 midterm elections 72.5 million people voted, 2.5 million fewer than in 1996. According to Steven Weisman (Weisman, "Election Turn-out Is at Historic Low," *New York Times*, 16 November 1998), voter participation was the lowest percentage of those eligible since 1942 and the lowest outside the South since 1818. The drop-off in Republican votes from those gained in the 1994 midterm election was 19 percent. This time, according to polls, voter nonparticipation was motivated by a wide rejection of Washington and the press's preoccupation with the Clinton/Lewinsky scandal. The failure of Republican Conservatives at the national level to present issues in the campaign, which cost Speaker Gingrich his position and led to his resignation from Congress, many Americans saw as confirmation of Republican Conservatives' belief that they could increase their power base as a result of the scandal. Nor could it be claimed, of course, that Democrats flocked to the polls, though they gained unexpected political strength in the election at both state and national levels.

The surprising voter participation in the year 2000 primaries (when thirteen of the eighteen states that held elections through "Super Tuesday" generated record voter turnouts in primary elections) was seen by most as a promising counter force. It was a largely non-partisan display of enthusiasm for political reform and perceived candidate integrity. After the elimination of challengers John McCain and Bill Bradley, analysts feared a return to voter apathy in the general election.

Evidence abounds that citizen alienation from politics and government grew progressively deeper in the 1990s. In August 1997, when President Clinton signed the bipartisan budget plan projecting an end to annual deficit spending, one of the most important legislative actions of his administration's second term, Americans in large numbers mistrusted both the budget agreement and its sponsors and saw little cause for celebration. John Cassidy expressed the doubts of many: "Far from ushering in a new era [as the president claimed], the budget agreement was simply a short term trade in which the Democratic and Republican leaders took advantage of an unusually bullish economy to distribute a number of dubious handouts and make themselves look good." It had "cheated" Americans, said Cassidy, and was nothing more than "a gaudy handout to the rich disguised in the burlap of virtuous thrift" (Cassidy, "The Budget Boondoggle," *The New Yorker,* 11 August 1997).

In October 1998, when the federal budget for 1999 was approved, the president and members of Congress again failed to address thoughtfully and coherently matters of importance to the people: funding for Social Security, broader provisions for health care and health insurance, improvements in the education infrastructure, and protection of the environment. Instead, in the closing session of Congress in October, when members were focused upon their own reelections, eight of the required thirteen appropriation bills were folded into a $550-billion *Omnibus Appropriations Act* that was drafted and agreed to, not by Congress itself following appropriate debate, but by half a dozen senior members and several White House staffers. Moreover, Americans saw clearly that both a $76-billion estimated surplus from the preceding year and the "balance" of the spending plan for 1999 resulted from continuing strength in the economy, not from needed spending disciplines that both parties claimed to have applied. When the 1999 *Act* was passed, only Wall Street cheered: It unabashedly prefers a government unable to agree about spending money, even for purposes that other Americans may see as the peoples' interest.

Perhaps ironically, Americans are cynical about their government and about their constitutional relation to it at a moment in history when the economic and military power of the United States is greater than in any polity since Rome, perhaps greater than Rome's, and at the conclusion of what many, following the example of the publisher Henry Luce, came to call "The American Century."

If we drop back from the disillusionments of the 1990s to midcentury, the period of American ascendancy at home and abroad after our leadership of the Allies' victory against Germany and Japan in World War II, we can see at once why today's debilitating cynicism and alienation have met with so little resistance. In the war years and after, Americans recognized the brutal effects of Hiroshima, Nagasaki, and the nuclear peril. We confronted the Holocaust. In the 1960s we were changed irrevocably by the horrors of assassination: John F. Kennedy as president; Martin Luther King Jr. as leader in the cause for civil rights for all Americans; Robert F. Kennedy as presidential aspirant.

During the war years and after, we saw dramatic misrepresentation of truth by many governments: among others, Nazi, Stalinist, Afrikaner, and, worst, our own. The U.S. government misrepresented both motive and progress to Americans in the tragic war in Vietnam. It sponsored corruption and abuse of power in the events that led to President Nixon's resignation in 1973, after the Watergate break-in. It faced charges of illegal government action in the 1980s under President Reagan in the Iran-Contra Affair and saw a larger number of presidentially appointed or elected officers of the Reagan government face indictment in a variety of cases and charges than in any previous administration.

Just as important in our quest to understand the context for today's mistrust of government is recognizing the successful effort led by President Reagan and his followers to discredit the federal government. Conservative ideologues since Reagan's election in 1981 have consistently added to Americans' disillusionment with their government by their constantly repeated message, institutionalized successfully by Reagan himself, that the federal government is the people's enemy. They believe, as Reagan so often asserted, that central government cannot solve the nation's problems, because it is the problem.

Throughout the 90s, Conservative Republicans persisted in their relentless, partisan attack upon President Clinton, spawning sometimes equally partisan response from Democrats who sought to defend him. In all of this, Americans countered by developing a roster of defensive responses about their own relationships to their divided, strife-torn, and recriminatory national government: disillusionment, distrust, and political apathy. Our attitudes seemed to prove an observation of the National Public Radio analyst Daniel Schorr, who observed that "every generation since the 1950's has become increasingly mistrustful of one another and of their institutions, starting with the federal government" (Schorr, "Americans Lose," *Christian Science Monitor*, 2 February 1996).

Many Americans believe that excessive, uncompromising partisanship has cared little for what Clinton called "the peoples' business." Clinton himself tried doggedly and often successfully to create his own defensive responses in Centrist politics. In his avowed Centrism, often described by his supporters as "the third way," Clinton added complexity to presidential politics after a Conservative Republican ascendancy in 1994. Clinton's middle ground was first and foremost a politically savvy response to political developments he had not foreseen, events that might have paralyzed a less skillful politician and student of human nature or thrown government into hopeless gridlock. In fact, a disappointed former Clinton labor secretary Robert Reich frequently termed Clinton the *most conservative* Democratic president of the century.

Nothing if not pragmatic, Clinton quickly acceded to Conservative Republican shifts of policy prerogatives away from the federal government and toward the states. In his 1995 State of the Union Address and frequently thereafter he declared that the "era of Big Government is over." In all of this, however, he continued to press for a largely Liberal social agenda that he argued activist national government should support: strengthening education, providing wider health insurance, and restoring benefits to the poor (in the latter case, after he had signed new legislation that withdrew support).

After the 1994 election, Clinton continued to follow his already established fiscal discipline, aimed at reducing annual deficit spending, and assigned Vice President Al Gore responsibility to make federal government more "efficient." Choosing his battles wisely, he then focused upon economic policy at home and abroad, leaning toward the Right as needed on issues such as welfare, immigration, and tax policy reforms. In some ways fortunate in his political enemies, he watched while Gingrich-led Conservative Republicans alienated many Americans of both parties in the uncompromising zeal with which they fought to implement their Contract with America in 1994 and 1995. Predictably, Liberals, usually Democrats, were angered by Clinton Centrist policies that appeared to sacrifice the agenda they had supported in electing him twice. For their part, Conservative Republicans quickly began to complain loudly that the president had co-opted their philosophy and intentions.

Following the president's 1999 State of the Union message, at the height of the Senate's deliberations about whether to remove Clinton from office, the Conservative Republican editor William Kristol remarked on ABC News's "Sunday Morning" that, whatever the outcome of the Senate's debate, he feared Clinton's Centrism might be here to stay. Would it not be possible for a new coalition, a new synthesis, to develop, he asked in horror, embracing Clinton's Liberal social policies *and* his fiscal Conservatism?

Clinton Centrists were frequently challenged to justify their progovernment differences from ideological, partisan thinking at either end of the conventional spectrum. Their politically pragmatic aim, unsatisfactory to ideologues on both sides of the political divide, was, as Kristol observed, to capture desirable goals of each partisan camp, as, for example, Liberals' calls for activist government and spending to support Social Security, education, and health care policy reform and Conservatives' insistence upon tax cuts, limited government, and limited government spending, to prevent fiscal deficit (an unpalatable motive for many Liberals).

Despite the opposition and suspicion that Clinton's middle-of-the-road approach engendered, however, we shall see that his political approach was constitutionally sound: It followed precisely the compromising course the Framers had anticipated for government in American democracy. Any party or faction or Congress or president would have to discover ways of working with the political opposition. The people would thereby be protected from hasty decision making and be well advised by opposing arguments on policy questions.

We argue, however, that, despite the constitutional soundness of Clinton's politically Centrist approaches, they contributed to the nation's loss of important ground in another tenet of the Constitution: the Framers' careful design of structural federalism. Clinton's Centrism went too far by abetting Conservative Republicans' antigovernmentalism, that is, their efforts to diminish federal government, in favor of localized decision making at the state level and through private sector initiatives.

Why does the nation require the Framers' specifically Federalist organization of government? What is sacrificed when national government is diminished, when mutually reinforcing relations among the federal, state, and local governments are lost? Competition for power and resources between the federal government and the states has always existed in the United States, generating sixty- to seventy-year cycles in the relative domination of each. But at this point in the current cycle, with the states so dramatically in the ascendancy, Americans have cause for great concern in the loss of essential balance and breadth in policy debate; in the loss of federal leadership, perspective, and oversight in matters that affect all Americans; and in costly failures of policy coordination and collaboration between federal and state sectors.

As a political Centrist, Clinton often described a middle ground in which all members of government might have brought forward ideas and proposals in the public interest. But because his strategies frequently embraced the agenda of Conservative Republicans as fully as the proposals of his own party members, he also alienated Liberals, usually Democrats.

Despite other legislative successes with a Democratic Congress, his high-profile, first-term effort to extend provision for health care failed, in part because extremists on both sides of the partisan divide were unused to a middle ground, mistrusted the president's aims and motives, and therefore could not occupy the space for debate that the president attempted to create for them. Later, after the Republican ascendancy in 1994, Clinton's Centrism became more politically strategic, many Liberals thought excessively accommodating to the partisan extremism of Conservative Republicans under Speaker Gingrich.

Even after Clinton's reelection in 1996, only about 10 percent of the members of Congress described themselves as Centrists, defined then as people whose concepts of government's responsibilities were not ideological and might therefore be amenable to compromise in bipartisan debate. The bitter acrimony that passed for congressional decision making after 1994 therefore made thoughtful public consideration of policy questions, which Americans need to hear and are responsible to assess, all but impossible. This lack of constructive bipartisan debate, characterized by the now predictable absence of resolve to bridge political and ideological differences and infected by the lingering bitterness of the impeachment battle, only added to public alienation, mistrust, and apathy. For example, it is effectively impeding legislation to support Social Security for the long term. Similarly, provisions to improve public education and health care or to address urgent questions in immigration and immigrant policy are entrapped in partisanship, in single-issue politics, where the "issue" is political ideology.

Americans remember that after the Republican electoral victory in 1994, Speaker Gingrich passed over Republican moderates with reputations for conciliatory approaches, in distributing leadership positions in the House, occasionally actually stating that a representative was "just not mean enough" to qualify for appointment. Following Gingrich's lead, in 1996, his Conservative colleagues in the Senate adopted a new party rule requiring party leaders and committee chairs, now confirmed by secret ballot, to pledge allegiance to a legislative agenda at the start of each session, thereby precluding even the possibility of meaningful bipartisan debate about the priorities of the session. These blatantly partisan strategies to control congressional debate and action, reasserted by Gingrich after the 1998 election (only days before his resignation), exacerbated the deep divisions in government in the 1990s and precluded effective government response to issues such as those we discuss in the chapters that follow.

The political divisiveness resulting from Liberal and Centrist opposition to an uncomprising Republican Conservative agenda runs specifically counter to citizens' views about what government is for and how it should work. This was clearly demonstrated in the midterm election of 1998. As Democrats surprised even themselves with victories in congressional races, governorships, and voter decisions on an array of referenda, a powerful recognition emerged in both parties: voters had supported candidates who described themselves and their intentions as moderate or Centrist. Weary of partisan acrimony, ideological extremes, personal attack, and scandal, the Americans who voted, albeit a small percentage of those eligible, succeeded in persuading the candidates of Election 2000 to think again about their priorities and strategies, to seek a middle path that includes the possibilities of compromise. Of course, the fact of differing interests between Liberals and Conservatives exists and must be acknowledged, but in constructive debate that can reach compromise about how governance might proceed.

Republican Conservatives' relentless propagation of a well-orchestrated ideology, and their dimunition of the federal government as we've known it, were successful political strategies in the '90s. In fact, they have dislodged a long tradition of American Liberal politics while virtually controlling public discourse about government and policy-making for nearly two decades. But political moderates of both parties, including those who call themselves "New Progressives," (whether they supported the Clinton political agenda or not) argue that the most compelling challenge to our federal and Federalist government is to reduce intractable single-issue conflicts between entrenched, partisan political ideologies in order to strengthen government (Dionne 1996). Many believe, as we do, that this will be most fully achieved when the balance among federal, state, and local governments that the Framers envisioned (and that antigovernment Conservative Republicans have seriously disturbed) has been recaptured. It will be achieved when political debate is strengthened by anticipated coordination among government initiatives at all levels and in the private sector.

Despite evidence that divisions in the Republican Party are perpetuating intellectual disarray, Conservative Republicans' rhetorical and legislative successes warrant Americans' concerned reexamination of their efforts and the results, our topic in the chapters that follow.

By way of further introduction, it may be helpful to consider several leading ideas that the Founders of American democracy brought to their discussions about how American Federalist democracy could be made to work. They remind us that, beginning in 1789, the Framers of the Constitution warned that citizen disengagement from the affairs of government, the very dilemma we have today, would constitute the greatest threat to our democracy. James Madison, in particular, insisted until his death that the security of American government and the protection of citizens' freedoms would depend upon our engagement in what he came to call "the public sphere" (Cornell 1999, 241–245).

Like ours, the Founders' debates about governing centered in arguments about who, if anyone, could be trusted. At the same time, more insistently than any of those in government who've come after them, the Founders emphasized the necessity of citizen knowledge of, and opportunity to, affect government, even as they could not hide their concern about the quality of citizens' preparedness to cope with complicated issues. Recognizing the failures of the nation's first governmental design, the states-based Articles of Confederation, the Framers of the Constitution created a representative, Federalist government with several important characteristics. Among others, these included a strong but necessarily responsive central government; clear delineation and division of powers, both in central government and between federal and state (including local) governments; and the opportunity for electing to government at every level broadly representative and knowledgeable citizens accountable to their constituencies.

The Founders' insistence upon citizens' leadership and wide participation in government responded to the expectations of a people who had risked revolution to gain the rights of self-determination. Just as important, however, it grew out of their mistrust of the motives and actions of any individual or group. Political parties as we know them now did not yet exist, and several of the Founders, including George Washington, specifically warned against them as potentially dangerous to the development of the nation now newly committed to Federalist ideals and to a strong central government.

Concern about the wide distribution of government's powers to assure broad and balanced perspective was perhaps most fully developed in the thinking of James Madison, whom many recognize as the most influential contributor to the Constitution. His essays in *The Federalist* (1788), a series variously written by Madison, Alexander Hamilton, and John Jay to advocate the ratification of the Constitution, tell us more than any other source about the issues Americans faced in deciding whether or not to approve the proposed government.

In *Federalist* No. 10, Madison explained how the Constitution would assure the freedoms of individual citizens, as well as the nation's stability. Both, he emphasized, would require protection from the divisive factions that were sure to develop, possibly even to attain majority support. He acknowledged his fears, shared by many others, that "the public good [would be] disregarded in the conflicts of rival parties" and that "measures [would be] too often decided, not according to the rules of justice and the rights of the minor party, but by the superior force of an interested and over-bearing majority" (Madison, *Federalist* No. 10, 57). For readers of these words today, Madison's warning highlights the dangers of contemporary partisan extremism.

To prevent such distortions, Madison wrote, the new Constitution would protect the roles, responsibilities, and interests of citizens, not only by assuring free elections, but by its many provisions to keep the powers of individuals and groups separate and the roles and responsibilities of the central government distinct from those of the states. This division of powers would always require extensive public debate about policy matters before decisions were made. With Thomas Jefferson, Madison foresaw the continuing need for citizens to "inform their discretion," to learn about the questions facing the nation, so that they could participate in the sort of public debate that would serve the public interest by linking principle and action.

Deeply committed to the democratic processes they had devised for the new government, the Founders wisely placed their confidence not in anyone but in everyone. Then, as now, efforts to exclude or ignore those holding citizenship from governance and policy-making were unacceptable to American ideas of democracy. To be sure, the concept of citizenship then was far less inclusive than we have since made it. Restrictions of the franchise originally limited the power of the ballot essentially to white male property owners. Nevertheless, failure on the part of those qualified by law to seek involvement with, and to assume responsibility for, the conduct of the peoples' business through their elected representatives at all levels was unacceptable. This public charge placed before Americans themselves responsibility for the quality and responsiveness of government from the beginning.

Many of the major issues we face now were already central preoccupations of Americans by 1787, when the Constitution was written. They are questions we will consider in parts 1 through 4 of this book:

- How should American democracy be organized today to achieve the broadest and wisest representation of the peoples' will?

- What should be the roles of government in the economy of a democracy committed to "free enterprise"?

- What principles should guide our relations with other sovereign nations?

- Who should be encouraged or permitted to come as immigrants to America and with what formal understandings?

Part I

Organizing Government in America

Chapter 1

What's at Stake?

In framing a government which is to be administered by men over men, the great difficulty lies in this: You must first enable the government to control the governed; and in the next place to control itself. A dependence on the people is no doubt the primary control on the government; but experience has taught mankind the necessity of auxiliary precautions. . . .

Justice is the end of government. It is the end of civil society. It has ever been, and ever will be pursued, until it be obtained or until liberty be lost in the pursuit.

—James Madison

Two days before President Clinton's second inauguration in January 1997, the historian Garry Wills wrote a cover story on the president [Wills, "Does He Believe in Anything? (Actually, Yes)," *The New York Times Magazine*, January 1997]. What the president believed in, according to Wills, was *government*. An astonishingly flat conclusion? Not at all when considered in context. Given citizens' well-documented mistrust of government's ways and Conservative Republicans' determination to treat government as the peoples' enemy, the president's reported faith in it was a controversial matter of great importance to the nation.

Among government observers, not a few are gravely concerned about the probable long-term effects of the current Republican Conservative agenda to reorganize government, to redistribute, minimize, and, some fear, to virtually dismantle federal government as we've known it. They are

17

especially alarmed at Conservatives' enthusiasm for "outsourcing" social policy studies to the private sector and "devolving" decisions about creating or implementing most policy actions to states and localities. Since 1996, decisions about policies as diverse as education spending, welfare reform, access to health care by the poor, immigration and immigrants, and environmental protection statutes and enforcement have, by and large, been moved from federal responsibility to the states. In the week before the 1998 midterm election, the *Washington Post* columnist David Broder stated on the television program "Washington Week in Review" that the congressional elections were now "not very important," since most public policy issues are decided by the states.

Even those who concede the need for productive change in the distribution of responsibilities and powers of government are calling now for caution as we think about the kinds of devolution from federal to state control already implemented and proposed. Whatever our political allegiances (Conservative or Liberal, Republican or Democrat, or now, perhaps, Centrist) Americans must understand this: The current debate about minimizing government or about redistributing it from federal responsibility to the states goes straight to the heart of our beliefs and intentions about government's very purposes.

For excellent reasons that we will discuss in chapter 2, the organizers of American democratic government insisted upon a balance of power between the states and localities, on one hand, and the federal government, on the other. Our Federalist approach means that individual states control many aspects of public life through their own constitutions and statutes. They also collect the taxes to meet their individual priorities. In fact, almost half of all spending for domestic purposes (not foreign and military spending) is paid from taxes raised through state and local governments. But states subscribe to superseding federal law, as established by the federal Constitution or by federal courts-approved statutes consistent with it.[1]

The Constitution assumes both elected and appointed offices at every level. It stipulates what kinds of responsibilities and powers belong to the federal government and then, in the Tenth Amendment, whose application has generated vital debate since its inclusion in the Bill of Rights, states that all powers not specifically assigned to the federal government belong to the states or to the people.

The themes of the Consitution are almost always protective against the possibility that any individual, group, or political entity might acquire too much power over any other. Thus, it is primarily about limiting power, not awarding it without safeguards against its misuse. This approach has proven over and over again to serve well in a representative democracy, where federal government is controlled, not only by regularly scheduled elections, but by established differences among terms of office, separation of executive (presidential) powers from those of the legislative and judicial branches, and nearly absolute freedoms of the press and of public assembly.

The strength of America's government by law, under which everyone is to be treated equally, derives from Americans' respect for the systems of government that the Constitution prescribes. In turn, the Constitution derives its strength and resilience, not only from the principles of democracy it represents, but from the balance of powers it describes. From the beginnings of government under the Constitution in 1791, the nation has seen nearly constant tension about whether the states or the federal government should set and administer domestic policy and about how questions of jurisdiction should be decided. Approaching Election 2000, Conservative Republicans successfully shifted the weight of argument away from the federal government and toward the states. They have continued to create imbalances that require thoughtful reconsideration.

"What is at stake in this debate," wrote Linda Feldmann after the Conservative Republican electoral victory in 1994, is "the role of the federal government in Americans' lives—how big the government should be, what functions it should perform, and whether the federal government should provide a safety net for the poor and elderly" (Feldmann, "Historic Debate Over Federal Role," *Christian Science Monitor*, 20 November 1995). Former senator Carol Mosely-Braun (D-IL), in a succinct declaration bringing to mind arguments about the character of American federalism that predate the Constitution, summed it up this way: "We [must decide] again whether or not these United States are one country or a conglomeration of fifty separate entities" (ibid.).

So important is the distribution of power issue to our national well-being that virtually all the questions troubling us now may be seen as in some way related to it. The broad debates about it rapidly turn into more specific but equally confounding considerations that dominate the headlines as our most pressing particular policy questions: Who should create policy to govern health care? See to provision for the poor and the elderly? Bear responsibility for improving public education and protecting the environment? Who can address the problems that will increasingly grow from persistent imbalances in wages, wealth, and personal security among

American workers? Who should develop policies to regulate immigration and clarify government's responsibilities to immigrants, once they're in the United States? The *Personal Responsibility and Work Opportunity and Reconciliation Act of 1996* (also called the Welfare Act), which moved most governmental provision for the poor and for immigrants from federal oversight to the control of state governments with widely varying problems, priorities, and resources, is just one illustration of the immediate effects of this structural redistribution on peoples' day-to-day lives.

Recently, new concerns are complicating these already difficult questions: Will a substantially smaller and therefore weaker federal government have sufficient strength to defend and advance the interests of the nation in a world increasingly shaped by immensely powerful, technology-supported transnational associations and interest groups, and by global interdependencies in politics and in the marketplace? How much reduction in our federal government is too much? Might we go so far in redistributing the federal government's powers that we prevent it from maintaining the regulatory and stabilizing characteristics that our society (and our markets) require to function?

For all of the reasons implicit in such questions, making fundamental changes in the organization and roles of our government requires us to understand whether and why change is in our interest. If Americans are to be activists, not mere spectators in matters of governance, we must participate in this debate. Given Conservatives' particular assault upon federal government, Liberals and moderates of both parties must insist on asking, What purposes of government will be better served if responsibility for them is moved from the federal government to the states, localities, or the private sector? And, the inevitable corollary, What purposes might be neglected, or even lost?

What's at stake in the reorganization of government is the possibility of careless change from what Americans have believed about its purposes.

Chapter 2

A Nation of States:
Creating the Constitution

*No morn ever dawned more favourable than ours did, and no day was
ever more clouded than the present.*

—Washington

ON THE WAY TO INDEPENDENCE

Most Americans today cannot imagine the drama of the Revolutionary
War years and succeeding decades, and their confusion and uncertainty.
Knowing little about the intensity of efforts required to create a sense of
nationhood and shared purpose among the settlers of thirteen disparate
colonies, we have lost the threads of connection between the first Americans' chaotic experiences and our own ongoing efforts to sustain a sense of
community and common goals.

The result has been dis-ease, for many fear that our nation is drifting
away from the originating principles and purposes of American democracy.
Others believe that ignorance of these originating principles and purposes
creates the insecurities that prevail when people have no basis for current
analyses in real knowledge of the options, their own or the nation's. In fact,
the sense we make of our national origins helps to define for us the values,
purposes, and acceptable characteristics of our current political institutions
and cultural life.

From their earliest settlements in this New World, the colonists had emphasized their commitments to self-governance, liberty, and equality. On their long journey to America, *Mayflower* passengers designed the government they intended to live by, and for much of the seventeenth century the British granted the colonists self-determination in affairs of local governance, which varied considerably from place to place.

As the colonies prospered, however, the British increasingly treated them as possessions of the Empire, while other European powers, France and Spain in particular, also sought to exploit America's riches to their advantage. For over a century, through the 1760s, Britain's Acts of Trade and Navigation imposed progressively more arbitrary and constraining trade regulations so as to profit from colonial imports and exports. By 1765, the year of the Stamp Act, angry Americans were calling for resistance to the Crown's excessive taxation, clearly intended, they believed, to subvert the rights and liberties of the colonies. Although Britain repealed the Stamp Act the following year, subsequent legislation reaffirmed their sovereignty and intention to control American life at the colonists' expense.

Gradually Americans began to believe that separation from England was inevitable, though many still hoped this could be accomplished without an actual revolution. In a first demonstration of the powers of a free press, leaders such as Benjamin Franklin published pamphlets and letters redefining the appropriate relationships between England and the colonies. Others soon joined them in an earnest search for grounds of resistance that would be both moral and legal. Many, including Stephen Hopkins, questioned Parliament's role in limiting the opportunities and freedoms of people who had been loyal to the Crown. Writing to an English friend, Massachusetts governor Thomas Hutchinson captured well the colonists' frustration as British actions threatened their hard-won freedom:

> The people of New England fled for the sake of civil and religious liberty; multitudes flocked to America with this [confidence], that their liberties should be safe. They and their [families] have enjoyed them to their content, and therefore have endured with greater cheerfulness all the hardships of settling new countries. No ill use has been made of these privileges; but the domain and wealth of Great Britain have received amazing addition. Surely the services we have rendered the nation have not subjected us to any forfeitures. (Becker 1942, 83)

Paradoxically, Americans' rejection of British government derived in large measure from political and philosophical developments in England. By the 1740s, public discontent with their government had led many British citizens to conclude that power was itself evil. The American historian Bernard Bailyn puts this development in contemporary terms: "A populist cry against what appeared to be a swelling financial-governmental complex that was fat with corruption, self-satisfied and power hungry had swept over England in the early 18th century" (Kurtz and Hutson 1973, 9).

Given colonial leaders' and many citizens' close human and cultural ties to England, which included great admiration for Britain's Constitution and legal system, these developments powerfully influenced our own thoughts about separation from the Crown. In a massive failure of trust during the pre-Revolutionary War decades, the colonists' representatives in England came to believe that English politics were so grossly corrupt that no one in the King's Court could be relied upon to act fairly or rationally on the colonies' behalf. Scarcely anyone welcomed this recognition, and indeed, some colonists continued all along to hope for some sort of negotiated settlement.

But the colonists' arguments for separation had a deep philosophical, as well as pragmatic political basis: John Locke's concept of "Natural Law," as widely promulgated in seventeenth- and eighteenth-century England. Locke's *Two Treatises of Government* (1690) insisted that the ultimate concern in the resolution of political issues must be respect for human nature, cultivated to virtue and wisdom through education. Emphasizing the inherent rights of individuals, Locke refuted not only the divine right of kings but all theories of government derived from faith in supernatural sources of power or religious belief systems likely to become absolutist. In his rational, humanist universe, political power, understood as "the right of making laws . . . for the regulating and preserving of property . . . and the defense of the commonwealth from foreign injury . . . for the public good," was to benefit people, not rulers (Becker 1942, 63–73).

For Locke, individual rights in a civil society included the right to own property, a relatively new concept in his day. Two contemporary economists Robert Heilbroner and Lester Thurow emphasize that land, labor, and capital, the so-called factors of production in a market society, became broadly accessible as late as the sixteenth century and then only in Europe, when "a vast revolution undermined the world of tradition and command and brought into being the market relationships of the modern world" (Heilbroner and Thurow 1994, 15).

Furthermore, Locke asserted people's right to expect that political power would be used to preserve individual property ownership, along with the rights of free thought, speech, and worship. In exchange, citizens would abide willingly by the civil law, finding their freedom in voluntary obedience to laws they helped to create for the common good. In all, these were principles the American Founders would grasp enthusiastically, and upon which they would build. By the time Jefferson was drafting the Declaration of Independence, he could assume that most colonists understood and agreed with them. A colleague of Jefferson's, James Wilson, writing before the Declaration of Independence, expressed his "Lockean" vision of government's purposes:

> All men are, by nature, equal and free; no one has a right to any authority over another without his consent: all lawful government is founded in the consent of those who are subject to it: such consent was given with a view to ensure and to increase the happiness of the governed, above what they would enjoy in an independent and unconnected state of nature. The consequence is, that the happiness of the society is the first law of every government. (Becker 1943, 108)

By July 1776, the Continental Congress was ready for a radical step: formal acceptance of a Resolution of Independence, drafted by Henry Lee of Virginia. The Resolution declared boldly that "these United Colonies are, and of right ought to be, free and independent States, that they are absolved from all allegiance to the British Crown, and that all political connection between them and the State of Great Britain is, and ought to be, totally dissolved." A committee to "prepare a declaration to the effect" of the Resolution was quickly appointed; its chair was Jefferson.

Members of Congress knew that the situation required a powerful public explanation. They would have to show that the king and Parliament were responsible for their decision to declare independence, not willful Americans seeking rebellion against established law to serve their self-interests. They needed to demonstrate that their decision incorporated a morally and legally persuasive theory of government in its rejection of kings that was fully justified. This would be accomplished by showing how their treatment at the hands of a tyrant had irreparably violated the principles of natural law. Within one week, on 4 July 1776, the committee presented its draft declaration to Congress for acceptance. The purpose and high intentions of the Declaration of Independence are set forth in its opening paragraph:

> When in the course of human events, it becomes necessary for one people to dissolve the political bands which have connected them with another, and to assume, among the powers of the earth, a separate and equal station, to which the laws of nature and of nature's God entitle them, a decent respect to the Opinions of mankind requires that they should declare the causes which impel them to the separation.

Over time, Jefferson's formulation of Locke's principles, by then part and parcel of Americans' belief in all peoples' entitlement to freedom, has become the universal principle for all peoples struggling toward basic human rights. It also remains an unforgettable declaration of the purposes of government:

> We hold these truths to be self-evident, That all men are created equal, that they are endowed by their creator with certain unalienable rights; that among these are life, liberty & the pursuit of happiness; that to secure these rights governments are instituted among men, deriving their just powers from the consent of the governed; that whenever any form of government becomes destructive of these ends, it is the right of the people to alter or to abolish it, and to institute new government, laying its foundation on such principles and organizing its powers in such form, as to them shall seem most likely to effect their safety and happiness.

The Declaration did not specifically influence subsequent documents in the new government, serving rather as the sort of statement that might issue from the White House today (given a Jefferson in our midst), explaining and building support for actions of the federal government. Later, closer to operational realities, the challenge would be to translate its principles into a workable body of civil law incorporating the Revolutionaries' aspirations for the new nation. A gigantic task. Consider just one among many discords between principle and actuality clear to us at the end of the twentieth century: the long decades before civil law actually accorded all Americans, African American men and then all women, the rights of freedom and equality that the Declaration had promised.

BALANCED GOVERNMENT

Working furiously to define a new national government as the Revolutionary War began, leaders envisioned a political federation of thirteen member states, the United States of America. Given their experience with English rule, many Americans had with good reason come to fear and mistrust a powerful central government. The states' desire to retain virtually all of the autonomy each had known in its separate relationship to England made envisioning an effective central government extraordinarily difficult. Thus, a first task, still at the center of debate about the purposes and functions of government, was to determine what powers would belong to the states and what powers to "the united states in congress assembled." This dilemma, unresolved in the nation's first effort to create a government, ultimately caused the failure of the Articles of Confederation, ratified in 1781, nearly six years after the declaration, as the Revolutionary War was ending.

The Articles protected the powers of the states, yielding very little authority to the central government. Even where the latter had jurisdiction, its actions were subject to prior approval by at least nine of the states, or by other groups assembled from time to time to consider proposed actions. Although Congress was given the authority to determine the expenses of the Union and to both borrow and appropriate funds for its support, including the support of the war, it was not empowered to tax the states. Congress was required to submit requests for funding to the states, which had sole rights of taxation, and were not obligated to grant congressional requests.

Inevitably, many problems developed for the new nation under these fragmented arrangements. By war's end in 1783, the government was $40 million in debt. General Washington's soldiers, who had not been paid for months, threatened insurrection. Although the beloved and respected general was able to prevent this disastrous action, he later became one of the most persistent advocates for a strong federal government with powers to tax as well as to govern.

All in all, the years between 1776 and 1781, among the most difficult in the nation's history, were a rocky period of trial and error with a potentially disastrous outcome. Despite a steep national learning curve and a dizzying rate of development, it seemed likely that our "great experiment" would fail. The major hurdle was Americans' tendency to view themselves still as citizens of essentially separate, sovereign states. To the degree that they supported central government at all, most assumed that it existed primarily for their protection.

By war's end, citizens more sympathetic to centralization, the Federalists, saw that the future of the new nation, including its credibility and credit in Europe, required new ways of bringing citizens' and states' divergent interests together for the progress of all. Alexander Hamilton, in particular, spoke for the need to centralize revenue management and trade policy to enable the national government to enter into advantageous agreements with other countries (Lind 1997, 17–25). Americans, he insisted, needed their combined strength to develop as the Revolutionaries had envisioned. Even internal management was imperiled by the very real possibility that, without a strong central government to bind interests together, the states might split apart irrevocably into sectional and rival interests. The United States needed national policies to guide her growth and to achieve political and economic stability (Lowi 1996, 7).

Despite these powerful Federalist arguments, leaders working to solve the nation's problems with decentralized governance in 1787 tried first to amend the Articles of Confederation. When this quickly proved to be an unworkable approach and they could no longer avoid acknowledging the failure of the Articles, they moved quickly to propose to a weary but hopeful people a new organization for their government. The circumstances were desperate. Then as now, public confidence in government was low. Equally important were the ever present tensions between the claims of moral and social idealism on the one hand, and economic and political realities on the other. Then as now, most Americans wished to satisfy both sets of possibly irreconcilable claims. Perhaps most important, the conflict between Federalists supporting a stronger central government and anti-Federalists, whose loyalties resided more fully with the states, was increasingly bitter.

To grasp today the intensity and range of disagreement that prevailed concerning the rights of states in the new national government envisioned by the Framers of our Constitution, we must recall that many loyal Americans then, too, feared and mistrusted the power of "Big Government." Among these, of course, was Jefferson. Intent from the beginning upon both preserving the nation and protecting the individual freedoms it promised, Jefferson was not an anti-Federalist. Nevertheless, he led a cohort of leaders and ordinary citizens who believed that democracy could be most fully achieved and tyranny most fully avoided in the primarily agrarian nation they foresaw if most affairs affecting citizens were addressed at state and local levels.

The Framers were required to justify the proposed Constitution, and ultimately to make various compromises, in response to what we would now call "Conservative points of view." Among the dissenters from prevailing Federalist intentions about the powers to be assigned the central government were ordinary citizens, including some of the Framers themselves, whose support was required for ratification. Compromise with these dissenters was especially evident in language that limited powers of the federal government while specifically protecting those of the states and the people, as in the Tenth Amendment. Some historians claim that the dissenting spirit of the anti-Federalists—that is, their original sympathies for states' rights in the national government—has been more vital to the spirit of American politics than have Federalist arguments supporting a strong central government (Cornell 1999, 1 and n. 1).

As we assess this dissenting spirit in the extremism of today's Conservative Republican politics, it is important to recognize its complex lineage and political tradition. Political Conservatism is neither inherently pathological, as several historians of American politics have suggested, nor an alien spirit sprung full blown from the minds of its advocates in the 1990s. Rather, as Theodore J. Lowi shows in his excellent study *The End of the Republican Era*, today's political Right is the current expression of a "genuine American tradition" which, by design, had always been most active in state and local government before the election of Ronald Reagan (Lowi 1996, 19–23).

In addition to tracing the origins and developments of the anti-Federalist, states' rights emphases in modern Conservatives, Lowi shows that, among both "patrician" and "populist" groups, Conservatives have always included the Christian Right, as well as a "traditional Right" that has found particular wisdom in historical precedent. No matter what their political party affiliation over the years, Conservatives have always been political activists. From their perspective, the justification for government has been "to intervene against conduct deemed good or evil in itself" and to "impose morality" in order to create a communal society of equals with shared values, who accept that "the right" can be known and must be prescribed by government (19). Since the Reagan years, as Conservatism in the Republican Party has evolved at the national level from a political movement to entrenched statism, it has sought also to internationalize its values.

Another recent study, *New Federalist Papers: Essays in Defense of the Constitution*, by Alan Brinkley, Nelson W. Polsby, and Kathleen M. Sullivan, argues that anti-Federalists felt justified in opposing the Constitution because they considered it a "betrayal of the principles of the American Revolution" (Brinkley, Polsby, and Sullivan 1997, 1–2). After all, in shaping a representative, republican government, the Constitution "quite deliberately created a buffer between popular will and the exercise of public power." Brinkley and his colleagues state that Federalists also "feared excessive centralized power . . . but feared inadequate national power even more, convinced that without it there would be no protection against chaos and disunion" (2). These differences are with us still; their persistence gives rise to the need for renewed citizen debate about, and vigilance to, guard the essential elements of constitutional federalism that concern us throughout this book.

Those of us fretting in the year 2000 about the complex challenge of expanding opportunities for everyone's freedoms, security, and economic advancement while supporting necessary government services, remaining free of deficit spending, and protecting free enterprise, should be encouraged by the awareness that these very preoccupations were present in the earliest days of this democracy. As the Framers grappled with the philosophies and strategies of an inadequate government, Americans faced questions: How could we manage the $40-million Revolutionary War debt? How could we create and support a central government strong enough to guide the domestic and international future of the nation, without inhibiting the freedoms or the spirit of opportunity and enterprise among individuals and states? What could we do about the developing disparities in people's incomes? (James Madison had already recognized the widening gap between the rich and the poor as a serious danger to the nation's stability.) As we have already seen, Americans were thinking hard about the organization and responsibilities of our government. Should these questions be addressed by a national government? If so, how?

Despite continuing intense disagreement, our Constitution, one of the world's great political documents, was hammered out in the sweltering Philadelphia summer of 1787, a long six years after the end of the Revolutionary War. The most difficult challenge that muggy summer was to demonstrate that a strong central government need not endanger the liberties of individuals. The Constitution had to show that such government could, despite and because of its strength, protect the political liberties of individual citizens and minority factions. The substance and creativity of the Framers' debate is vital information for all of us thinking about government today. So intense was the clash of opinions about how to "fix" a government that was not working that the new nation almost certainly would have split apart if George Washington had not agreed to preside over the Constitutional Convention and then to lead the new government it created. From Philadelphia that summer he wrote to a friend: "Demagogues, men who are unwilling to lose any of their State consequence . . . will oppose any general government. But let these be regarded lightly, and justice, it is to be hoped, will at length prevail" (Van Doren 1948, 106).

With Washington as convener and Franklin, then past eighty, in attendance, Madison led the exceptionally talented representatives of all thirteen states to describe ideals of democratic governance never before seen. Government would be placed in the hands of the people through fairly apportioned elected representatives. With two houses, each with responsibility for policy-making and legislation, the delegate apportionment concerns of larger states would be met by basing representation in the House of Representatives on population. To reassure the smaller states fearful of losing power, each state would have the same number of senators, regardless of size.

Americans today still rely upon the vision Madison, in particular, introduced into the Framers' thinking about the functioning of a republican, Federalist form of government in a highly diverse, widely dispersed society. To assure many perspectives in balanced debate, while also protecting minority voices against the potential tyranny of a united majority, Americans must "extend the sphere" of government, said Madison, and "take in a greater variety of parties and interests." In this way, it will be "less probable that a majority of the whole will have a common motive to invade the rights of other citizens." If they have a common motive, it will be "more difficult for all who feel it to discover their own strength, and to act in unison with each other." People will also be protected by their "distrust" of each other, "in proportion to the number whose concurrence is necessary" (*The Federalist*, Nos. 10 and 64).

A broad distribution of powers would sustain the nation in a kind of dynamic balance. Multiple tensions, among the states, between the state and federal governments, and between the houses of Congress and among the three branches of government, would serve to protect and enrich American democracy. In *The Federalist*, Nos. 10 and 51, Madison explained how government so widely distributed would protect the people from "violent factions" and from anyone's excessive ambition, whether for power or property, by ensuring the widest inclusion of ideas in public discussion and decision making. The larger the American Republic became, the more satisfactory its representative, Federalist government would be.

Madison was well aware of the fact that conflicting economic interests would be responsible for most of the skewed domination and factionalism government was to prevent, or at least to contain: "The most common and durable source of factions," he wrote, "has been the various and unequal distribution of property. Those who hold, and those who are without property, have ever formed distinct interests in society." Yet, in a uniquely democratic paradox, he held that government must protect, not diminish, the very "faculties" that create differences in individuals' ability to acquire property: "The regulation of these various and interfering interests forms the principal task of modern legislation, and involves the spirit of party and faction in the necessary and ordinary operations of Government" (*The Federalist*, Nos. 10 and 59). The Framers consistently placed their greatest confidence in achieving freedom and opportunity for the people in the requirements they set for the broadest, most inclusive debate in a government accountable to the people.

Realizing that no one could know which of the states would comprise the nine required by the Constitutional Convention for ratification, the Framers decided not to include the names of the individual states in the Constitution's Preamble but rather to focus upon the nation and its citizens. "We the PEOPLE of the United States. . . ." thus replaced "We the people of the states of Virginia, New Hampshire, etc." eloquently proclaiming that the states form one nation, whose people are citizens of both the nation and a particular state. Especially in *The Federalist* Numbers 10, 37, 39, and 51, Madison explained and justified the government that the Framers envisioned. No explanation better serves the ideas of American democracy, the how and why of its functioning.

The most bitterly debated among the many new questions was this: Should the new Constitution include a Bill of Rights? Its advocates wanted to specify individual rights that would be protected in the new national government. Those opposed emphasized that most states already had Bills of Rights; its inclusion would cause more wrangling and confusion about the distribution of powers. There was fear that it would undo one of the most carefully constructed compromises already reached in the draft Constitution: language giving Congress the authority "to make all laws which shall be necessary and proper" to carry out its responsibilities. Once any specific powers not claimed by the federal government were enumerated, as in a Bill of Rights, what about responsibility for those rights not mentioned? Would fear of excessive congressional power reopen the entire lengthy debate about even having a national Constitution? Would there be endless wrangling about which specific powers were to go to the states? In his darkest hours, Madison thought this might happen.

In the end, by prior agreement (insisted upon, significantly, by Jefferson among others), Congress added a Bill of Rights, the first ten amendments to the Constitution, in 1791, two years after constitutional ratification by the states. The Tenth Amendment stated clearly (and forever problematically in the minds of many), that powers that the Constitution does not specifically grant to the federal government would belong "to the states, respectively or to the people."

Ultimately, the new Constitution, a "product of historical contingency, competing philosophies, and political competition," as the historian David T. Konig wrote recently, was also, miraculously, a totally unprecedented enlargement of the possibilities of democratic government (Konig 1995, 2):

- It replaced the clear and deliberate emphasis upon the states in the articles of Confederation by a new opening salvo: "We the PEOPLE of the United States, in Order to form a more perfect Union, establish Justice, insure domestic Tranquility, provide for the common defence, promote the general Welfare, and secure the Blessings of Liberty to ourselves and our Posterity, do ordain and establish this Constitution for the United States of America." The new government expressed the will of the American people, not, primarily, that of the states;

- It granted the federal government powers to tax and regulate commerce;

- It created genuinely shared responsibility for government by locating power in both state and federal governments and eliminated the states' earlier rights to approve, or disapprove, virtually all actions taken by Congress.

- It made provisions to assure that governmental functions would be shared by many units unlikely to consolidate as sources of undue power—likely, in fact, to compete and thus to bring varied perspectives before the people;

- It created a federal government made up of three branches—legislative, executive and judicial—so that each could complement the power of the others and all would find it necessary to work deliberately, in concert; and

- It listed specific circumstances in which the federal government would not act, both in the Constitution itself and in the first ten Amendments, the Bill of Rights.

A great victory had been won. Yet the old arguments were not gone, and difficult issues kept arising. In his book, *The Price of Federalism*, Paul E. Peterson recounts the Federalist/anti-Federalist debate that continued after ratification of the Constitution (Peterson 1995, 6–10). The Civil War, which we consider in some detail in our next chapter, marked the end of early federalism: more clearly than ever before, governmental sovereignty was placed in the authority of the central government. By then, however, the still young nation had confronted many new questions. Who, for example, should govern the vast expanses of land that had come to some states as grants from the king? How should Indians and slaves be counted to determine proportional representation in the newly constituted House of Representatives? Just as today, there seemed to be no end to the challenges. We will look at other such crucial episodes in the story of Americans' early experience with constitutional democracy in chapter 3.

A SECULAR BALANCE

The tendency to usurpation on one side or the other, or to a corrupting . . . alliance between them, will best be guarded against by an entire abstinence of the Government [from religious matters], beyond the necessity of preserving public order.

—James Madison

In the thirteen chaotic years between the Declaration of Independence and the ratification of the Constitution in 1789, Jefferson, Madison, and their colleagues envisioned a democracy deriving its legitimacy from the consent of the governed. Among many impassioned disagreements standing in the way of such consent, none was more perilous than that concerning the appropriate relationship between politics and religion. Given today's Conservative Republican agenda for the nation, strongly influenced now as in the past by the Christian Right, this argument is, of course, as perilous as ever (Lowi 1996, 24–25).

Religious liberalism, represented by Jefferson and Madison among others, was vigorously opposed by the conservative Patrick Henry and by others inclined toward more traditional views. Today, they would almost certainly place themselves among Conservative Republicans' "moral majority." Thus, as today, the earliest debates about the purposes of American government frequently revealed deeply held differences among the Framers as to whether the federal government was to be strictly neutral in matters of religion, or specifically committed to encouraging systems of morality and ethics drawn from the Judeo-Christian tradition. Ultimately, the language of the First Amendment developed a compromise position on how best to fit religion into the body politic, emphasizing consensual human rights:

> Congress shall make no law respecting an establishment of religion, or prohibiting the free exercise thereof; or abridging the freedom of speech, or of the press; or the right of the people peaceably to assemble, and petition the Government for a redress of grievances.

In effect, the national government is barred from establishing one church over others and from restricting activity in any of them. Everyone is free to bring his or her own religious convictions to bear. In an 1802 letter to Baptists in Danbury, Connecticut, Jefferson reaffirmed his faith in a government protecting the religious liberty of individuals, not legislating them: "Believing with you that religion is a matter which lies solely between man and his God . . . that the legislative powers of government reach actions only, not opinions, I contemplate with sovereign reverence the act of the American people . . . building a wall of separation between church and state" (Malone 1970, 108–109). This separation has been hailed as among the most important political developments of the millennium.

Carefully separating itself from "revealed" or religious truths, American secular government places particular responsibility upon citizens to engage actively in policy debate to assure the quality of their government. Our failure to do our share in this responsibility, whether from alienation or ignorance, dangerously diminishes the plurality of viewpoints that the prevailing Framers considered the best protection of American freedoms and the surest guidance to right action. Significantly, in the beginning the language of the First Amendment to the Constitution aimed to protect the freedoms of religion from government. Today we recognize that it is equally important to protect the freedoms of secular government from religion.

Chapter 3

The Union Challenged

A Majority held in restraint by constitutional checks and limitations and always changing easily, with deliberate changes of popular opinions and sentiments, is the only true sovereign of a free people. Whoever rejects it, does, of necessity, fly to anarchy.

—Abraham Lincoln

POLITICAL CRISES: THE PAST AS PROLOGUE

Challenges to the Constitution's vision of federalist government came thick and fast in the crowded years between ratification (1789) and the outbreak of the Civil War (1860). They came, not as neatly separate and separable issues, but in tightly interwoven bundles, mixing ideology, ambition, and practical concerns. Economic motives, national, sectional, and individual, were deeply imbedded in almost every major controversy.

Looking again at early tests of the still new Federalist, national government, we realize how very brief our nation's history actually is. We see, as well, how persistent the early challenges have continued to be, and how closely they resemble problems we face today:

- partisan extremism and failures to compromise;
- wavering confidence in the federal government and insistence on states' rights;

- the challenge of creating opportunities for business at home and abroad;
- a large national debt;
- the urgency of devising policies to guide international relations;
- the pressures of living with a national press which, by 1800, was directing—often distorting—people's perceptions of government;
- political betrayal and conflicted political ambitions.

The complexity and fragility of the nation in its first seventy-five years under the Constitution caused wide uncertainty about whether the Republic would survive. Each political crisis produced extreme reaction, just as it still does. What were crisis points in the first decades? How were they resolved? What did they teach us about government, its functions and purposes?

IN THE NAME OF STATES' RIGHTS

In 1798, under Federalist president John Adams, a proponent of strong central government in the tradition of his predecessor George Washington, our government, fearing anarchy, joined with several European monarchies to oppose republican revolution in France. Might popular resistance to strong central government in Europe spread like wildfire, even across the seas? The Adams administration feared so. Predictably, however, by making common cause with monarchies against antiroyalist citizens, the Adams government fed the fears of American critics, usually anti-Federalist states' rightists, that our own leaders might also be harboring monarchical aspirations.

The still insecure federal government rushed to adopt a series of so-called Alien laws, ostensibly to protect the new nation. They raised the eligibility requirement for naturalization to citizenship from five to fourteen years, permitted the detention of persons from an enemy nation, and authorized the president to expel anyone he deemed a danger to the nation. The laws' primary targets were French and Irish immigrants, most of whom just happened to belong to the opposing political party, led by the states' rights advocate Thomas Jefferson. The "Sedition Act," passed soon after, made it a crime to publish false or malicious statements about the government, or to incite opposition to any act of the Congress or the president.

How rapidly the Adams government had moved from protecting citizens' rights of free expression to suppressing them. What confusion about the purposes of government these actions in the nation's first decade revealed. And, indeed, how foresighted the Framers had been to insist that citizens be ever vigilant to safeguard their freedoms against the will of political leaders.

Ironically, public outrage at these actions, intended to forestall citizen dissatisfaction with government, precipitated one of the most far-reaching early challenges to the very concept of our constitutional system. Jefferson and his fellow Republicans, opponents of Adams's Federalists in this instance, fought the Alien and Sedition acts as unconstitutional, giving the president unwarranted power over individuals, and violating the freedoms of speech and press that the First Amendment guaranteed. Their combat strategy was to invoke the states' rights to reject an allegedly unconstitutional action of the federal government.

Paradoxically, Jefferson, moving to safeguard important democratic principles, argued with disconcerting ease that the Constitution was after all only a "compact" among the sovereign states. Together, he and Madison persuaded the state of Kentucky to nullify these allegedly unconstitutional congressional acts, while their home state of Virginia, acting more generally, reaffirmed the right of states to interpose their own decisions against any act of the federal government they considered unconstitutional.

In any event, the Alien and Sedition acts lapsed harmlessly after about two years, following Jefferson's defeat of Adams in the presidential election of 1800. What did turn out to have extremely important and unintended consequences in America's subsequent history was Jefferson and Madison's method of opposing them. The success of their line of argument meant that a state's right simply to reject an action of the federal government remained in play up to the Civil War. It became almost routine to invoke this threat whenever the federal government took an unpopular step. About the only means of forestalling such threatened disruption were painstaking compromises with the opposing political party.

In 1800, when Jefferson stood for the presidency against Washington's Federalist ally and successor, John Adams, he referred to the election as "the Revolution of 1800." There could hardly be a more dramatic early instance of public debate about the constitutional limits of central government than this campaign (Hofstadter 1960, 144). In the end, at Alexander Hamilton's insistence, the Adams administration had begun to amass an army, supposedly to defend against a feared invasion by the French. Had the army been organized, some scholars believe it might have been used against the Virginia militia to resist the transition from Federalist to anti-Federalist government after Jefferson was elected (Wood 2000, 68). There was real danger that the peaceful transition of government from one political party to another might not have occurred and our democracy not passed its first critical test (Peterson 1995, chap. 1, n. 14).

Over time, states' rights became the central tenet of Jeffersonian democracy. We've seen that, although always supportive of the Union, he considered a broad application of states' rights the essential guardian of individual liberties against excessive federal power. He intended thoughtful balance, but unhappily it was only a short step for extremists of every stripe to move from his characterization of the Constitution as a mere "compact" to their own periodic threats of secession from the Union. Even today, most states rightists, now usually Conservative Republicans, look to Jefferson's argument and example to support their position. In a grotesque misunderstanding of his intentions, one of the men arrested after the 1995 bombing of the Federal Building in Oklahoma City was wearing a shirt boldly emblazoned with Jefferson's picture.

THE TUG OF SECTIONALISM

Creating citizens' identification with, and loyalty to, the newly constituted nation, rather than primarily to states and regions, continued to be a major challenge throughout the early 1800s, as an increasing number of new states petitioned for recognition.

President John Adams's appointment of John Marshall, a committed nationalist as chief justice of the Supreme Court (1801-1835), was an important victory for those favoring a strong central government. Marshall had argued for the Constitution and national government in the Constitutional Convention in 1787. The Court's rulings during his lengthy tenure established the primacy of national interests and of the new federal judiciary to the extent Marshall deemed consistent with the Constitution, often to the chagrin of Adams's successor, Jefferson. Since his defining tenure, states can no longer simply reject duly passed and signed federal legislation. When Americans allege that actions of the federal government are unconstitutional, the case is argued in court and may be decided by the Supreme Court, which has ultimate jurisdiction. Overall, Marshall's influence strengthened public belief that a strong federal government was essential to a strong nation and that regional- and state-based interests would have to advance within that context.

Yet clashing sectional interests continued as a major force in American politics. Regional and state constituencies then were primarily concerned with securing their own economic advantage, as, indeed, they still are. People expected that the government, state or federal, would act to protect the growth of economic opportunities wherever they happened to be. In the South and West, that typically meant protecting the interests of farmers, whereas mercantile and other aspects of a developing market economy dominated the political agenda in the Northeast as early as the 1830s. Farmers typically leaned toward Jeffersonian politics, favoring a limited, decentralized government sensitive to states' rights and to assuring opportunities for most Americans. With some exceptions, the urban opposition tended to favor a strong central government whose approach to tax policies and finance would be closely allied with business interests, in the tradition of Alexander Hamilton.

A telling early example of sectionalism's power to undermine national interests occurred in the context of the War of 1812. The New England states bitterly opposed this war against Britain, which they considered unfavorable to their economic interests. In 1814, the legislature of Massachusetts actually called for a convention of the New England states "to make a radical reform of the national compact." New England Federalists, previously consistent supporters of a strong central government, stood ready to disrupt the Union to advance their own economic interests.

As it turned out, their convention accomplished very little, though its intransigence may have helped seal the death warrant of the Federalist Party. Nevertheless, New England's sectionalism continued to exacerbate already divided impulses and loyalties throughout the third decade of the Republic. It is not impossible to imagine that under slightly different circumstances their actions might have led to a northern secession from the Union as early as 1814.

Instead, it was the tragic sectionalism dominating political thinking in the South during the first half of the nineteenth century that finally became the greatest threat the nation has ever faced. Its most dramatic expression was Southerners' persistent defense of the institution of slavery as an economic necessity in their agrarian culture and as a matter exclusively within the jurisdiction of each separate state. These intractable issues finally caused the Civil War of the 1860s.

EARLY DEALS

In 1789, the Constitution had assigned responsibility for monetary policy and for the production of coinage to the federal government and created federal responsibility for the management of free and secure interstate commerce and for all trade agreements with foreign nations. With these important exceptions, it was assumed that the federal government would maintain a hands-off relationship to the developing economy. But so precarious were the new nation's finances that Congress almost immediately asked President Washington's treasury secretary, Alexander Hamilton, for a report on the state of public credit.

Hamilton's recommendations included a highly controversial proposal to create a first Bank of the United States, a federally managed institution specifically charged to create financial solvency. In Part II we will consider the Bank further, for it was, indeed, a brilliant solution to the nation's debt problems. At the moment, let us examine the opposing positions in the lengthy debate that preceded congressional chartering of the Bank in 1791, the same year the first stock market opened in Philadelphia.

Hamilton and his supporters intended to do more than just relieve the national debt. They believed in a stronger federal government that would play an active role in advancing free market goals. Their strategy for the Bank called for a partnership between the national government and the nation's wealthiest individuals, based on shared interests favorable to business. The government would shape trade and tax policies to support investors' economic interests, and together they would develop commercial enterprises in the United States and abroad.

The alliance would assure the government the support of America's richest and most powerful citizens. Then, as now, some Americans were bitterly opposed to these assumptions and goals as aspects of government's purposes. They fought the centralization of economic power; distrusted policies that seemed to favor the wealthy few at the expense of the less privileged majority, most of whom were farmers; and held that market initiatives should belong to the people privately, not to the federal government.

Among the Bank's fiercest opponents were Jefferson and Madison, who campaigned vigorously against it in the press, anticipating sentiments and strategies characteristic of many populist leaders today. They charged Hamilton with forgetting the purposes of the Revolution, and caring more about commercial enterprise than about opportunity for all Americans. They saw the federal government's expanded power over financial policy-making as seriously disadvantaging states and local communities, as well as American workers.

Despite the furor, Hamilton's Bank endured until its charter expired in 1811. As president, Jefferson mourned the loss of American innocence that the Bank seemed to represent but recognized the impossibility of turning back the clock. In a letter to a friend he wrote: "When this government was first established it was possible to have kept it going on true principles, but the . . . ideas of Hamilton destroyed that hope in the bud. We can pay off his debts in fifteen years, but we can never get rid of his financial system. . . . What is practicable must often control what is pure theory" (Hofstadter 1958, 35).

There would be many other such moments in the early years, when the government faced questions that the Constitution had not provided for. One of the most dramatic and profitable presented itself in 1803, during Jefferson's first term as president: the Louisiana Purchase. Concerned with protecting Americans' access to the inland waterways for commercial purposes, Jefferson saw a danger to American merchants in the possible loss of the Port of New Orleans, controlled either by Spain or France over the years. When Napoleon unexpectedly offered to sell the United States the port, as well as all the vast territory previously held by Spain and France, quick action was called for.

Jefferson, who believed profoundly in strict adherence to constitutional limitations of federal power, held that a constitutional amendment was needed to authorize the government's acquisition of the territory. However, when political problems arose that might have imperiled the transaction, he moved quickly, setting aside his own and others' concerns about his constitutional authority to act. In order not to lose the opportunity, he changed course, denying that the Purchase was, indeed, a matter requiring congressional approval.

In the end, Congress acted quickly to approve the purchase of a land mass that doubled the size of the nation, for what turned out much later to have been a price of about three cents per acre. During the months required to complete the transaction, former president John Adams, a Federalist, insisted without success that an amendment to the Constitution was necessary to legitimize this or any other such assumption of power not specifically authorized to the president. Late in his life, Adams wrote with considerable irony that the Purchase, whose dimensions neither sellers nor buyers knew at the time, had required Jefferson to assume greater powers, with greater consequence, than all the assumptions of power in Washington's and his own years in the presidency combined. It had obligated the government to a known cost of $11,250,000 (ultimately, over time, $27,267,622) and brought dramatic changes to the nation's prospects and fresh conceptions of itself as an aspirant to transcontinental power.

For all its success, the Purchase left many constitutional questions unanswered, How strictly would the federal government be expected to live by the letter of constitutional law? Were powers not explicitly given the government, such as this land acquisition, assumed to be outside its authority? Ironically, in convincing President Washington that the first Bank of the United States was constitutional, an argument Jefferson had opposed, Hamilton had created a precedent for Jefferson's own actions. Writing several years after the Purchase, Jefferson mused provocatively:

> A strict observance of the written laws is doubtless one of the high duties of a good citizen, but it is not the highest. The laws of necessity, of self-preservation, of saving our country when in danger, are of higher obligation. To lose our country by a scrupulous adherence to written law, would be to lose the law itself, along with life, liberty, property and all those who are enjoying them with us. (Malone 1974, 277–278)

Jefferson's actions in the Louisiana Purchase are also important as an early, controversial demonstration of presidential power. Though perhaps the early American statesperson most concerned about the dangers of an overly powerful central government, he in fact added greatly to the actual or assumable power of the presidency. Later, presidential power was also notably increased by Abraham Lincoln (for whom Jefferson was a kind of exemplar) and by Theodore Roosevelt and Franklin Roosevelt. In our own day, thoughtful Americans seeking to sustain the dynamic balance of our three-part organization in federal government must remain vigilant to assure that the powers of the presidency, like those of central government itself, are not endangered.

CIVIL WAR: THE UNION'S SEVEREST TEST

Despite these challenges to American constitutional democracy and others equally important to the development of our government, Americans must pause again before the questions that led us to Civil War. What happened to bring us so near the brink of tragic dissolution? How could Americans, under the Constitution and given the Union, ever have taken up arms against each other? Given our wide political differences and the repugnance of partisan extremism as we know it today, we must work to understand as fully as possible the dangers such conflicted politics once possessed: the power to sectionalize and factionalize us beyond the capacity of every good intention to save us from ourselves. Conceivably, some fear, they could do so once again.

As state after state petitioned to join the Union following the 1803 Louisiana Purchase, and it became evident that the United States would eventually control all territory in the continental expanse, American democracy was tested as never before or since by questions concerning the rights of states to hold slaves. Not that the issues and circumstances that finally made Civil War unavoidable were new. Rather, they were long-standing problems of America's social and political life, simmering just under the surface, ready to erupt. Even when the clouds of armed hostility finally gathered in the winter and spring of 1861, sectionalism, angry assertions of states' rights, political demagoguery and partisanship, cultural differences, and racist attitudes persistently blocked rational public discourse that might have resolved the crisis.

After decades of debate and prior threats of secession by Southern states, and despite periodic, carefully negotiated compromises that permitted slavery to continue where it already existed, while protecting citizens' rights to decide the issue for themselves in the new Western states, the presenting cause of the conflict was, after all, the unrelenting defense of the indefensible, the institution of slavery. Would the federal government guarantee the protection of slavery in the new territories being settled? This was the question everyone asked. As moral indignation about slavery grew outside the South, most Americans found it unconscionable to imagine its extension beyond the slaveholding states. Yet the Southern states were demanding just that extension, both to vindicate the practice of slavery and to assure future protection for their way of life.

The proslavery *Dred Scott* decision of 1857 and the discussion that ensued, especially in the famous debates between Abraham Lincoln and Stephen Douglas, represent another telling period in the evolution of federalism. After years of earlier public debate around the slavery issues that finally converged in the *Dred Scott* case, the Supreme Court interpreted federalism in this instance to mean that no boundaries could be placed on the movements of masters and slaves. As property duly acquired by an owner, a slave did not become free when taken into a free state. Furthermore, the decision stated that Congress could not bar slavery from a territory, nor could Blacks be citizens. The *Dred Scott* decision helped Northern Republicans in 1860 to commit support to the antislavery candidate Abraham Lincoln for president, which, in turn, convinced Southern whites that their freedoms of decision were more important than the Union. Thus the *Dred Scott* decision turned out to be one of the presenting, immediate causes of the Civil War.

When President Lincoln was elected in 1860, the slaveholding states, in an unprecedented move, refused to accept the election results. Seven states seceded immediately afterward, moving quickly to create a new Confederate government that would protect their rights to extend slavery by armed force. Most of their actions to this end defied constitutional assumptions, while lacking any other public authorization. In effect, the citizens opposed to secession in these states were voiceless. Some found a degree of comfort in the notion that the seceding states might obtain better assurances of their rights from a position outside the federal government. Many Southerners expected to return to the Union, following an act of legitimate civil disobedience once these rights had been assured. After only six months of the war, many of the southerners who had never supported secession were crying out for negotiations to end the conflict.

In the brief interval between the secessions and Lincoln's First Inaugural Address early in 1861, a number of men who had been prominent in state and federal government, including nineteen former governors, gathered in Washington in a last minute effort to reach a compromise that would prevent dissolution of the Union and almost certain war. Even in hindsight, it is hard to see what compromises either side might have offered at the ill-starred Peace Conference. The Republicans, the president's party, claimed no jurisdiction over slavery in the states where it already existed (professing to support states' rights in the matter), and the South, never having won the right to extend slavery into the territories, could not surrender it. Thus entrapped, the nation needed statesmanship and a will to creative resolution, as never before.

In the event, Republican legislators newly elected on a platform opposing slavery were not amenable to compromise in any form. (We may pause to think about the unwillingness to compromise that newly elected Republicans brought to national politics in the 1990s. . . .) They considered the Acts of Secession an intolerable challenge to their stated principles and perceived an opportunity to both preserve the Union and to rid it forever of slavery. In their fervor, which admitted no conciliating moderation, they parted company with Lincoln, who still sought a gradualist, some would say Centrist, approach to solving the problem that would in due course, he believed, end slavery without a war.

For as long as he could, Lincoln encouraged nationalist loyalties and the spirit of compromise that had saved the Union in the past. Not until the Confederate army had initiated armed confrontation by firing upon Fort Sumter, a federal naval installation in South Carolina, did the president authorize a military response. Still hoping for settlement, intent upon reassuring the rebellious states of their rights under the Constitution, and unwilling to recognize the constitutional legitimacy of secession, Lincoln used his 1861 First Inaugural Address to develop the rationale for his passionate commitment to preserve the Union as his most important presidential responsibility.

Three points lay at the heart of his argument: no constitutional right had as yet been violated, no constitution can foresee every future problem, and no Union can hold without opposing parties' absolute determination to transcend conflict by compromise. In an extraordinary step, stating that "the central idea of secession is anarchy" and that once accepted, it would recur whenever differences developed, Lincoln simply declared secession unconstitutional.

The First Inaugural Address is Lincoln's agonized appeal to the American South to uphold the Union:

> Will you hazard so desperate a step while there is any possibility that any portion of the ills you fly from have no real existence? . . . while the certain ills you fly to are greater than all the real ones you fly from? Will you risk . . . so fearful a mistake?
>
> All profess to be content in the Union, if all constitutional rights can be maintained. Is it true then, that any right, plainly written in the Constitution has been denied? I think not. . . . Think, if you can, of a single instance in which a plainly written provision of the Constitution has been denied. . . . All the vital rights of minorities, and of individuals, are so plainly assured to them . . . in the Constitution that controversies never arise concerning them. But no organic law can ever be framed with a provision specifically applicable to every question which may occur. . . . No foresight can anticipate . . . all possible questions.
>
> Shall fugitives from labor be surrendered by national or state authority? The Constitution does not expressly say. May Congress

prohibit slavery in the territories? The Constitution does not expressly say. Must Congress protect slavery in the territories? The Constitution does not expressly say.

From questions of this class spring all our Constitutional controversies, and we divide upon them into majorities and minorities. If the minority will not acquiesce, the majority must, or the government must cease. There is no other alternative; for continuing the government is acquiescence on one side or the other. (Lincoln 1953, 266–267)

The Constitution had been built upon an apparently solid, Federalist foundation that assumed mutually reinforcing public policy between state and federal government, as well as upon the expectation that political compromise in the common interest would prevail. In this terrible instance, both failed, leaving the new president in a desperate situation. He faced secession and possibly war against citizens of the country that had elected him, and members of his own political party rejected his leadership on how to proceed.

The war marked the end of early federalism, placing governmental sovereignty more clearly than ever before under the authority of central government. But the tests to constitutional government were no less severe after the war. Just five days after Confederate General Lee's surrender in April 1865, President Lincoln was assassinated. The efforts of Andrew Johnson, his successor, to hasten and ease the reformation of the Union were thwarted by Republicans in Congress, who refused to recognize newly formed state governments previously authorized by Lincoln and claimed the sole right to direct future federal policy toward the South. Johnson was impeached by Republicans, who found his efforts to apply Lincoln's previous understandings with Southern states unacceptable. He was saved from dismissal by only one vote.

Dishonesty and prejudice of all sorts, especially virulent racism, were rampant, along with intractable political partisanship and demagoguery. With the issue of voting rights for Blacks now at the center of controversy, and highly partisan Republicans reluctant to see the restoration of Southern Democrats to any positions of national authority, the decade of acrimony and manipulation that followed, Reconstruction, heaped humiliation and waste upon the South and upon the nation.

Blatantly hypocritical, Republican leaders in Northern states refused to establish voting rights for Blacks in their bailiwicks, even as the Republican

Congress, seeking to dominate postwar national politics with the support of Black votes, was requiring Southern states to do so. In 1867, the defeated states were placed under military rule, allowing Congress to carry out political and social programs of its own in the ravaged region. With the election of Gen. U. S. Grant to the first of two presidential terms in 1868, Reconstruction Republicans were also in control of the White House.

Three Constitutional amendments, the Thirteenth through the Fifteenth, emerged from the blood-soaked years 1865–1870. Respectively, they established the freedom of slaves; described their citizenship; and declared that citizens' voting rights would not be "abridged on account of race, color, or previous condition of servitude." Political and social equality, however, were still far away. The Fifteenth Amendment, in particular, left room for states to establish other requirements that for decades effectively prevented many Blacks from realizing their right to vote. As enforced, it perpetuated a tragic retardation in the role of Southern states in national politics until well beyond the Civil Rights movement of the 1960s.[1]

The postwar Reconstruction years were a time of national emergency and a period of consolidation of U.S. Federalist governance, during which interest in anti-Federalist political ideals as such all but disappeared from the national scene.

Chapter 4

Organizing Government in the Twentieth Century

The Federal Constitution forms a happy combination . . . the great and aggregate interests being referred to the national, the local and particular, to the state legislatures. . . . Extend the sphere, and you take in a greater variety of parties and interests; you make it less probable that a majority of the whole will have a common motive to invade the rights of other citizens.

—James Madison

THE FRAMERS AND GOVERNMENT NOW

James Madison's insistence in *Federalist* No. 10 that factions will inevitably exist and must be included in the "ordinary operations of government" is reassuring for Americans observing today's acrimonious factional debates about which aspects of government belong to the states and which to the federal government. Madison insisted that the success of American democracy ultimately depends on including the many sparring voices within a field of force unified by shared commitment to the concept of a single democratic nation. He showed why a Federalist Republic such as ours gives the best opportunity both to tolerate and to capitalize upon dissent.

These earliest visions of organizing American democracy contain many ideas vital to the nation now. Among the most powerful is the argument for distributing the responsibilities of government among federal, state, and local elected representatives. Yet, Americans of every era are responsible for asking to what extent the Framers' convictions about this Federalist ideal are still viable. Today, for example, we must consider the huge size of our nation and our government: 50 states, 3,000 counties, more than 80,000 other units of government, and an ethnically diverse population projected at 300,000,000 (Anton 1989, 208–209). Do we still believe that the tensions created by the wide distribution of government's powers, and having at least the potential to include the greatest number of voices in public debate, are creative tensions, encouraging inventive problem solving, defending everyone against anyone, and contributing positively to American life? Or, might their importance be even greater now, as we face the multiple challenges of re-creating effective democratic government for an increasingly pluralist society?

As former revolutionaries, the Framers of American democracy were preoccupied with distributing the powers of government in order to prevent such violations of liberty as they had experienced under the British Crown. They thought relatively little about distributing the responsibilities government might someday assume, except to assert that they knew American government would be a necessarily dynamic, evolutionary process, changing as times and circumstances changed. Late in life, Thomas Jefferson said:

> I am not an advocate for frequent and untried changes in laws and institutions. But I know also that laws and institutions must go hand in hand with the progress of the human mind. As that becomes more developed, more enlightened, as new discoveries are made, new truths disclosed, and manners and opinions change with the change of circumstances, institutions must advance also and keep pace with the times. (Malone 1981, 349)

The Framers gave us a blueprint, not a prescription, to show how government could work, not what it might actually do.

It was left to future citizens, now to us, to fill in the details that would best realize their and, later, our own visions of *e pluribus unum*, from many (now, very many), one. For Madison, the tenor and effects of current debates about shifting power from the federal to state governments would surely confirm the Framers' wisdom in distributing government broadly, thereby helping to protect Americans against hasty policy decisions such as those about reorganizing and diminishing the federal government that Conservative Republicans seek today.

PROGRESSIVISM AND ACTIVIST GOVERNMENT

We've seen that, during the Civil War the nation experienced unprecedented centralization of government at the expense of states-based initiatives and that this centralization continued during the decades of postwar Republican Reconstruction, as the federal government imposed its will upon the defeated Confederacy, we may say, "with a vengeance."

The period of hectic economic expansion that followed the war, especially in the North and West, crested in an era of flamboyant, uncontrolled capitalist expansion, popularly known as "The Gilded Age" (1890–1920). Soon, huge increases in corporate power and startling income disparities, coupled with a strong and, many thought, increasingly insensitive federal government, called forth an opposing, grassroots populism. Its champions spoke out passionately against the perceived corruption of a too-powerful central government, in league with "Big Business." In the beginning, this grassroots movement championed localized, citizen-led government that would implement policies specifically favorable to farmers and workers.

By 1900, urban Americans were joining this originally rural movement in full force, creating a national Progressive movement that sought specific response to the needs of ordinary citizens and came to dominate American politics throughout three of the most turbulent decades of our history. Its most far-reaching effects, in the New Deal of President Franklin Roosevelt, are a major contextual element in current debates about the goals and organization of government. They have much to teach us.

From the beginning, Progressives supported an activist government at both state and federal levels. They wanted to limit the power of corporate wealth and to protect workers, public lands, the environment, and opportunities for small businesses and farmers. They blamed unregulated capital for most of the corruption in public life, and were convinced that structural changes in government would assure renewed government integrity in cities, states, and the nation. They drew strength for their battle from the ideas of two popular American philosophers, William James and John Dewey, who emphasized the peculiarly American opportunities of change and experimentation in all aspects of national life.

Wisconsin, where Robert La Follette had been elected governor in 1900, was the site of the first Progressive triumphs. Within six years, La Follette's administration had established direct (rather than party-controlled) primary elections; a demonstrably more efficient civil service; a state income tax (the first of its kind in the United States); and state commissions to regulate railroads, banking corporations, and natural resources. Other states soon followed Wisconsin's example, establishing local controls and extending government regulations to banking, insurance companies, and other business corporations. The many successful reforms carried out by states between roughly 1900 and 1916 also demonstrated clearly the uniquely valuable contributions states may make to the national enterprise as experimental laboratories for governing.

During the administrations of Republican Theodore Roosevelt (1901–1909) and Democrat Woodrow Wilson (1913–1921), Progressive thinking began to shape the agendas of the federal government, laying the groundwork for Democrat Franklin Roosevelt's famously infamous New Deal, launched in 1933. Like those in politics today, each of these men claimed a determination to retain or re-create for ordinary Americans the freedoms and opportunities envisioned by the Founders. Building upon the successes of the states, some would say climbing upon their bandwagons to thwart political corruption and the excesses of capitalism, all three claimed for the federal government Progressive ideals: an activist government to assure a primary, though not exclusive, focus upon the well-being of citizens, rather than principally upon the prospects for "Big Business." Forceful, capable, and yet idealistic even to a fault, they supported Progressive directions in domestic policy. The Roosevelts in particular gave the nation renewed confidence in government by and for the people.

Theodore Roosevelt was especially skillful in adapting his presidential agenda to the popular causes of Progressivism. In actions perhaps more likely in a Democratic than a Republican administration, he used the powers of the presidency and the federal government specifically to enforce the public interest against corporate trusts. For example, his suit against the Northern Securities Company, a railroad holding company put together by the capitalists J. P. Morgan, John D. Rockefeller, and others, was brought in order to curb the corporation's monopolistic excesses and to bring about competition to reduce costs. In another dramatic confrontation, TR forced the end of a miners' strike in the Northeast by insisting that operators and union members meet and submit to binding federal arbitration.

TR's use of the federal government's power to mediate between contesting parties, not just to protect property and capital, was a significant move in relation to balance of power issues. During his second term, TR won additional legislative victories against capitalist monopolies, created such federal agencies as the Pure Food and Drug Administration, and introduced new approaches to preserving public land for the people's use. In all of these activities he captured for the people and the presidency the Progressives' insistence upon a government responsive to the needs of ordinary Americans.

These measures set important precedents for the administration of Democrat Woodrow Wilson (whose terms in office were separated from TR's only by that of Republican William Howard Taft, 1909–1913). Whereas TR had emphasized primarily national aims, Wilson's New Freedom platform stressed greater individual freedom and aspiration through renewed public confidence in the integrity of government and legitimate competition. Riding the tide of Progressive reform, Wilson's nationalist agenda continued his predecessor's "trust-busting" crusade. With Congress, whose interests were more often local than he wished, Wilson lowered import taxes to stimulate economic competition, created a graduated income tax, established the Federal Reserve Bank to stabilize currency and regulate the banks, created the Federal Trade Commission to control illegal business practices, and won passage of the Federal Highways Act.

By the time Wilson left office in 1920, citizens could draw upon a clearly defined, congressionally supported legacy of Progressive action, tilting once again toward greater centralization of activist government both within states and in the nation. Its generally Liberal supporters justified Progressive aims as best serving broad popular priorities, especially opportunities for everyone to achieve a decent standard of living. Its critics, usually Conservatives, de-emphasized these gains and instead warned, as they do today, of the perils for liberty and economic expansion that "excessive" government brings.

FDR AND THE NEW DEAL

Democrat Franklin D. Roosevelt came to the presidency in 1933, following the Republican administrations of Warren Harding, Calvin Coolidge, and Herbert Hoover. Before his death in office in 1945, a month before the surrender of Germany and five months before the end of the war with

Japan, he had led the nation out of both its worst depression and its most comprehensive military challenge.

In all these efforts, but especially in the massive New Deal legislation intended to lift the country out of economic depression, FDR added even more than his predecessors to the by then largely reestablished public support for centralizing government, especially in times of great distress. At the same time, he conformed to Madison and the Framers' belief that state governments and the federal government, though separate, should not be thought of as rivals for power. Rather, they could work together coopera- tively, using the legitimate tensions of different perspectives to forge a stronger nation. This concept guided FDR's development and implemen- tation of public policies that would see the nation through more than a decade of economic depression and world war. Convinced that Washing- ton and the states could be partners in meeting ultimately shared responsi- bilities, FDR utilized existing state programs wherever possible, inventing and coordinating direction that united the nation in ideals of social relief and promise.

How extensively the legacy of the New Deal will influence Americans' current and future decisions about organizing government is still uncer- tain. The New Deal was, after all, a strategy for government in years of ex- treme economic hardship. Nevertheless, no one can doubt its significance as a component of our debate about how to govern, in all of the years since its inception almost seventy years ago. Let us review briefly some of the es- sentially Progressive actions that Americans took under FDR's leadership:

We strengthened the Federal Reserve System to ensure government regulation of the banks, created the Federal Deposit Insurance Corporation to protect citizens against loss of deposits, and took steps to regulate the stock market through the Federal Trade Commission and the Securities Exchange Act, all to help avoid a recurrence of the market collapse and eco- nomic depression the nation was experiencing when FDR came to office.

We developed and implemented, under the National Industrial Re- covery Act, the most comprehensive legislation the nation had ever seen on behalf of both business and labor, including price supports, stimulation of the economy through a public works program, and, for workers, wages- and hours-protection and the right to bargain collectively.

We awarded, through several public relief programs, funds to feed the hungry, employ young men whose families were on relief, provide farmers the support to renegotiate loans, and householders the opportunity to refi- nance mortgages. We also granted loans to both large and small businesses.

We supported the Works Progress Administration, which substituted jobs for direct relief.

We established the Social Security system, which at the time provided assistance for the elderly, retirement annuities, unemployment insurance, aid for the blind or crippled, and aid to dependent children.

With this much change underway, excesses of feeling and action, both among those who supported and those who opposed FDR and the New Deal, were inevitable. As early as 1934, Conservative critics, usually Republicans, called for repeal of much of his legislative program, in order to reduce or abolish the government's role in economic and social initiatives. They advocated, instead, a return to what *they* saw as more balanced federal/state relationships, by which they typically meant restoring the prerogatives of states to decide, one by one, whether and how to support social programs. In this effort, they provided an example for today's Conservative Republicans, who are working to devolve most authority to the states, especially for social programs. Eventually, FDR's Conservative Republican critics largely prevailed, in part because our strong post-World War II economy allowed them to argue convincingly that a national commitment to programs for social provision was no longer necessary.

Extending the legacy of the Progressives, the New Deal assumption that government's responsibilities include social welfare seemed to foresee the bitter partisan divisiveness in the nation now. The political columnist David Shribman observed that the New Deal and its later, sister program, President Lyndon Johnson's Great Society "cast megalithic shadows across American life and politics," shadows that most politicians and voters not only accepted, but "venerated." Shribman asked: "Were those two attempts at social programming part of a grand progression in our history, or were they aberrations?" (Shribman, "Will There Be a *New* New Deal," *The Boston Globe*, 4 February 1996). At present, they seem to have been aberrations, victims of both the Conservative Republican agenda and the Clinton administration's Centrist pragmatism: Facing a Conservative Republican Congress after the 1994 midterm election, Democrat Clinton frequently declared that national priorities would have to be met within the reality that "the era of Big Government is over."

Now the operative question in Conservative Republican efforts to reduce and reorganize American government is, Will Americans dismiss the Progressives' legacy of activist, collaborative government, as Conservative Republicans would have it, or will we explore and utilize Progressive thinking, adapting and reinventing strategies for an activist government, including federal and state government partnerships, as needed? Must we choose between activist federal government or reliance upon state and local decision making? Or largely abandon both and rely instead upon private sector leadership wherever possible, as Conservative Republicans have proposed in response to the social agenda that Liberals support?

We'll look more fully at the New Deal as we consider developing relations between government and the economy in Part II. The aim here: to recognize the New Deal as a watershed in the ongoing debate about American federalism, about the purposes and organization of American government.

HIGH STAKES PING-PONG: ORGANIZING GOVERNMENT IN THE LATE TWENTIETH CENTURY

As we reach the beginning of the twenty-first century, and as many Americans look with increasing alarm at what sometimes seems to be the wholesale transfer of responsibility and power away from the central government, we must also recognize a seeming nonchalance, even ignorance in some quarters, about why any of it matters. In this context, there is comfort in appreciating again the slow pace of political change and the divisions of responsibility that our Federalist system was so carefully designed to require.

Consider, for example, the following: Republican President Dwight Eisenhower, elected after the Truman administration's unsuccessful efforts to preserve and elaborate the social provisions of the New Deal (as, e.g., in a national health care program) was convinced that the central government had become too big, costly, and intrusive. To his surprise and disgust, the Commission on Federal and State Government, which Congress established at his request in 1953 to recommend reductions in the federal government, while providing guidance for its future relations with the states, found no evidence that Washington was usurping state powers, nor that it was any threat to the states' freedoms. Indeed, the commission called for more cooperative partnerships between state and federal governments, declaring: "There are few activities of government in which there is not some degree of national interest" (Anton 1989, 215–216ff.).

Not easily deterred, Eisenhower tried again in 1956, with Vice President Richard Nixon at the helm of a two-year Federal/State Action Committee. Again, the group reached no agreement about how to redivide or clarify government responsibilities at each level. Actually, only two federal programs were recommended for transfer to the state governments during Eisenhower's two terms in office, while more than a dozen new federal grant-in-aid programs were enacted, including the federal highway system, the largest ever.

Yet, there were harbingers of change. By the late 1950s, the single remaining social program of universal import was Social Security. In effect, as the sociologist Theda Skocpol points out, the New Deal's social programs had been dismantled: "The postwar United States was not to have universal social provision, except for retired elderly wage earners." Southern Democrats and Republicans, acting together, had managed to eliminate public employment programs and to defeat, or significantly cut back on, all other social provisions. Gone were "national standards of public assistance, . . . the temporary nationalization of unemployment insurance . . . and proposals for governmentally guaranteed full employment" (Skocpol 1995, 301–302). Initiatives for national health insurance, championed by President Truman, were roundly defeated. Only the GI bills after World War II and the Korean War were exceptions to the pattern.

Not surprisingly, the pendulum reversed direction in the 1960s and early 1970s, as Democratic presidents renewed the call for activist central government and social provision. In New Deal tradition, Presidents Kennedy, Johnson, and later Carter, oversaw the birth of hundreds of new programs, among them those of Johnson's Great Society, to create opportunities for those people left behind in the generally prosperous postwar era: the poor, children, and most African-Americans. Theodore J. Lowi portrays a "First Republic" in which national and state governments function according to the definitions and restrictions of the Constitution, and a "Second Republic" after 1961 (Lowi 1996, 17, 36). He shows that the successes of Liberalism through "Big Government" in the New Deal caused the federal government to extend its power far beyond anything the Constitution had envisioned.

Unlike Republicans Eisenhower and Nixon, Democrats Kennedy, Johnson, and Carter were not much interested in process questions about the distribution of governmental authority. They assumed responsibility for social justice at the level of the federal government and anticipated state and local collaboration. Though most of their ambitious goals were not fully realized, the establishment of Medicare under Johnson in 1965 and the subsequent indexing of Social Security benefits to the inflation rate in the Carter administration in 1972 significantly improved the lot of the nation's elderly. And, of course, the Civil Rights movement in the Kennedy and Johnson administrations led to extensive new federal legislation supporting human rights and attempting to assure that access to education and employment, among other entitlements in American democracy, would be protected against race- and gender-based discrimination. (Today, much of this legislation is under threat of dissolution by Conservative Republicans at both state and national levels.) Under Carter, discrimination against the elderly and the handicapped was also made illegal.

Widespread public criticism of "Big Government" in the Kennedy and Johnson years helped Richard Nixon to win the presidency in 1968. His frustrations during Eisenhower's administration still fresh in his memory, he again attempted to formulate strategies for redistributing powers among federal, state, and, local governments, while also trying to reduce the number of federal social programs. To Nixon's credit, his intended scheme would have returned power to the states and localities through block grants supporting social programs that linked federal and state objectives. State and local governments would decide together how grants were to be used. His administration also developed proposals calling for revenue sharing by government at every level, as well as for consolidation and devolution of powers to the states in functional areas, such as education, transportation, employment training, and urban assistance (Anton 1989, 217).

Although Nixon intended to reduce the federal government, federal programs actually continued to grow during his administration. And, of course, they continued to do so under his successor, Jimmy Carter, when the federal government expanded to unprecedented levels. The Carter years (1977–1981) saw increased federal assistance to the states, a larger federal government, and a host of new programs to ameliorate social ills, such as food stamps, Old Age Assistance, Aid to the Blind, Aid to the Disabled, and the Supplemental Social Security Income Acts (218).

By 1980, federal assistance programs were three times what they had been at the decade's start. Once again, citizens seemed less worried about governance structures, or even about the huge sprawl of the federal government, than about underlying social problems. With federal officials now involved in virtually all of the responsibilities of state and local governments, discussions about how levels of government should relate to each other became extraordinarily tangled. Yet the overall pattern seemed to demonstrate Americans' continuing approval of an activist central government.

But did we approve? In 1981, citizens elected Conservative Republican Ronald Reagan to the first of two terms. His agenda for Americans derived from the conviction that government could not solve social problems. In fact, Reagan went further than most, proclaiming that, in its efforts to act instead of insisting upon citizen leadership in the private sector: "Government *is* the problem." His words have remained a rallying call for Conservative Republicans and Libertarians, who have done so much to discredit government by insisting that it is, indeed, the enemy of a free and enlightened citizenry. A free people, they say, will take care of themselves, and competitive requirements of the marketplace will assure the effectiveness of their efforts.

Once in office, Reagan immediately launched a proposal that would have turned forty-four federal assistance programs over to the states, with reduced federal funding planned to expire as states decided whether or how to continue them. But, like Eisenhower's efforts, the plan failed, not only because of the inherent difficulty of disestablishing entrenched programs, but also because Reagan's top-down plan lacked workable funding mechanisms and was not supported by broad public understanding or sympathy.

Undeterred, Reagan continued to press for national rejuvenation in his vision of the Framers' "nation of states." Many Conservatives in the private sector gladly joined his efforts to limit and redistribute to the states many purposes and functions of the federal government. In 1984, with private support, The National Conference on Social Welfare formed a bipartisan Committee on Federalism and National Purpose to achieve these goals. However, the group's report, "To Form a More Perfect Union" (1985) emphasized lack of agreement about "what the philosophical basis of change should be," echoing similar findings during Eisenhower's term and anticipating subsequent divided opinion during the Bush years. By 1985, at the end of Reagan's first term, all of the strategies that Nixon had created to limit federal government's involvement with programs in states and localities were gone, except for the greatly reduced Community Development Block Program.

In sum, even when initiated by Conservative Republican presidents, broadly based, bipartisan efforts to diminish federal government in favor of state, local, or private sector leadership have never produced a rationale that the American people found persuasive. Recent successes with this agenda, as we shall see, are part and parcel of Conservative Republican political initiatives and Liberal or Centrist political compromise. In fact, a recent study by National Public Radio, the Kaiser Family Foundation, and Harvard University's Kennedy School of Government found that "most Americans want *more* government involvement and regulation to solve the nation's problems," not less ("Americans Distrust Government, but Want It to Do More," nprONLINE, 28 July 2000).

RECENT LEGISLATION FAVORING THE STATES

Observing the shift in powers from federal to state governments underway at present, many Americans, Liberals, moderates of both parties, and some Centrists, still believe that a philosophical basis for this redistribution has not been persuasively stated. But Conservative Republican leadership for it is powerful not only in Congress, but in the Supreme Court, as well as in many states, including those that rejected the Reagan initiatives of 1982.

Two congressional actions of the mid-'90s illustrate the success of Conservative Republicans' leadership in reducing and redistributing government: *The Unfunded Mandates Reform Act* (1995) and *The Personal Responsibility and Work Opportunity and Reconciliation Act* (1996). These legislative actions are part and parcel of the Reagan legacy. What are their implications?

The Unfunded Mandates Reform Act limits federal power by making it illegal for the federal government to impose any mandates on the states for which it will not assume all costs above a specified threshold. The *Act* also suggests that private entities, such as businesses, may recover costs incurred as a result of a federal mandate, as, for example, in pollution control. This legislation passed with bipartisan support, as Liberals and Centrists climbed on the Conservative bandwagon, much as Theodore Roosevelt's Republicans had embraced Liberal Progressivist causes in 1901–1909.

But what of the effects this time? Knowledgeable observers see the *Act* as significantly reordering federal/state relationships, by reducing the power of the national government to initiate or to require state support for needed social or other legislation in the public interest (Fort 1995, 727). The effects of the *Act* will be, they fear, to leave social policy initiatives, broadly defined, to the states. Eager to minimize their costs, states, in turn, may leave the social agenda unattended or, in time, develop it through a patchwork of autonomous initiatives that create massive inequities in policies and programs throughout the country. In any case, critics point out, social provision and all other legislation is now, as James Madison warned in 1788, at greater risk of falling victim to local factions as the sphere of governmental leadership grows smaller.

In sum: *The Unfunded Mandates Reform Act* raises extremely important issues for citizens' consideration. If the power to take social initiatives in the public interest is effectively yielded by the federal government, will needed legislation occur? Can needed initiatives be adequately coordinated? Will some Americans be less well served by social policies than others?

An illustrative case in point: *The Personal Responsibility and Work Opportunity and Reconciliation Act of 1996*, the Welfare Act, was signed into law by President Clinton in August 1996, shortly before the presidential election. It gave states new power to develop and administer their own welfare and work programs. After a five-year "bridging" period in which the federal government pledged continued support to such programs as food stamps, emergency financial assistance, and job training, states will assume the authority to make decisions about continuing such programs, as well as assuming the lion's share of responsibility to fund them.

There is in the Welfare Act a clear financial incentive for states to reduce the numbers of people who receive public assistance. It rewards them for reducing the number of welfare claims. Moreover, if the targets set for each year's per capita work requirement are not met, federal funding for state-based welfare programs will be cut. The Act stipulates that by the year 2002, half of all persons receiving welfare must be working.

These are high stakes for state treasuries, and reduction in the numbers of people on welfare is occurring. According to Jason DeParle, as of March 1999 the nation's welfare rolls had dropped 47 percent from the 1994 peak (DeParle, "Leftover Money for Welfare Baffles States," *New York Times*, 29 August 1999). What is not clear yet is what is happening to the people who are no longer being helped. Many have found jobs in this period of historically low unemployment (and the private sector is being encouraged by tax incentives to hire them). Questions remain about whether they can sustain employment when the economy is not as robust as today. Meanwhile, in the 1999 *Omnibus Appropriations Bill* (see chap. 3), the states saw their budgets for federal support to social services reduced by 17 percent; they were funded at $1.9 billion, $390 million below fiscal year 1998. The greatest losers were the most populous states: California, New York, Texas, and Florida. As we'll see in Part IV, these are also states with large immigrant populations, whose public support was specifically curtailed by the Welfare Act and by other, accompanying legislation.

The aim in the Welfare Act was to move individuals and families, both native born and legal immigrants, from welfare programs to work and self-sufficiency. In President Clinton's terms, it would "end welfare as we've known it" and eliminate the "culture of dependency" that had limited aspiration in generations of Americans. The agreed upon strategies of the Act were a five-year time limit on support to any family, strict penalties for noncompliance with any regulation of the new law, and work requirements.

In fact, the Welfare Act ended the sixty-year-old federal guarantee of cash assistance for the nation's poorest, including children, a last vestige of New Deal legislation. By April 1999, particular concern had developed about the loss of health insurance by the working poor, people formerly on welfare who had been covered by Medicaid as a part of their welfare provision and who, under the Welfare Act, frequently lose eligibility for Medicaid once they are employed. According to Robert Pear, this development is an unintended consequence of the Welfare Act (Pear, "Poor Workers Lose Medicaid Coverage Despite Eligibility," *New York Times*, 4 April 1999). Not mandated by federal legislation, it is a result of state-based regulations for welfare reform. This as yet unanswered concern is a consequence of disparities in the administration of federal funds from state to state and general slippage in the transition from older welfare provisions to the Welfare Act.

It was reported that this damage is severest among children, who are eleven million of the roughly forty-four million of uninsured Americans. In the twelve states with the most uninsured children, "health coverage losses have canceled out many of the gains made earlier through the Clinton Administration's Children's Health Insurance Program" (*Boston Globe*, 21 October 1999). In New York, Mayor Rudolph Giuliani announced in October 1999 a plan to require all adults in homeless shelters to work unless they are evaluated and found physiologically disabled. Parents who did not comply faced removal of their children to foster homes.

Citizens favoring these revisions in our social welfare legislation, Conservative Republicans and many Centrists, are largely motivated by Americans' traditional faith in the morality of work. They believe that earlier welfare provisions had allowed dependents of government to become ever costlier burdens upon taxpayers, contributing neither to the economy, nor to society. By contrast, the Welfare Act not only requires claimants for assistance to work but, at least in theory, may help enable them to do so.

Not surprisingly, the Welfare Act has passionate opponents, usually Liberals. Some are concerned that insufficient reliable data will lead to unrealistic projections of the legislation's impact on poor families, understating its deleterious human effects. They worry that states may be tempted to remove many persons unable to work from the eligibility rolls. Furthermore, they argue that assuring provision for the disadvantaged is a responsibility of a just national society, not of states only, and a main purpose of its government.

Opponents also make the structural argument that goes to the heart of issues surrounding Conservatives' shift of power and responsibility from federal to state governments in this as in other aspects of government. In particular, they believe that income redistribution programs under any guise, for any purpose, should be conceived and managed at the federal level or through close federal/state coordination of intent and implementation, to assure fairness to all citizens (Peterson 1995, 186–195).

However, vast differences among states in the implementation of the Welfare Act are being reported. States are awash in money many don't know how to spend. Meanwhile, since the states themselves, not the federal government, are setting forms and levels of support for the needy, inequities of service and opportunity feared by Liberals and by many Centrists abound. Wisconsin, a leader in advocating the shift from federal- to state-based responsibility for administering social provision in the United States, has reduced the number of its claimants for public support by more than 80 percent. It has strengthened benefits for those who remain eligible. However, it has had enough federal antipoverty money to "shift more than $100 million into a tax cut for the decidedly non-poor" (Jason DeParle, "Leftover Money," *New York Times*, 29 August 1999).

As this piece also reported: "The states slowest to spend [federally supplied] anti-poverty dollars include some of the neediest" (ibid.). In Mississippi, for example, the nation's second poorest state had spent less than two-thirds of the federal antipoverty dollars available to it as of August 1999. State records did not distinguish "between $14 million spent to raise welfare payments (now $170 a month for a family of three) and $35 million spent on new computers for Mississippi officials" (ibid.). Many states have dramatically reduced their numbers of welfare claimants and simply stockpiled their antipoverty funds for the proverbial rainy day.

It is impossible to assess how many needs are going unmet, as states have accepted requirements of the Act to reduce welfare costs and now insist they must save federal dollars to be prepared for economic recession or to direct them to other purposes that may or may not address needs of the poor. Moreover, it seems likely that, given unspent dollars, the Conservative Republican-led Congress will continue to reduce welfare funding, as it did in the 1999 *Omnibus Appropriations Bill.* This, in turn, will very likely lead to a "spend it or lose it" approach in the use of available federal dollars. Ill-considered state-based welfare expenditures to retain the money (and thus the chaotic, disparate results in social provision that many Liberals abhor) and outright misappropriation of federal dollars, as states use the funds to sponsor pet projects at the local level are probable. Peter Edelman, former under secretary of health and human services in the Clinton administration and an outspoken critic of the Welfare Act, argues that, at the very least, the legislation must be amended to respond to citizens' demonstrated needs, even if, as seems likely, its basic tenets remain in place for some time to come.

As the political scientist Richard P. Nathan suggests, the changes being effected by the Welfare Act go significantly beyond our usual pattern of cyclic shifts in the distribution of government and government funds. Removing so much of the safety net from federal government responsibility for the needy was a momentous move, signaling a far-reaching and difficult to reverse Conservative Republican-led redefinition of the purposes of the central government. It is at best a "great experiment," which concerned Americans are watching carefully (Nathan 1995, 50).

Post-1994 Conservative successes in actions such as the *Unfunded Mandates Reform Act* and the Welfare Act did not draw support for the Conservative Republican cause in the 1998 midterm election. Speaker Gingrich, the Conservative architect of Republican failure in the election, consequently lost his leadership position and resigned. But, although the 1998 elections were a disappointment for congressional Conservative Republicans, state elections extended the party's domination of the nation's governorships, a powerful expression of developing political support for their intention to devolve more policy decisions to the states.

Voters' alienation from excessive political partisanship and especially from Conservative Republican efforts to oust President Clinton in 1998–1999 mandated a more moderately Conservative presentation of the Republican agenda in Election 2000. Nevertheless, there is no reason to believe that the agenda, especially the Conservative plan for reorganizing government, will be more moderate. Liberals and moderates of both parties will need to reassert actively the vision of balanced federalism and the responsibilities of the national government.

THE SUPREME COURT AND
FEDERAL/STATE RELATIONS

Concurring with the Conservative agenda of the Reagan administration, Chief Justice of the Supreme Court William Rehnquist has worked steadily since President Reagan appointed him in 1986 to enforce redistribution of federal government in favor of the states.

A 1992 Supreme Court decision in *New York v. United States* (488 U.S. 1041) cited the Tenth Amendment to the Constitution in affirming the right of states to strike down a federal law. In deciding in favor of the states in this challenge to federal authority, the Court ruled that the federal government could not force states to be responsible for the removal of low-level radioactive waste generated within their borders. This decision was wisely regarded by close observers of the Court as signaling the Court's willingness to review other cases challenging the powers of federal government.

Prior to this decision, the Tenth Amendment had not been used by the Court for many years to contravene earlier Court decisions that assumed a legitimate federal jurisdiction in matters affecting the nation as a whole. Rather, decisions supporting the legitimacy of federal jurisdiction had been supported by the Court's broad interpretation of federal responsibilities under interstate commerce law. Referring in the decision on *New York v. United States* to the Constitution as a dividing power "among sovereigns," Justice Sandra Day O'Connor wrote that the federal government could not "commandeer" the states "into the service of federal regulatory purposes."

In 1996, in *United States v. Lopez* (514 U.S. 549) the Court ruled for the first time in sixty years that Congress had exceeded its authority under the so-called Commerce Clause when it made carrying a gun within one thousand feet of a school a federal crime. This controversial ruling also has the potentially far-reaching consequences for federal/state powers foreseen since 1992. As the Supreme Court reporter Linda Greenhouse wrote, federal jurisdiction under the Commerce Clause has gradually expanded to become an "umbrella law," encompassing "much of modern legislation" (Greenhouse, "Justices Curb Federal Power to Subject States to Lawsuits," *New York Times*, 28 March 1996) in such sensitive areas as affirmative action, civil rights, environmental protection, and public safety.[1] The Supreme Court's willingness to reverse earlier assumptions about federal jurisdiction indicates the vulnerability to the reversal of most social legislation in the second half of the twentieth century. This would mean that states, not the federal government, would be empowered and responsible to decide whether to establish laws in these areas.

Writing for the Court in *Lopez*, Chief Justice Rehnquist emphasized the fact that to support the government's case that carrying firearms near a school should be considered a federal offense, the Court would have had to conclude the absolute impossibility of distinguishing "what is truly national and what is truly local. . . . This," he declared firmly, "we are unwilling to do."

Also in 1996, a Rehnquist Court decision reinterpreted the Eleventh Amendment. In 1795, the Eleventh Amendment grew out of states' fears that they might be sued for Revolutionary War debts. It prohibits suits against a state by other states, and also by citizens against their own state except under very special circumstances. The Court's decision in the 1996 case, *Seminole Tribe v. Florida* (517 U.S. 44) was that the Seminole Tribe, whose rights are protected by federal statutes governing Indian affairs, could not sue the state of Florida to gain its compliance with federal laws regulating gambling on their reservations. It thus called into question the authority of Congress to guarantee that citizens (the Seminoles) can defend federally guaranteed rights in federal court.

Since then, in June 1999, the Court rendered three decisions many believe reconfigured the federal/state balance of power. In decisions that seem to indicate the direction of future Rehnquist Court action where federal/state powers are at issue, it determined in *Alden v. Maine* (119 S. Ct. 2240) that states are immune from suits by state employees for violations of federal labor law; and in *College Savings Bank v. Florida* (119. Ct. 2219) that states are immune from suits by patent owners for infringement of patents by state universities and agencies, and by people alleging unfair competition from states' activities in the marketplace.

The first of these decisions effectively disrupts vital state/federal cooperation in federal law enforcement, leaving enforcement of federal labor law, for example, to individual federal agencies. It was followed in January 2000 by the Court's decision in *Kimel v. Florida Board of Regents* (98-791) that state workers cannot sue a state for discrimination under federal law requiring non-discrimination on the basis of age. Late in the term ended 28 June 2000, in *United States v. Morrison* (99-5), the Court struck down the damages provision of the federal *Violence Against Women Act*, thereby denying suits in federal court by victims of crimes "motivated by gender." These rulings give greater weight to constitutional protection of the states against suits, and diminish people's entitlements to rights established by congressional legislation (Greenhouse, "States Are Given New Legal Shield by Supreme Court," and "The High Court Rules, America Changes" *New York Times*, 24 June 1999 and 2 July 2000).

Conservative supporters of the Supreme Court and other federal courts' rulings in these cases welcome the new constraints that will keep the federal government from interfering in matters they consider appropriate to exclusive jurisdiction by states or by other local bodies. Opponents worry that protections for national initiatives and standards esssential to the spirit of the Constitution and to the people's well-being are being eliminated in favor of individual states' powers to decide. At greatest risk from Conservative courts as we write are civil rights and affirmative action regulations, won for nonwhites and women during the Civil Rights movement of the '60s and '70s, and federally mandated environmental protection laws.

CONCLUDING THOUGHTS

Today, many Liberal and Centrist observers call attention to significant parallels between characteristics of our era and the converging factors that gave rise to the Progressive movement as the twentieth century began: income disparity; a perception that a Conservative government favors the wealthy and Big Business; and widespread feelings of mistrust and alienation from government. Today's Progressives, recalling the peak of government responsiveness and political action in the New Deal, see in these similarities hope for new citizen advocacy on behalf of a strong federal government. They envision a federal government collaborating with the states and the private sector, not competing with them; and a return to a mutually reinforcing federalist government, coordinating policy to safeguard opportunity for all in our dynamic and globally interconnected society.

And, indeed, advocacy for a second Progressivist era in American politics seems to be gaining momentum. Recently, a Progressive Caucus, attempting to respond to ideologically driven Conservative Republicans, emerged in Congress. Comprised of moderate Democrats and Republicans, the caucus seeks to make common cause with mainstream America, proposing, for example, the elimination of corporate tax loopholes and subsidies, deeper cuts in defense spending (actively opposed by the Clinton administration, as well as by Conservative Republicans), and increased resources to support education, still seen as the indispensable source of opportunity for most Americans. The Progressive Caucus may also be a hopeful sign as a bipartisan effort sympathetic to pragmatic, Centrist approaches to governing.

In his book *They Only Look Dead: Why Progressives Will Dominate the Next Political Era*, the journalist E. J. Dionne Jr., argues that, far from proving the futility of politics, as many allege, the twentieth century in its entirety might yet emerge as a "history of the triumph of democratic politics" (Dionne 1996, 312). For Dionne, America's most urgent problem is not excessive government, nor has the nation run out of the economic and technical inventiveness that has time and again advanced national prosperity. The real peril we face, says Dionne, is "decay in the sort of *social and political* inventiveness and organization" that empowered ordinary citizens, created widely shared prosperity, and undergirded a strong democracy. What the nation desperately needs now, he argues, is "a new engagement with democratic reform" (312–313). We concur and find the "organization" needed to regain "social and political inventiveness" present and awaiting rediscovery: in bipartisan reconsideration of federalist government as envisioned by the Framers.

Other proponents of a reborn Progressivism or Liberalism also have particular goals in mind. They call for new, government-based measures to address the specific social needs of people who cannot help themselves. The truly disadvantaged, they argue, lack the means to compete for jobs in a high-tech society and access to even the most basic opportunities for self-reliance. In *The Bridge Over the Racial Divide*, the sociologist William Julius Wilson argues throughout for "affirmative opportunity," an approach to assistance for the needy that would avoid the current taint of quota systems. Absent education, reasonable health care, and the opportunity to work, these Americans have little prospect of becoming contributors to society. Wilson is convinced that with the necessary public assistance, which, he concedes, would undoubtedly consume a disproportionate share of the nation's resources in the short term, they would ultimately become able to return value to the nation's coffers. Wilson and many who think along similar lines are calling for public works programs and training in the tradition of the New Deal.

We agree with Derek Bok, former president of Harvard University, who wrote in *The State of the Nation* that Americans must rely on a strong activist government to overcome barriers that will otherwise keep our country from moving ahead. Comparing recent social progress in the United States in such vital areas as overall prosperity, quality of life, personal security, and social values with achievements in other developed nations, he finds, not surprisingly, that we do very well in areas depending on individual initiative and competition, but significantly less well when the need is for cooperation among private and public sectors and when outcomes cannot be quantified in market terms. Strong at "ingenious solutions," Americans founder when it comes to expanding them to make an impact nationwide, partly because our systems offer no discernible inducements or models that encourage public and private agencies to share information and to learn from each other.

We believe that achieving this kind of collaboration is a responsibility of government and that success in achieving such collaboration is a reflection of government's quality. It is a major factor in determining Americans' ability to achieve the social progress that has always been part of the American Dream. As Bok writes, when President Reagan declared that "government is the problem in the United States," he failed to see that "government must also be the solution" (424). Bok calls on citizens to insist upon and to craft a government with the strength to lead us beyond our current dilemmas and divisiveness. That government must perpetuate the balanced distribution of responsibility and power between federal government and the states envisioned in the Constitution, together with imaginative collaboration between government and the private sector.

Inevitably, the relative optimism of such liberally inclined visions of American possibilities as these are countered by gloomier predictions. These contend the impossibility of a grassroots movement such as the United States saw at the turn of the previous century, and we call for here, given current bitter divisions: deeply conflicted political ideologies, racial antagonisms, white middle-class resentment of affirmative action and welfare, and a fully mobilized Christian fundamentalism. They suggest that, in these days of intractable political partisanship and single-issue politics, those speaking for Progressive causes will have to be content with relatively modest local gains in specific problem areas like the environment, education, and the most egregious disparities in wealth and income.

Perhaps so, but it would be foolish, indeed, for citizens to succumb to premature faintheartedness or to failure of will, even in the face of alienating political conflict in government. We are, indeed, at one more fork in the contentious, evolutionary road to full realization of democratic government in the United States. In November 1998 and again in the March 1999 primaries the people registered their hope of an Election 2000 that would be centered on issues, not on scandal or ideological zealotry, an election that would be responsive to their visions and needs. Now we must insist upon thoughtful, bipartisan approaches to government at every level. In this possibility may also lie the opportunity for rediscovering the essential principles and organization that the Constitution spells out for American democratic federalism.

Part II

Government,
the Economy, and Citizens

There was a time when the limitation of governmental power meant increasing liberty for the people. In the present day, the limitation of governmental power, of governmental action, means the enslavement of the people by the great corporations.

—Theodore Roosevelt

Chapter 5

What's at Stake?

The final measure of an economy is the well-being of the people.
—Adam Smith

In modern capitalism, government is a major factor in the economic system. More and more, we make *our history, rather than just waiting for it to happen.*
—Robert Heilbroner and Lester Thurow

The business of America is business.
—Calvin Coolidge

Most Americans would say that the primary responsibility of government is to keep the nation safe by protecting it against war, aggression, and terrorism. With only slightly more reflection, we'd be likely to add the roles of government in also protecting us against economic disaster. But beyond preventing disaster, government's intentions and actions in the economy have almost limitless consequences for the kind of nation Americans are and aspire to be.

As we saw in Part I, the "American Dream" has always embraced opportunities for everyone's economic advancement. It is one of Americans' most deeply held beliefs that, by our resourcefulness and hard work, most of us can achieve a good life for ourselves and for our families. Yet, translating the dream into reality is not, and never has been, a simple matter. The Framers of our Constitution knew it would not be, that inequities of property and income would immediately develop among citizens, in fact, that they had already done so by 1787. After all, people's inherent talents were unequal. The realities of these material differences would, however, be an incipient cause of danger to the Republic. Nevertheless, in creating what they thought would be an environment generally favorable to business and to individual opportunity, the Framers provided few specifics about government's relation to the economy. Later legislative actions, some of them subsequently repealed, provided more specific rules for the ways in which government might act to strengthen both the economy and individuals' access to success.

Questions about the roles and purposes of government in the economy have always been and continue to be at the center of political debate in the United States. Because so much is at stake for us, individually and collectively, citizens need to understand how and how fully government participates in the economy. What are its roles and purposes? What might they be, ideally?

Not surprisingly, those entrenched in politically partisan positions respond very differently to these questions. Believing, as we've seen, that government is often a barrier to creative problem-solving by competent citizens, Conservative Republicans generally seek a minimum of government participation in, and regulation of, the economy. As a matter of economic principle, not just preference, they also seek a minimum of taxation, in order to retain control of resources in the private sector. They prefer to see the laws of supply and demand, not government, provide discipline for both businesses and individuals.

For Republican Conservatives, unfettered competition is the force likely to provide the fairest, most lucrative opportunity for everyone. Usually, they are loath to enforce antitrust legislation designed to protect small businesses. Many would say that there are few public services that would not be better and more efficiently performed under competitive private ownership than by government: mail service is a good example, the administration of prisons another. The question of government's role in protecting service to passengers in now deregulated airlines is yet a different debate: Conservative Republicans believe there is no responsibility in this sphere that markets will not handle best. Although some are more moderate in their outlook and support a somewhat greater role for government oversight in the economy, a tendency deeply imbedded in our two-party political system usually impels them to cling to dominant partisan positions.

Clinging to ideological, often partisan views of their own, Liberals argue that in economic matters, as in many other aspects of our public life,

Americans need their federal government today as never before. They point to overarching policy issues too complex to be dealt with piecemeal: tax policies; the imperatives of controlling inflation; dramatic inequities in the distribution of income and wealth; quality of life and work issues, such as health care, provision for children and the elderly, education, and environmental protection, and the complexities of the global marketplace. And Liberals usually support activist antitrust action in the Justice Department.

Issues of this magnitude, Liberals hold, can be addressed only by government, whose concerns extend to all citizens, and whose responsibilities include the wise investment of public capital in workers and in their opportunities, for the public good. Deeply distrustful of unrestrained corporate greed, they favor legislation and regulation to redress what they see as destructive and unfair economic disequilibrium in our society. Often, they call specifically for government to protect individuals who, for whatever reasons, do not compete successfully in the workplace. Government assistance may come through fair employment statutes, including affirmative action programs; or through job training or social welfare programs funded by taxpayers at national and state levels. Liberals often distrust private initiatives to provide needed social services; they want to assure equity of quality and access for all who require assistance.

In simplest terms, in contrast to Conservative Republicans' positions, the entrenched Liberal argument sees an activist national government as necessary to provide leadership and oversight to assure both individuals' access to the American Dream and wise direction for economic policy questions that affect everyone.

Between these opposing positions, Clinton Centrists, together with moderates and pragmatists from both parties and many Independents, wanted to reduce partisan conflict, diminish antigovernmentalism, and create new syntheses about government's responsibilities in the economy, as in other aspects of national life. Under Clinton, government was the active partner of business and, many Liberals thought, was guilty of excessive capitalism. At the same time, as we'll see, it was active in protecting consumer interests and in advocating support for workers.

Questions about the roles of government in the economy are difficult. The stakes are as high as they can be. Americans' vigilance and active participation in shaping the economic purposes and strategies of their government are critical. So is their support of a balanced, federalist government that can protect the economic security and opportunities of all Americans.

Chapter 6

Hands-Off (Mostly)

THE FOUNDATION: *WEALTH OF NATIONS* AND *THE CONSTITUTION OF THE UNITED STATES*

Americans' expectations that they would prosper were fundamental from the arrival of the earliest settlers. More than a century and a half later, in the months when constitutional democracy was being invented, Thomas Jefferson's declaration of each citizen's rights, not only to life and liberty, but also to "the pursuit of happiness," included most prominently the opportunity to acquire wealth and property. Americans expected then, as now, that government would protect both opportunity and the gains opportunity yielded. As we noted in Part I, it was the British philosopher John Locke who, in the seventeenth century, declared individual property ownership an individual right, and protection of individual property an important government responsibility.

Was it destiny or happenstance that 1776, the year of Americans' Declaration of Independence, also gave the world a new vision of government's purposes in an economy regulated for the most part by the laws of supply and demand? In his *Wealth of Nations* Adam Smith, a Scottish professor often hailed as the Father of Capitalism, also set forth certain limited but essential responsibilities for capitalist government: maintaining defense against foreign enemies; providing for law, order, and the administration of justice (to include the granting of patents and copyrights and enactment of tariff protections to infant industries); and protecting citizens against dangers to commerce.

Smith also believed that not everything people needed to prosper could or should be left to the marketplace: capitalists—investors, themselves—were likely to run amok. Often overlooked in his laissez-faire proposals calling for a minimum of government regulation in business is Smith's insistence upon related responsibilities of government in a capitalist society: to create "public institutions" and "public works" which, "though in the highest degree advantageous to a great society, are, however, of such a nature, that the profit could never repay to any individual or small number of individuals," the expense involved (Smith 1937, 681). Because these components of society are essential to the well-being of the people, including the strength of the economy, but are not, in the usual sense "profitable," said Smith, they must be provided by government. No one should expect to rely upon private enterprises that require profit as a direct result of investment to supply the "public institutions" or "public works" that a great society would need to perpetuate itself.

The economists Robert Heilbroner and Lester Thurow emphasize the extraordinary impact of Smith's work on American and world development when they write: "It is not easy to say which document is of greater historic importance. The Declaration sounded a new call for society dedicated to 'Life, Liberty, and the pursuit of Happiness.' The *Wealth* explained how such a society worked" (Heilbroner and Thurow 1994, 27).

As we saw in Part I, the always-impassioned colonial debates about the distribution of powers between state governments and the new national government from the beginning were at their most fervent when the issues were economic. With thirteen states accustomed to thinking of themselves as separate sovereignties, that balance tilted heavily toward individual states in the Articles of Confederation. However, it was soon apparent that such decentralization was costly and impractical, leaving the new Republic hampered in developing coherent trade and foreign policies and deeply in debt.

The Constitution corrected the articles' most significant weaknesses by its provisions for a stronger central government, but with a few notable exceptions, left unanswered many questions about the government's role in the economy. Smith's influence on the document is clear: in general, government should do no harm, but assure the fundamental order without which no economy can function: national defense, the administration of justice, and support to public works and institutions that are fundamental to successful commerce (Smith 1937, part 5, chap. 3). The Framers gave their contemporaries a blueprint for the conduct of democratic government, not a prescription. Citizens in each generation would decide what the government might at any point actually do on their behalf, especially in relation to the economy.

However, the Constitution makes clear that the federal government, acting through Congress, not the states, would be responsible in the following economic areas: regulating trade with foreign countries and Indian tribes; assuring uniform national policies for such matters as bankruptcies, patents, and the production and valuation of a national currency; and using its powers of taxation to support the work of the government, assure national solvency, and gain advantages for businesses in import and export. It stipulates further that Congress will institute no measures in the "Regulation of Commerce" favoring one state over any other.

Clearly, regarding government's purposes in the economy, the idea was to maintain what we now call a "business environment" that would give each state and its citizens a stable, equitable, and relatively unregulated context in which to prosper. In fact, however, our government's role in the economy, has always been important. For all our talk about a "free economy," ours has always been mixed, with limited regulation usually, but not always directed toward the creation and support of partnerships between government and the private sector. Guidance for such initiatives has been provided by federal officials whose ideas about what to do with the economy have over time produced dramatically varying and not necessarily fair results.

EARLY CONTROVERSY: THE NATIONAL BANKS AND THE AMERICAN SYSTEM

At the close of the Revolutionary War, the nation faced an immediate financial crisis in deciding how to retire its huge war debt. (With a single exception, every president since George Washington has also faced the formidable, frustrating task of deficit reduction or elimination.) How would we eliminate the federal deficit and pay for government services? This was already one of the most urgent, hotly debated issues as Americans originated the Republic and set about shaping its government. We've seen that, under the Articles of Confederation, with the states essentially sovereign, the national government, such as it was, could not enact policies without the express support of at least nine states. Perhaps most important, the federal government could not tax the states, even to pay for the war, without their individual consent, which usually was not forthcoming.

This period in American history is important here because it illustrates the protracted difficulty Americans experienced in their early efforts to govern themselves and in learning to think nationally, not only locally. It illustrates the essential functions of a strong federal government, a case that has required remaking, as now, at relatively frequent intervals in Americans' political experience. Delegates to the Constitutional Convention quickly saw that a radical reconceptualizing of our government was needed, with special attention being devoted to the economics of the nation, including its significant war debt. But dealing with the debt was only the tip of the iceberg, as Treasury Secretary Alexander Hamilton was quick to state. It was vital to think now also of government's roles in the economy. We saw in Part I that Hamilton's "Report on the Public Credit" recommended the highly controversial creation of a national bank. The bank would assume the states' financial obligations and sell bonds to retire them.

This was, indeed, a brilliant strategy to address the country's debt problem, but to Hamilton a United States bank was critical to his other plans for the economy, as well. It would lend strength to the still fragile federal government, in part by creating an unprecedented alliance between the government and the country's wealthiest men. The latter would purchase the bank's bonds and, in return, the government's trade and tax policies would favor their interests. Together, they would work as allies to develop thriving commercial enterprises both at home and abroad. Capitalism would be born in the United States at last, with the government in a position to help envision and to support the development of American businesses.

In these plans, we see the birth of mutually reinforcing government/business partnerships that have continued to be fundamental and controversial in the nation's economic development throughout our history. But, then as now, there was no lack of serious objections to such partnerships between private entrepreneurs and government. Didn't the bank contradict the widely shared assumption that government was to keep a hands-off relationship to the economy? Wasn't the newly reconceived democracy, pledged to protect everyone's "pursuit of happiness," unduly favoring business and the rich? There was concern, too, that the bank and its attendant financial policies were setting fundamentally new economic directions for the nation: the bank seemed to support the acquisition of wealth by speculation, as well as by marketing products and services for sale, rather than for use.

In sum, the First National Bank appeared to many to represent the federal government's commitment to business enterprises at the expense of most citizens, farmers still, and to exacerbate the peril of excessive income gaps among Americans generally. States' Rightists who had known only the Articles of Confederation, were, in any case, bitterly offended by the expansion of federal power and campaigned in vain to arrest these developments The First National Bank nevertheless continued its controversial existence for two decades, from its chartering in 1791 to the charter's expiration in 1811.

But the debate did not end then. Only a few years later, in 1816, two enormously ambitious members of Congress, John C. Calhoun and Henry Clay, succeeded in winning congressional approval for a Second National Bank of the United States. Like its predecessor, the Second Bank was jointly owned by the government and by private sector interests. Its powers were even greater than the First Bank's: as the fiscal agent of the Treasury Department, its notes were the national currency, over which it thus had control. Suspicion that private interests were manipulating the nation's finances for their own ends was widespread. The national bank and its actions were again a focus of ongoing controversy and clashing convictions about appropriate roles for government in the economy.

Matters came to a head during the serious financial panic of 1819. Threatened with collapse, the Second National Bank managed to survive, but only by permitting the failure of many state banks and businesses: it called in loans and refused to extend credit. The legacy of suspicion that this "betrayal" created, haunted American politics throughout the presidency of Andrew Jackson (1828–1836), who was its fiercest antagonist. Jackson believed that the Bank extended privileges to the wealthy, rather than workers and ordinary Americans. He finally brought the Second National Bank down near the end of his term by depositing federal funds in state and local banks, a strategy that yielded failures of coordination many believed caused the serious financial panic of 1837.

There followed several decades of uncertainty about the roles of banks and of government, federal, state, and local, in controlling them. Significant financial panics occurred in the nineteenth century, both before and after the Civil War. Various U.S. Treasury and national banking systems were tried, especially in the years 1863–1913. None of these, however, was a central banking system such as the one finally created in 1914 under Woodrow Wilson: the Federal Reserve System.

As early as the administrations of Presidents Madison and Monroe, another interesting, ultimately unsuccessful, economic initiative occurred. Building on the Second Bank, and, like the Bank, a brainchild of Sen. Henry Clay, a proposal called the "American System" tested whether Americans would support specific government regulation of the economy. Clay's idea was to unite all sections of the nation in a union of economic interest embracing agriculture, industry, and commerce. The cornerstone of his vision was a protective tariff—that is, a federal tax on imports competing with American businesses—which Congress approved in 1816. Thus united and protected against competition by import taxes, American industries would expand until they could furnish all of the manufactured goods the country needed; and farmers, assured of a home market for their produce, would no longer be dependent on exports. The United States would, in effect, be self-supporting and would not need to rely on foreign-based commerce of any kind. Guidance and financial support to this protected American economy would be provided by the Second National Bank of the United States.

Although Clay continued to fight for the idea of the American System up to his death in 1852, no attempt to implement it was ever made. The immediate cause of the plan's failure was that the South, claiming states' rights, refused to accept federally mandated trade restrictions. But the American System was probably doomed from the start. Americans, it turns out, almost always resist the idea of increasing government regulation when the economy is strong. In the heady years following the War of 1812, America was not in the mood for increased government intervention in the economy, much less its control. The country was high on unfettered free enterprise and capitalist opportunities, the air abuzz with ideas much closer to Smith's laissez-faire prescription for economic policy.

Chapter 7

Abiding Issues for Government in a 'Free' Economy

PROTECTING BUSINESS

Questions about whether and how government should protect or otherwise regulate business in the United States have never been more controversial than they are now. This is true, in part, because, in pragmatically supporting aspects of both Liberal and Conservative agendas, a Centrist Clinton administration often paradoxically generated new conflicts. These conflicts frequently included the charge from both sides that the president was simply without any principles that he was willing to defend consistently.

Under "Clinton the Liberal," for instance, we saw a strengthened Justice Department charged to become significantly more active than in recent Republican administrations in the pursuit of antitrust cases. These efforts were designed to protect small businesses and individual entrepreneurs against mergers or business practices that would thwart competition. In a period of proposed and actual corporate mergers that helped to fuel almost unparalleled rates of growth in corporate profit, the Clinton administration investigated and/or brought to trial antimonopoly cases involving industries as varied as telecommunications, banking and related financial services, insurance, automobile manufacturing, retail sales, and network computing. Its case against Microsoft was touted as the most important antitrust case since the government forced John D. Rockefeller's Standard Oil to break apart under Teddy Roosevelt's protégé, William Howard Taft, in 1911.

In addition, at both state and federal levels, the Clinton administration led federal and state governments to bring suits against tobacco companies that resulted in significant regulation of tobacco companies' business practices and multibillion dollar settlements to the states, to assist with the costs of health care for smokers and other expenses to be decided by the states. Perhaps the most significant failure of domestic policy-making in the 1990s, the Clinton national health insurance plan was defeated, as it had been in at least two earlier administrations, by lobbies against it mounted by the American Medical Association, private insurance and the pharmaceutical companies, and small businesses, all supported in Congress by Conservative Republicans. In these efforts and in others affecting the perceived freedoms of private business enterprise, a Republican-led Congress, supported by powerful private lobbies and funding, opposed such government "intervention" in the economy.

On the other hand, also in an effort to protect U.S. business opportunity, the president joined forces with this same Republican-led Congress to support corporate America in developing the global economy. The president and Congress worked together to eliminate annual deficit spending by the federal government (whatever one may think of the budget strategies agreed upon). This action was essential to economic growth as we saw it in the Clinton years, in part because it liberated public and private funds from rising interest payments on the national debt, for investment in the economy. Clinton's commitment early in his first term to eliminate annual deficit spending by the government also strengthened the confidence of international investors in U.S markets: American businesses quickly became not only more solvent, but also more profitable and more productive than in recent decades.

Republican Conservatives also joined their Centrist president by supporting renewal of so-called fast track negotiating authority for the president in creating international trade agreements to reduce or eliminate trade barriers between the United States and other nations. This authority was blocked by members of the president's own party, who said he was not concerned enough about American workers or environmental protection. By contrast, the president supported fellow Democrats who voted to reduce Conservative Republicans' use of economic sanctions (as unfairly penalizing business interests at home and abroad) against governments whose political or other activities appeared to warrant U.S. opposition. He also stood fast with fellow Democrats against Republican Conservatives' persistent calls for tax reductions, insisting that the first priority for the use of discretionary resources must be extending funding for Social Security and support to Medicare. In this debate, the president's pragmatic, Centrist instincts were vividly captured when he then once again resisted his own party and called for partial investment of federal funds for Social Security in the stock market, long a priority of Conservative Republicans.

On the whole, government's protection of business interests, especially the interests of "Big Business," is closer to the Conservative Republican agenda than to that of Liberals. Moreover, Republican Conservatives typically focus upon government's protection of opportunity for success through individual initiative and reward in the private sector. To this end, they advocate among many other activities at home and abroad, government investment in basic research too expensive for business to undertake alone; tax advantages and monetary policies that support new product development and small businesses; and tax policies that protect corporate and personal profit when success occurs. If appropriate, Republicans argue, privately held dollars will find their way into social programs through private initiatives and philanthropy.

By contrast, Liberals, usually Democrats, see government's role as contributing to both private and public welfare when an activist government protects American consumers, including their jobs, usually from business itself. As we'll see in the remainder of Part II and in Part III, the forms of consumer and job protection Liberals advocate extend into many areas of potential consumer exploitation by business interests and, beyond these, to job protection for American workers in a global economy. To this end, Liberals support government-sponsored educational and job-training programs, among many other initiatives.

With these important differences in mind, we may say that both Conservative Republicans and Liberals see protectionist roles and responsibilities for an activist government in the economy. How have Americans' ideas about the responsibilities of government to protect both business and consumer interests evolved? Is this history relevant today?

The American protectionist tradition in government was launched as early as Washington's administration, when Treasury Secretary Hamilton imposed a federal tariff on imported goods until American manufacturing could take hold after the Revolutionary War. (Not surprisingly, Jefferson and Madison initially opposed this step, as they had the National Bank, as inappropriate and excessive power-wielding by central government.) Since then, proposals favoring or objecting to many forms of economic protectionism have been at issue in virtually every American administration.

For example, debate has almost always surrounded the question of whether tariffs, import taxes, are genuinely helpful and, if so, helpful to whom and for how long. The *McKinley Tariff* (1890), written by Progressive movement leader Robert La Follette to protect farmers, was a high point of economic protectionism in the nineteenth century. Many such tariffs have been imposed since then and dropped. In the twentieth century, perhaps the most egregious was the *Hawley-Smoot Tariff Act* of 1930, signed by President Hoover over the vigorous protests of economists. This tariff, created to protect farmers and industries in the Great Depression, was levied on all imported goods and materials. It aroused such deep resentment abroad that, within two years, twenty-five countries had established retaliatory tariffs against U.S. goods and products. These developments aggravated the Great Depression in the United States and created economic hardships in Europe that many believe ultimately helped give rise to World War II. More about this topic in Part III.

In the last half of the twentieth century protective tariffs have been much less widely used. Today, by wide agreement, they are largely out of favor, though the Clinton administration decided inexplicably in 1999 to threaten their use in Europe (over bananas) and in Japan (over the alleged dumping of Japanese steel into the American marketplace, suppressing prices and causing worker layoffs). Today, the U.S. government seeks, or claims to seek, open markets and competition, worldwide, as the path of economic development, not only for the United States but for other countries that American business leaders envision as trading partners. In the Clinton administration, government protection of U.S. business interests was seen to reside primarily in its support of a global economy and, through it, world political, economic, and monetary stability.

We should note that government's general rejection of tariff-based protectionism, as in the Clinton administration, was also explicit early in this century under President Woodrow Wilson (1913–1921). Prior to World War I, seeking to strengthen competition in American business, Wilson limited protective tariffs and opened American markets more fully to international trade. Protective but not "protectionist" in his assumptions, he was also certain that our advanced technologies promised advantages in a broader market. In language very like Clinton's and that of other global market proponents today (including sponsors of recently approved international agreements such as a new General Agreement on Trade and Tariffs

[GATT] instituted in 1997, and the North Atlantic Free Trade Association [NAFTA]), Wilson sought both to gain advantages for American consumers and to develop international commerce in open markets that the United States would surely lead.

As it turned out, Wilson's economic vision was never realized, because the outbreak of World War I dashed prospects for world trade. After the war, America had had enough of Europe. The nation's retreat into traditional political unilateralism was accompanied by a tragic revival of economic protectionism as a cherished priority of people and government. Economic historians agree that, by 1935, still mired in the Great Depression brought on in part by misplaced U.S. economic protectionism, Americans looked to the rest of the world much as Japan appeared in the '80s and early '90s: we seemed to be a paragon of economic nationalism whose ill-conceived domestic self-interests nearly paralyzed global trade and caused widespread economic collapse everywhere.

Not until a decade later, after the government reenvisioned and redirected America's economic and political policies abroad toward supporting the European economies and societies shattered by World War II, were the consequences of our extreme protectionism and the mistrust it had caused in the 1920s and 1930s at least partly overcome. The Marshall Plan, an elaborate system of economic and political partnerships, was the most successful of our post-World War II efforts: in partnership with all of the countries involved, we rebuilt Europe's economies and infrastructure; helped to assure ourselves and other nations of viable trading partners; enabled nations that might otherwise have allied themselves with, or been co-opted by, communism and the political agenda of an aggressive and developing USSR, to remain on the free side of the Iron Curtain. (In Part III, we will revisit the Marshall Plan in context of the development of close relationships between American economic and foreign policy in the post-World War II era. After 1945, our government invented new, complementary roles and purposes for itself in both the world economy and in global political leadership.)

Of course, there are, and always have been, many strategies in addition to trade policies that the government can use to protect and support business. Among these are several forms of direct financial payments, which make clearer, perhaps, than any other strategies we have mentioned that Americans' accustomed language about their "free" economy perpetuates a myth. Government provides both direct subsidies and tax credits to corporations engaging in research and development judged to be important to the further development of the economy. It sometimes rescues individual enterprises from failure, as in the controversial bail out of the Chrysler Corporation in the early 1980s, the strategies employed to rescue depositors' dollars after the failure of savings and loan associations in the Reagan and Bush presidencies in the 1980s and early 1990s, or the government-engineered protection of Long-Term Capital Management, a "hedge fund," in 1998.

Government is also a major purchaser of private sector goods and services, both to support its own operations and to assist other consumers through the income transfer programs it administers, that is, through welfare and health care support to the poor and disabled. In exercising its powers of eminent domain, which it did as early as the colonial period, government may appropriate land and other natural resources, assigning them to private businesses engaged in such enterprises as building railroads, canals, and bridges, all judged important to the economy and in the public interest.

Government support to business also includes reliable management of the money supply, that is, of both interest rates and liquidity, by its central bank, the Federal Reserve Bank; specific aid to small business development; and maintaining a strong and reliable currency through oversight of the economy and skillful debt management. These responsibilities of government in the U.S. economy are essential to economic performance. "Private" enterprise depends upon a strong and vigilant government in order to do business. Americans are thus well advised to think further about the difficulty in drawing pure distinctions between "private" and "public" economic enterprise in the United States today, as Conservative Republicans would have us do. And we must further consider the dangers to the economy in Conservative Republican antigovernmentalism: businesses, workers, indeed, all Americans require a strong, vigilant government to protect individuals and the economy.

An illustrative case in point: In October 1998 and again in 1999, the Conservative Republican-led U.S. Congress declined to consider President Clinton's proposal for a so-called Patient's Bill Of Rights. It would have given citizens rights of legal appeal about their health care in privately owned Health Management Organizations (HMOs). Failure to win a Patient's Bill of Rights came about, as was widely reported, because of the fierce political battle among Conservative Republicans, Liberals, and Clinton Centrists over the roles of government in so important a private enterprise as health care.

PROTECTING CONSUMERS

Government's regulatory functions, including the enforcement of antimonopoly and fair business practice legislation as directed by the Justice Department, are also about protecting citizens, consumers in this context, from business. These functions are performed through agencies of the federal government, in the 1990s under more or less constant attack by the Conservative Republican-led Congress. For example, a Consumer Protection Agency requires fair disclosure and admission of product liability. The Federal Food and Drug Administration requires independent scientific verification of claims and testing of drugs, sanitation standards in the preparation of all consumables sold in the United States, and truth in advertising. The Environmental Protection Agency guards against pollution and against other misuse of natural resources that for-profit interests are historically likely to cause.

Oversight of fair hiring and labor practices is administered by the Commerce Department and stipulated by a large body of Labor Relations law. At state and national levels, government regulations require that, based upon the number of employees, businesses must provide not only Social Security benefits, but also access to health insurance and unemployment assistance.

Americans' history with these kinds of protections for consumers against business is essentially a product of the twentieth century. They were hard won and came first in the antitrust reform and new legislation demanded by the Liberal Progressive movement at the turn of the century, which insisted that government restore needed balance in its roles and purposes in the economy. It must be concerned about consumers, as well as about supporting business interests.

Driving the development of antitrust legislation, beginning with the *Sherman Anti-Trust Act of 1890*, was a claim upon government protection by consumers who had seen their opportunities to participate in the economy blocked by large corporations with the power to dominate and control markets. At least in law, if not always in reality, antitrust legislation, usually passed in periods of comprehensive social reform, responds to this claim and to other effects of proposed business mergers: its concerns are to legitimize promised corporate efficiency and to assure the likelihood that consumers will benefit through anticipated corporate cost benefits. Antitrust legislation also protects the values of competition by preventing anyone from having a monopoly, that is, sole control, in the production of an essential product that could be used to gain profits from American citizens that would not be available in a competitive situation.

How was it that at the beginning of the twentieth century a government as generally business friendly as ours came to move in a direction so opposed to its usual priorities? In the hectic post-Civil War era American businesses had surged as never before. Leaders of industry whose names are synonymous with American fortune-building, names such as Rockefeller, Morgan, and Harriman, amassed unheard-of power and wealth. They were able to rout competition, control access to capital as well as prices, and exploit consumers. With the pendulum swinging so far in one direction, ordinary people felt abandoned by the government. Inflamed by muckraking journalists and bitterly resentful of the provocative excesses of a Gilded Age that excluded them, Americans blamed unregulated capital for most of the corruption in public life and sought redress.

We saw in Part I how Americans' urgent demands for reform were first recognized by activist intervention at the level of state government, with Robert La Follette's Populist agenda in Wisconsin leading the way. Refusing to accept a role for government subservient to that of business and industrial leaders, Theodore Roosevelt (1901–1909) subsequently used the powers of the presidency and the federal government specifically to enforce the public interest against corporate trusts. The most important of the antitrust cases won during his administration was the suit brought in 1902 against the Northern Securities Company, a railroad holding company put together by an alliance of capitalists including Morgan and Rockefeller. The intent was to curb the corporation's monopolistic excesses, reinvigorate competition, and reduce costs to benefit the public. In this case, the government under TR attacked the very citadel of U.S. finance, capitalism, and corporate business.

Following the victory against the Northern Securities Company in 1904, the *Sherman Anti-Trust Act* was used vigorously for the next seven years against some of the nation's greatest industrial organizations: U.S. Steel, Standard Oil, and more than thirty other industrial combinations were ordered into court. Size alone was not, in TR's view, an evil; rather, it was the effects of "Big Business" upon the public interest that mattered to him. Most basic was his demand for government regulation of industry. He was the first U.S. president to envision the federal government as an umpire, upholding the public interest in the conflicts among "Big Business," big labor, and the consumer. In these convictions, TR had an unusual impact upon the evolution of Americans' thinking about the roles and responsibilities of government, especially in the economy.

TR set essential precedents for the activism of fellow Progressive Woodrow Wilson, who defeated him (and Taft) in 1912. Also riding the tide of Progressive reform, Wilson acted immediately to protect consumers from corporate domination in several important ways, among them working variously to stimulate competition that would help to lower prices to consumers, and signing the *Clayton Anti-Trust Act*, which prevented government from interfering in labor disputes unless irreparable damage to national welfare was threatened and also proclaimed that strikes and boycotts were not violations of federal law.

In the aggregate, our government's interventions to control "Big Business" in the early years of this century, whether achieved by judicial decisions or by legislative antitrust actions, permanently changed the parameters of the U.S. economy. Consumers are better protected now than they were at the close of the nineteenth century. But it is also true that government's record in actual antitrust enforcement has been sporadic at best, though more consistent in Democratic than in Republican administrations. Elected officials contemplating antitrust actions inevitably lose political support from one side or the other: from corporate leaders on one hand, or from consumer advocacy groups on the other.

All too often the resolution of these conflicting interests reflects an ugly half secret of our democracy: it is easier to overlook the concerns of those who are most vulnerable economically, who lack an effective, well-financed political organization to exert pressure on their behalf. In the absence of principled government intervention, reforms giving priority to ordinary consumers rather than business interests face an uphill battle. Because of Conservative Republicans' primary alliances with "Big Business" and their emphasis upon protecting its interests, government under their leadership is usually reluctant to launch antitrust prosecution and to maintain active enforcement.

Today, Conservative economists argue that the need for antitrust interventions by government has virtually disappeared in a developing global economy so huge and far-flung that it is almost impossible to gain a monopoly in the production and sale of any essential good. Liberals are more likely to see excessive power among huge transglobal corporations, products of an unprecedented spate of international corporate mergers and industry consolidations, which, unchecked by government, will mean virtual control of goods and services in an unregulated, increasingly uncompetitive private sector.

Meanwhile, many Americans are uneasy, increasingly aware that now, more than ever, we need our government to assure sound policies and accountability in the rapidly changing world of globally interdependent business, banking, and securities exchanges. When activists disrupted the World Trade Organization meetings in Seattle in 1999, the crucial roles of government oversight in protecting consumers by protecting their jobs, and by helping to maintain a level playing field for workers were at issue. Many Americans worry that a pervasive public preoccupation with corporate profits imperils even government's power to help ordinary Americans and threatens its integrity. They argue that government must assert the case for consumers, as it did a century ago.

THE WEALTHY AND EVERYBODY ELSE

An economically unjustified, socially dangerous, historically unprecedented and morally unacceptable income gap has opened up between the wealthy few and the worried many . . . and politicians of both parties ignore it at their peril.

—Edward Kennedy

As we write, ours is the strongest economy in the nation's history and the envy of the world; yet the gap between those at the top of our economic ladder and the other 95 percent or so of Americans has widened dramatically in the last quarter-century. Will our economic successes eventually include all, or even many, Americans, as some observers insist? Or will income and wealth disparities, always a national problem, become even wider? Should government intervene? How?

Current concerns about these disparities are hardly new. As the United States was being reorganized under the Constitution, the Framers considered excessive disparity in income and wealth the most obvious threat to U.S. stability and prospects. Madison and Jefferson, in particular, foresaw that even if all citizens were equal under the law, differences of talent and fortune among us would surely lead to unequal distribution of wealth, a disparity inevitably putting the nation at risk. They were convinced that only as property holders with reasonable prospects, that is, with a stake in the system, would citizens accept responsibility for the nation's values and well-being. With the possible exception of Hamilton, no one thought that the government could be blind to this problem, or justify favoring the wealthy over the poor, as had been done in England.

Robert Coram, a contemporary of the Framers with views rather like Jefferson's, quoted a Yorkshire physician in his harsh indictment of a society that lets the poverty of some of its people go unchecked, while others prosper: "Poverty makes mankind unnatural in their affections and behavior. The child secretly wishes the death of the parent, the parent thinks his chidren an incumbrance and has sometimes robbed their bellies to fill his own . . . and the most scandalous practices are often the effects of . . . poverty" (Konig 1995, 191).

Indeed, we have a long history of turning to our government in this context, proposing intervention strategies and policies that might remedy ills. In 1781, the American economist Samuel Blodgett wrote that in order to help the government address disparities of wealth, "the rich must accept a sufficient tax on their income." Jefferson, writing to Madison in 1785, suggested that "one means of silently lessening the inequality of property is to exempt all from taxation below a certain point, and to tax the higher portions of property in geometrical progression as they rise." Noah Webster supported the equal division of inherited property by doing away with the practice of primogeniture. He hoped this change in the law, to which he assigned greater importance than even to the Magna Carta, or the protections afforded by a free press and habeas corpus, would keep interrelated powerful families from dominating less-privileged citizens, as they did in England: "Let the people have property and they will have power," he said (Konig 1995, 191–196).

And now? Despite a strong economy that saw unemployment fall in 1999 to its lowest levels in thirty years and virtually remain there, an almost imperceptible rate of inflation, and a continuing rise in the number of wealthy Americans, some citizens are understandably reluctant to affirm that all is well, economically.

Until recently, rates of annual growth in the income of most Americans were nevertheless continuing a twenty-five-year pattern of decline in purchasing power. Indeed, a 1999 study by the Economic Policy Institute in Washington showed that, despite the historic economic expansion of the 1990s, middle-class workers were only slightly better off than they were ten years earlier: "At $44,468, the annual median income of the American family (using late 1999 data) was less than $300 above 1989 levels (Bernstein et al. 1999). In a still expanding economy, these figures were adjusted upward in January 2000 to $46,737 (Louis Uchitelle, "107 Months and Counting," *New York Times*, 3 January 2000). Americans at the top of the salary and wealth pyramid have gained prosperity in this expansion beyond anyone's expectations. Nevertheless, most Americans' experience of the touted '90s economy has "not been as good as the 60's and no better than the 70's and 80's in inflation adjusted output" (Louis Uchitelle, "A Clearer View of the Economy," *New York Times*, 29 October 1999).

Similar 1999 findings were published by the Center on Budget and Policy Priorities (CBPP), a Progressivist center for economic analysis, using data provided by the nonpartisan congressional Budget Office. As reported by Thomas Oliphant (*Boston Globe*, 7 September 1999), the CBPP showed that, since 1977, "the average household income for the least well-off fifth of the American public, after taxes and inflation, has gone down by nearly ten percent. For the middle fifth, it has increased 8 percent, or a half percent per year." Meanwhile, as of 1995, the last year for which complete figures were available from the Federal Reserve, "the top twenty percent of households, while receiving more than half the after-tax income, were also holding eighty-four percent of the wealth, meaning stock portfolios and home equity."

Income gaps between rich and poor in America are "as wide as they have ever been in our statistically recorded history," the CBPP reported. Significantly, the growing income and wealth gap between the rich and everyone else in America is being exacerbated especially by the effects of tax cuts that benefit the wealthy: For the top 1 percent of households, the average tax cut since 1977 is worth more than $40,000. This is $9,000 above the entire after-tax *income* for the average household in the middle fifth of the population spectrum today. Put differently, according to the CBPP in 1999, income disparity will mean "the best-off 1 percent will have as much after tax income as the bottom 38 percent combined; 2.7 million people will have the same combined income as 100 million people. The rise in income at the top will exceed the total income of the bottom 20 percent of Americans."

In March 1999, Reuters News Service reported that, at retirement, Americans who do not own their homes retire with an average $800 in savings. Homeowners average only $115,000 in retirement savings. Not surprisingly, as consumer spending continues to exceed earnings in the United States, the typical married couple with children now works a full six weeks longer than they did in 1989 (Bernstein et al. 1999). Some interpret these developments to signify primarily that the economy is, after all, producing jobs and that "consumer confidence" is high.

There are other concerns, as well: Many sociologists and economists fear for the future of jobs in America, wondering what kinds of employment will be available in an increasingly technologized world, especially for those lacking the skills to function in the so-called New Economy. Recent studies establish a high positive correlation between citizen optimism and levels of education, with college graduates far more assured of their futures than less privileged contemporaries. Moreover, in the late '90s, several developments intensified the plight of laid-off, inadequately prepared, or otherwise unemployable workers: the political precariousness of Social Security provisions; the failure of prospects for government-sponsored national health insurance; and disparate, state-based applications of the *Welfare Act* of 1996, which removed the expectation of federal government assistance beyond a specified time period from even the neediest citizens and from many noncitizen immigrants. Under these circumstances, what lies ahead for the hardcore unemployed, whose prospects seem to be increasingly hopeless?

Nowhere in this study of the responsibilities of government is the current, remorseless, partisan confrontation between Liberals and Conservatives more dramatic than in the debate about government's role in addressing extreme income and wealth disparity and the needs of disadvantaged citizens, including actually and potentially displaced workers. Since Conservative Republicans gained control of Congress in 1994, emphasis upon government investment in citizens' well-being has been largely replaced by their advocacy of:

- diminished government participation in social policy, including health care and civil rights;
- local-, or state-based, rather than uniform, equitable federal supervision of social provision for citizens and immigrants as expressed in the 1996 *Welfare Act*;
- tax reform to serve the wealthy (as in 1998 capital gains tax reductions), while those at the lower end of society see dramatic cutbacks in government support.

In favoring business interests, and in their opposition to activist government, Conservative Republicans, often joined in new legislation by a Centrist president, dismantled government provisions through which the welfare of the people has usually been addressed in our society. They both reduced federal responsibility in favor of the states and shifted social investment largely from a public to a private concern. Private dollars, not public funds, they argued, should, wherever possible, support needed investment in human resources. They charged government programs with undermining the dignity of the poor and interfering with private charitable giving. Under fire were minimum wage laws, restrictions on advertising, licensing of the professions, and zoning laws.

Since 1994, the Conservative Republican-led Congress has also attempted, unsuccessfully thus far, to starve or eliminate several federal agencies and offices with responsibility for quality of life issues in the nation: the Food and Drug Administration, the Occupational Safety and Health Administration, the Environmental Protection Agency, the Department of Education, and the Antitrust unit of the U.S. Department of Justice, among others. Americans have seen specific efforts to weaken clean air and water standards and to remove or weaken controls on pesticides and other forms of environmental pollution. We've also seen active congressional opposition to Justice Department antitrust cases, such as former house speaker Gingrich's public call for an end to the department's investigation of Microsoft in late 1998.

Of course, it is not that Conservative Republicans wish to perpetuate poverty or injustice. Yet, favoring a relatively insignificant role for government in most aspects of public life, they prefer to interpret even dramatic gaps in income and wealth as an inevitable outcome of a competitive process they view favorably. To the extent that they recognize these disparities as a danger to society, or as morally unjustifiable in American democracy, they find solutions in work and self-help. Rarely, if at all, they contend, should such matters become public policy questions or anticipate any other form of government intervention in the marketplace.

Liberals, Centrists, and moderates of both parties, some of whom refer to themselves nowadays as neo-Progressives, are likely to contend that our democratic society is seriously endangered unless an activist government, working collaboratively at every level, protects citizens' opportunities to succeed. They advocate government assistance through public investment in critically important public institutions like public schools, health care, housing, and environmental protection. They point to the immediate harm caused by need, failure, and hopelessness: crime, disillusionment, and dependency, human costs that alone make a more than persuasive case for government investment.

But their concerns extend beyond individual, or even group, misery. They see our government and our society paying dearly, in the long and short run, for social policy failures that perpetuate poverty and the division of society into "haves" and "have-nots." Far more serious than the direct costs of crime and of last-ditch measures to address human need, they contend, are the virtually incalculable long-term costs of our failing to develop America's social capital, that is, the talents of our people, upon whom the survival of our way of life will ultimately depend.

Between these two positions stood Clinton and the Centrists, who, at their best, argued for the "third way," the discovery of a middle ground. Buffeted by criticism from both Liberals and Conservative Republicans in this as in most other policy debates, they sought especially to meet a clear need among children, the elderly, and the poor. With little discretionary funding to apply until 1999, in some instances, they called for revenue-sharing strategies between the states and federal government. Elsewhere, they drew upon socially concerned corporations and citizens who brought to bear the resources of the private sector. Such collaboration persists, though with unsatisfactory results thus far, in diverse problem areas such as welfare, including food and housing for the poor; health care; and improvements in public education. It has been more successful in public/private scientific research designed to drive U.S. leadership in technologies, communication, and medicine.

Centrists, most Liberals, and many moderates are likely to know the work of the Progressive philosopher Herbert Croly, who argued in his landmark book, *The Promise of American Life* (1909) that the democracy the Founders envisioned for America was not necessarily limited to what a powerful central government could achieve, indispensable though its leadership and coordinative functions would be to national progress. State and local government and the private sector would also be needed: Only through their active creativity and collaboration with each other and the central government, would the ideals of a federalist, national government be most fully achieved.

The rock bottom conviction of these groups also echoes Jefferson, Madison, and such Progressive leaders as the Roosevelts: Acting through the federalist organization of an activist national government, Americans may bring their considerable power to bear upon the needs of ordinary citizens. This aim (which is progovernment, not antigovernment, as Conservative Republicans would have it) requires leadership and funding, if necessary through programs of enhanced income redistribution, that is, through taxes or reallocation of existing dollars to support public/private sector investment in people. To this end, Liberals and Centrists today are likely to heed

Croly's warning: "If the National Promise fails, it will be because confidence in freedom alone has resulted in a morally and socially undesirable distribution of wealth . . . in the prodigious concentration of wealth, and of the power exercised by wealth, in the hands of a few men" (Croly 1909, 23).

A final note: By tradition in America, Liberal government at every level has invested in the development of our social capital, in the knowledge, skills, and physical well-being of ordinary citizens. Conservative Republican government in America has usually, as now, been much less willing to do so, seeing these issues as matters for individual or private sector redress. When social capital is high, citizens have the education, health care, and opportunity to develop the relational skills and strategies essential to the perpetuation of a democratic society and a strong economy. Social institutions are then self-organizing and self-correcting, maintaining an environment of reasonable public trust that permits our economic and political organizations to flourish. Whereas high social capital fosters creative problem solving and innovation in all aspects of public life, including the economy, extreme, persistent disparities in income, wealth, and opportunity, unalleviated by public policies, do just the opposite. By barring many citizens from economic and social participation in our democracy, these disparities deprive society of their talents.

As Americans consider how best to correct or prevent extreme economic inequities in our democracy and support policies that will strengthen social and economic development, what specific measures seem promising? The Harvard sociologist and Clinton advisor William Julius Wilson has written widely about the high cost to the nation of systemic poverty in our inner cities and about the development of a "permanent underclass." Wilson calls for action in four policy areas, all requiring the kinds of collaboration between federal and state government and the private sector that are consistent with our federalist organization:

- Creating local and national standards in education to make sure that all young people have the opportunity to succeed;

- Improving child care by developing facilities for infants and children of working parents and income support to families with dependent children, as needed, as well as medical care for all children who require it;

- Shaping city-suburban partnerships, funded in part by restored federal support to cities, to prevent further deterioration of inner cities and to create jobs accessible to inner city residents; and, most controversially,

- Reintroducing a federal Works Progress Administration, like President Franklin Roosevelt's in 1935, both to provide jobs and to accomplish needed improvements in such public services as roads, bridges, and recreational facilities. (Wilson, "Work," *New York Times Magazine*, 18 August 1996)

Wilson's Liberal recommendations are more far-reaching than most, but many Centrists and moderates of both parties agree that citizens dare not leave matters as important as these to voluntary, private sector initiatives, as Conservatives Republicans believe. In their view as in ours, Americans need to insist on activist government leadership to assure broadly based creativity in the coordination of policy development that supports everyone's opportunities to learn and work.

In July 2000 President Clinton estimated a federal government funding surplus of $1.3 trillion over the next ten years. Liberals and moderates of both parties wondered under what circumstances, if ever, a Congress bitterly divided along partisan lines, as now, could be brought to consider the well-being and prospects of Americans who are not participants in the nation's prosperity and not likely to be.

Chapter 8

Your Money:
How Does Government Spend It?

There is never enough money to do it all. That's as true for government at all levels, regional, state, and federal, as it is for families. It is therefore very important to track government's choices about spending: what is being expended, by whom, and for what purposes. Nowhere are the divisive partisan ideologies that plague government today clearer than in the emphases that Republican Conservatives on one hand and Liberal Democrats on the other bring to the management of our money. President Clinton's Centrist agenda in budget-building, as in other aspects of governing, displeased both parties much of the time. Nor did he achieve the coordinated budget development among federal and state governments envisioned by the Founders for our Federalist government, and for so much that is needed in the nation now.

GOVERNMENT SPENDING AS
A PROPORTION OF GNP

As its name suggests, the GNP (Gross National Product) is the annual measure of national output: the value of all goods and services produced by the United States each year, including those produced outside the country, an increasingly important component to assess. Although not a comprehensive barometer of national economic performance, the GNP's direction tells us how things are going in the economy: a rising GNP is good, a falling one less so.

According to calculations issued by the government's Bureau of Economic Analysis in December 1998, measured in market prices, the GNP had grown dramatically over the previous five years. Its greatest percentage annual rate of increase was projected to have come in 1998: an estimated 7.42 percent, bringing the anticipated value of the GNP in 1998 to more than one and a half trillion dollars. If we exclude the negative net impact of goods and services produced outside the country, to calculate the Gross Domestic Product (GDP) only, the value in 1998 was projected to be even higher (Larkin et al. 1998).[1]

The GNP also provides one means for Americans to assess, at least in general terms, the extent of government spending in the economy. Along with consumer spending and business investment, government is now one of the three domestic sectors of our economy. Its purchases (largely at state and local levels) are the second largest element of the GNP, after consumer spending, and comprise about one-fifth of GNP total value.

What does the government purchase with all those dollars? To even begin to answer that question, we need information that the GNP does not give us, and herein lies a problem that more Americans should know about: The GNP's account of government spending of its tax-generated income does not differentiate between expenditures for consumption and expenditures for investment, a distinction always made in calculating private, nongovernment, spending. Thus, for example, we are able to determine the proportion of income a business invests for further growth (always of interest to investors), and to see what kinds of investments for further growth are being made, but we are powerless do so when it comes to the federal government (Heilbroner and Thurow 1994, 78–85).

Seeing only a lump sum representing all government expenditures, Americans have no ready way to ascertain how the government actually uses taxpayers' money: What does it buy? To what extent are our dollars being invested in the public interest? Where and by whom? Lacking ready access to such information, we are not well equipped to assess government spending for the public good.

A second characteristic of the GNP, the exclusion of government payments made as social provision, is another barrier to our clear thinking about government's actual expenditures. These so-called transfer payments are excluded because they are unrelated to any kind of production: the dollars are seen as transferred from some Americans to others, not spent. But because the rise in such transfers largely accounts for much of the increase in government spending as a component of the GNP since 1929, increases vociferously deplored by fiscal Conservatives, the omission is important. Its significance is truly striking when we realize that, with this single exception, the money that government releases into the economy has remained an almost stable proportion of the GNP for the past quarter-century. Government's main expenditures during those years? Federal support to defense and, at state levels, to education and roads.

SPENDING YOUR MONEY

We have seen that in *The Wealth of Nations* (1776), Adam Smith emphasized that government's responsibilities in a capitalist society include investing in essential "public institutions" and "public works," investments that no one else can be counted upon to make because they are not, in market terms, profitable. Americans have embraced this concept of federal support to public institutions over the years, though with varying levels of intensity and results. As we've seen, Liberals, usually Democrats, have typically supported policies and programs to provide public assistance, and Conservatives, usually Republicans, have been much less willing to do so. On the whole, however, as Liberals and Progressives emphasize, Americans have been more reluctant than the citizens of any other developed country to direct federal government spending for public works or public institutions, even as support to economic development, broadly defined.

Partisan divisiveness on this issue was more virulent than ever as the Clinton administration began to campaign for its relatively Liberal social objectives in the last budget it would propose to the Republican Congress. For example, noting in early 1999 that the nation's welfare rolls had declined to a thirty-year low in the wake of the 1996 Welfare Act, the president sought $730 million in new spending for job training, housing vouchers, and transportation for workers from urban areas to the suburbs, where jobs are more prevalent. He also sought $1.3 billion over five years to restore health and disability benefits and food stamps for legal immigrants, who had lost these provisions in the 1996 welfare overhaul. Republican Conservatives insisted throughout the budget process that government must not abandon welfare reform and once again begin "throwing money at social problems."

Federal government investment in public services since the 1980s has diminished as a component of the GNP and today includes primarily the obvious: roads (a major component of the projected 1999 budget);

education (though highly decentralized); public safety (thousands of additional police officers were hired in Clinton's second term); communications and technology systems; Social Security; basic health care for the poor and elderly; and applied research deemed too expensive for the private sector to support alone. As Clinton's presidency approached its end, defense spending was planned to increase at a greater rate than at any period since the Gulf War.

In all of this spending, as well as in the expense of supporting needed services to the people, Americans will generally look in vain for evidence of federal government efforts to coordinate with state and local governments both policy development and spending to support agreed upon priorities. As an element of rational, Federalist planning, such coordination is particularly important, as we look ahead. Efforts by the federal government both to avoid annual deficit spending and to meet budgetary obligations may mean that, as under Clinton, the federal government will have relatively little discretionary money to spend. The Clinton Treasury Department's "buy back" of government debt in the form of high interest bonds, initated in 2000, is planned to provide discretionary dollars for the future. But absent the capacity to agree or compromise about reallocation of support to carefully established priorities, and without federal and states' collaborative budget planning, resource limitations may continue to cripple the work many Americans believe government should perform.

Members of Congress remain locked in adversarial ideologies, first about whether federal government should support enterprises such as those we've cited, and if so, how and to what extent. In 1998–1999 the president and most congressional Democrats insisted that projected government surpluses remain unspent until strategies could be devised to bolster the Social Security system. Republican Conservatives, caught by a politically popular argument they could not successfully refute and to which they reluctantly acceded, nevertheless made no secret of their preference to cut taxes. Virtually universal aversion to tax increases (assumed to be unpopular with voters) or to politically difficult reallocation of funds to Social Security from existing programs prevailed. In the end, the budget debate brought little change from the agenda of a Congress dominated by Conservatives inclined to reduce, not strengthen, government's direct investment in people and in the economy.

What are the issues and options for Americans, as we consider future government spending in relation to purposeful support to the economy and citizens?

With the passage of the Republican Conservative-led federal Welfare Act in 1996, Congress set a course which, unamended, will continue to decrease federal aid to the needy and to legal immigrants. Moreover, beyond the five-year "bridge" funding they provided to states, Conservative Republicans have no stated plan for federal/state collaboration on policy development or funding to meet the need for social provision, or for any other related need, in the future. Their interest in federal/state collaboration, the Republican Platform in Election 2000 notwithstanding, has been limited to little more than discussion of "Federalist accountability" legislation that insists that the federal government must not intrude upon or obstruct states' rights to create and support their own social policies.

However, a serious disconnection between the Conservative Republican-led reductions of federal government responsibility and the agenda of many Americans revealed itself dramatically in the 1998 midterm election. Despite the Conservative Republican agenda, Americans list a number of policy issues they wish federal government to address on behalf of ordinary Americans. For most, these include providing universal health care, improving the public school system, protecting the environment, and developing strategies to support care-giving for both children and elderly, a matter of special concern to women. With no plan to respond to concerns such as these, Conservative Republicans lost in 1998 what had seemed to be a certain opportunity to gain important political momentum leading up to the election in the year 2000.

Another issue of increasing concern to many Americans is the absence of coherent immigration and immigrant policy, the topic of Part IV in this study. Legal immigrants, by tradition the lifeblood of American enterprise and hope for the future, were for the first time largely removed in 1996 from eligibility for federally supported public assistance. In a move that perpetuated the nation's traditional lack of coordinated federal and state policy development on behalf of immigrants, Conservatives in Congress required in legislation accompanying the 1996 Welfare Act that each state now differentiate among legal immigrants and American citizens, an unprecedented distinction, and arrange to provide only such support to immigrants (an ever larger proportion of the U.S. population) as each sees fit to offer. Obviously, problems, national problems, lurk in the inequities in support that are emerging among the states. Nevertheless, in March 2000 the U.S. Supreme Court predictably refused to hear an appeal to this legislation, an appeal that, significantly, was not supported by the Clinton administration.

Americans have persisted in expressing their desire for programs that can come only from activist, coordinated national government, focused upon supporting citizens and enabling everyone to prosper in a strong economy. In the present antigovernment, Conservative Republican drive to see the social responsibility of federal government diminished, that is, to deny federal—*Federalist*—government support to the peoples' agenda, ordinary Americans stand to lose.

Chapter 9

FDR's New Deal and the Fortunes of Capitalism Reconsidered

Pursuing Adam Smith's doctrine of capitalism based on enlightened self-interest, many Americans have accepted as an article of faith that, since everyone is similarly motivated to aim for economic advancement, everyone will understand the motives of everyone else, and all will ultimately be well. Yet this assumption has never ruled unchallenged. Time and again Americans have reexamined the concept of self-interest, and in so doing confronted ethical precepts and values that placed such responsibilities as care giving and social justice on a plane at least equal to that of strengthening the economy as an end in itself.

In matters of economic policy, the Clinton administration usually explained its "third way" as an effort to reconcile support to local governments and to the private sector with the social conscience of American Liberal tradition. Favoring Republican Conservative fiscal policies that limited federal government spending as fully as possible, it nevertheless called upon both the private and public sectors to mount socially progressive programs, responding to peoples' need for public institutions. Under Clinton, the federal government was comfortable with highly decentralized approaches. In its effort to appease the antigovernmentalism of Conservative Republicans, however, it often went too far in its willingness to relinquish federal responsibility for the socially advantageous programs and outcomes it advocated. In this respect in particular, the Clinton era recalled an earlier era of this century when the conflict between Americans' capitalist and humanitarian ideals was engaged, with a different responsibility envisioned for national government: the period of FDR's New Deal.

In the desperate 1930s, the Great Depression radically transformed Americans' ideas about the responsibilities of government and the directions, as well as extent, of needed government intervention in the economy. The result was the most activist period for government in the nation's history. This economic and social activism, largely abandoned as the nation entered World War II and only partially brought back in the 1960s, grew out of New Deal debate and legislation led by President Roosevelt.

Roosevelt added more than any of his predecessors to the by then largely established potential for centralizing government leadership, especially in times of crisis. Yet, facing desperate circumstances, he also saw the wisdom of Madison and the Framers' belief that federal and state governments could, and indeed must, work together to forge a truly national government. Employing bipartisan political leadership and seeking creativity also from private citizens, both before and during World War II, his administration utilized existing state programs wherever possible, inventing and coordinating collaborative federal/state policies that united the nation in achieving social relief and support to the war effort. Under FDR's New Deal administration, Americans transformed the nation's economic structures and processes. Here's what they accomplished:

- They strengthened the Federal Reserve System, created under Woodrow Wilson in 1913, to strengthen government regulation of the banks; created the Federal Deposit Insurance Corporation to protect citizens against loss of bank deposits; and took steps to regulate the stock market through the Federal Trade Commission and the *Securities Exchange Act*, all to help avoid new market collapse and economic depression such as the nation was experiencing when Roosevelt came to office.

- They developed and implemented under the *National Industrial Recovery Act* the most comprehensive legislation the nation had ever seen on behalf of both businesspeople and workers, including price supports, to stimulate the economy through a public works program, and gained for workers, wages- and hours-protection and rights to bargain collectively.

- They awarded funds through several public relief programs to feed the hungry, employ young men whose families were on relief, provide farmers the support to renegotiate loans and householders the opportunity to refinance mortgages and complete home repairs, and grant loans to both large and small businesses.

- They supported the Works Progress Administration, which substituted direct relief with jobs, to encourage workers and enable continuing public assistance to them from 1935 to 1941.

- They established the Social Security System, which at the time provided assistance for the elderly, retirement annuities, unemployment insurance, aid for the blind or crippled, and aid to dependent children.

Of course, with this much change underway, there were excesses of feeling and action, both among those who supported and those who opposed Roosevelt and the New Deal. As early as 1934 Republican Conservative critics called for repeal of much of the legislative program. Like Conservatives today, they sought to reduce or abolish the government's role in economic and social initiatives, in favor of the states' perceived rights to decide individually whether and how extensively to support social programs. After the war, America's new economic strength enabled Republican Conservative opponents of the New Deal to argue convincingly that a national state committed to coordinated economic policy development and support to comprehensive social provision was no longer necessary.

As we saw in Part I, the political legacy of the New Deal nevertheless retained imaginative life for Democratic presidents in the second half of the century: Harry Truman, Lyndon Johnson, Jimmy Carter, and, to a lesser extent, Bill Clinton. Universal health care, for example, was a failed agenda for Truman and Clinton; both supported it in the tradition of government social support achieved in the New Deal. Johnson and Carter invoked FDR repeatedly in creating federal programs to support civil rights and fair employment practices and to wage war on systemic poverty. Republican Richard Nixon also expressed a debt to Roosevelt in the former's own effort to establish national health care, an effort many Americans have forgotten.

Political support for an activist national government fell to its lowest level in the Republican Conservative administration of President Reagan (1981–1989). Yet, the New Deal has continued to be an important component of national debate about the purposes of government, whether we've supported or opposed its effects, for more than sixty years, up to the present. Recently, in two decades of Republican Conservative ascendancy, it has in many quarters been politically unfashionable to cite the Federalist character and achievements of governing under New Deal assumptions.

Will Americans dismiss the Progressivist legacy of activist government as we knew it in the New Deal and in the Great Society? Or will we choose to explore again both an activist government and the potentials of federalism, to reestablish responsive national government? A Centrist response to questions such as these might opt, again, for Clinton's middle of the road approach, or perhaps for the "compassionate Conservatism" that George W. Bush claimed as a goal in his run for the presidency in the year 2000.

It is worth noting in any case that, although only vestiges of New Deal programs now remain, an ever larger cadre of economic historians maintains that an activist national government under the leadership of FDR succeeded in both humanitarian and economic terms. Government's active stimulation of the economy through spending for public works, including jobs and emergency financial assistance, restored the opportunities of individual Americans after policy blunders during the onset of worldwide depression caused the so-called free market to fail us. The New Deal is now believed by many to have saved American capitalism as well.

Chapter 10

The Clinton Years

What Americans need in the economic and managerial purposes and policies of the national government at any given time is a well-coordinated, comprehensive approach that fosters improved prospects for all Americans, as well as for business. Achieving balance between these two emphases, which has seemed to be an inadequate objective to both Liberals and Conservatives at various times in our history, was a primary goal of the Centrist Clinton administration. According to Lawrence Summers, secretary of the treasury in the last year of Clinton's presidency and principal advisor to former secretary Robert Rubin, success required "not the invisible hand, not the heavy hand, but the helping hand of government" (Cassidy 1998, 58).

What were the elements of this approach? How well did it succeed? The Clinton administration addressed its responsibilities in the economy most significantly by the following, interrelated policies:

- Supporting the independent Federal Reserve Bank's unwavering commitment not to permit inflation, thus protecting the value of private assets already held and avoiding the devaluation of the dollar that accompanies upward spirals of wages and prices;

- Promoting concerted efforts to rid the government of deficit spending in order to balance the budget, reduce the national debt, and protect the rating of government bonds (and thus U.S. attractiveness to business investors from here and abroad);

- Strengthening the value of the dollar in foreign currency markets through these policies, thus encouraging corporate investment and growth in global markets, which helped to curb inflation at home;

- Encouraging open markets and currency exchange, together with public accountability among business and banking around the world, to enhance business opportunity;

- Leadership, often controversial, to the International Monetary Fund and to the World Bank to gain international assistance for struggling or failed economies.

Each of these policy elements expressed choices about government's responsibilities in the economy. We'll consider briefly those policy choices that had most to do with managing the U.S. domestic economy. In chapter 11 we'll conclude with some discussion of currency management and international markets.

FIGHTING INFLATION

Why was fighting inflation such a high priority for the Clinton government and for the Federal Reserve Bank? Is it likely to remain "job one" for the Federal Reserve, as we look ahead?

Inflation refers to a spiraling increase in prices and wages that erodes the value of current assets (including fixed incomes) and permits economies to spin out of control and beyond the pale of credible investment. Until the last few years, since World War II, the United States and other Western economies had been inflation-, rather than depression-, prone for at least two reasons: first, because of heightened spending by governments, including support to consumers through Social Security and other forms of financial assistance indexed to projected increases in the cost of living, and unrelated to production; second, because of significant changes in the private business sector. Until recently, the last half of the twentieth century had rarely seen either wages or prices come down, despite technologically created efficiencies in virtually all sectors of business and manufacturing. In fact, we had rarely seen wages and prices remain even relatively stable in relation to each other. Thus, until recently, the pressure and the expectation were that both wages and prices would continue, inexorably, to rise beyond rates of increase in the GNP, thus feeding an ever present fear of spiraling inflation.

Since the nation's last experience with serious inflation, peaking in the 1970s and early 1980s during the Carter and first Reagan administrations, and brought to heel by the painful remedy of high interest rates imposed by the Federal Reserve, keeping inflation at bay has been a primary purpose of government in the economy. Its success protects the value of the dollar and of current assets, requiring business to increase profitability, always the expectation, by ever greater efficiencies or by the introduction of new products, rather than by simply raising prices, thus setting off the dreaded price-wages spiral.

Most economists have believed that full employment creates inevitably inflationary pressure on employers to raise wages in order to attract workers. They therefore believed that maintaining an unemployment rate of about 6 percent was desirable. More recently, however, the prospects of a global economy and efficiencies and productivity increases finally being realized through technological advancements, apparently mean that fuller employment than 6 percent does not necessarily mean inflationary pressure in the economy. In the last quarter of 1999 U.S. unemployment fell to 4.1 percent, the lowest level in more than thirty years, in a strong economy characterized by essentially dormant inflation.

The agency that controls interest rates and thus, ultimately, the costs of capital that business needs to expand and consumers need for large purchases, is the Federal Reserve Bank, the nation's central bank. Created in 1913 in the Wilson administration to bring order and confidence to national banking arrangements that had been in periodic turmoil for more than a century, the Bank saw its regulatory powers and options increased during the depression years of FDR's first term. Independent of the administration in place, the Bank's stated charge is to achieve a stable, moderately paced economy without dramatic increases in wages or prices. Under the leadership of Alan Greenspan, this goal has largely been met.

The Bank has a variety of tools in its arsenal of possible actions to meet its objectives. For our purposes here, it's important to know that, to protect the economy against inflation, the Federal Reserve may slow the growth of business profits by raising interest rates, making it more costly for business or consumers to borrow money. To this end, it raised interest rates six times in 1999–2000. To ward off economic decline or to reestablish market stability during turmoil, it may reduce interest rates, also a Fed action of the late 1990s, making access to needed capital easier to gain for both businesses and consumers.

Significantly, the Bank was created in recognition of the fact that central banking could not be performed in the private sector, if public confidence in its principles and stability were to be maintained. Thus, management of financial stability for the nation was understood (reluctantly, by some) to be a responsibility of government. Although the Bank is managed centrally, its board members represent all regions of the nation and advise each other about policy, based upon their close knowledge of economic conditions and concerns throughout the country. In these respects, the Federal Reserve Bank is a model of Federalist governance and provides a good example of centrally coordinated policy development and action that other agencies of government would do well to emulate.

Despite the deleterious effects of inflation for individuals and for the economy, its strict control also has its detractors, who question inflation control as an overarching goal of Federal Reserve policy or an unequivocal good. How, they ask, does the Fed's emphasis on preventing inflation look from the perspective of the majority of Americans, workers without accumulated wealth to protect against erosion?

After all, when the Federal Reserve raises interest rates to prevent inflation, everyone is affected, not just businesses. Workers, whose wages had not until recently risen in real terms for almost twenty years, have been forced to pay more for borrowed capital: to buy a house or car, send children to college, or meet interest payments on credit previously extended. Moreover, since business attempts to sustain profitability despite higher rates of interest, these same workers have been more vulnerable to loss of employment.

How certain are we that maintaining near zero rates of inflation should always be a top priority of government? Is there anything at all to say for modest inflation, which might mean greater security and ease of access to capital for workers and their families? When prices are contained in an economy where inflation is essentially nonexistent, the wealthy, whose assets are protected by low inflation, also benefit from cost containment. This means that wealthy Americans are doubly served when stamping out inflation is the Federal Reserve's chief economic policy goal. Meanwhile, isn't everything made harder for workers: the economic middle class and the poor?

The answer is "yes." However, as inflation hawks quickly and correctly point out, everyone is hurt by runaway inflation: prices rise, assets are lost, the costs of capital to business and to individuals is high, and unemployment grows. Confidence in the economy is low and investment presents unacceptable risks. With only a little imagination, however, we may identify both an anti-inflation and a pro-inflation camp among Americans. Opposed to inflation are wealthy people, whose main concern is to preserve the value—the purchasing power—of the wealth they have accumulated. Rising inflation devalues these savings. The pro-inflation camp includes those who may benefit from an economy that thrives at the cost of some inflation. Among them are wage earners counting on raises; retailers and manufacturers counting on a little inflation to help raise prices; homeowners who like to see their property values rise; and people in debt, who find that inflated wages and salaries can make their old debts easier to repay.

Some economists argued, at least until the last two years or so, that the cost of maintaining inflation below 3 percent, as in the U.S. economy in the late '90s, would outweigh any potential gain: eventually a slowed economy would encourage layoffs and drive up the unemployment rate, with all the accompanying personal and economic costs. But, as we've seen, these effects did not appear in the economy in the '90s. Rather, improved rates of worker productivity and thus of business profit, together with the global extension of American markets and investment, indicate that the economy's previous experiences of inflation may in any case be irrelevant for the foreseeable future. This will be increasingly likely if Southeast Asia and Japan emerge from recessions and resume their roles as trading partners for the U.S. economy and for the rest of the world. We look in chapter 11 at some of the dangers and uncertainties interdependent global economies pose for Americans now and at policy questions that are emerging as a result.

Meanwhile, observers concerned about the victims of our current wide disparities in income and wealth argue that the United States ought to give growth a chance for everyone now. Forestalling inflation, they insist, must be a means to wider prosperity. The real issue, often repeated, is whether policies of the government, including the Federal Reserve, will help to sustain opportunities for all American workers to find jobs and thus to share in an historic economic expansion, by now the longest Americans have known. Achieving this aim, the fullest sustainable employment, is part of the formal charge by Congress to the Federal Reserve Board.

BALANCING THE BUDGET

Passage of the *Balanced Budget Bill* that President Clinton signed in July 1997 for the following year gave politicians of all persuasions a chance to claim victory over annual deficit spending. Agreement on a spending plan that achieved budget balance gave private investors at home and abroad new confidence in both the American economy and in the government's ability to manage political and financial stability. It thus helped immeasurably to assure domestic and foreign investment in sustained U.S. economic growth.

But former Clinton labor secretary Robert Reich noted the paradoxical nature of this success with wonderment: "The fact is that a lot of the deficit solved itself. . . . It was the one solution that no one thought of" (David Sanger, "A Booming Economy Made It All Much Easier," *New York Times*, 1 May 1997). Reich meant that it was the strong economy, performing in expectation of a reduction, if not elimination, of deficit spending, and responding as well to other elements of the government's coordinated direction, which provided the opportunity to create the balanced budget plan.

In Reich's observation there is cause for citizen concern. Like the revisions mandated by the 1996 Welfare Act, the balanced budget plans submitted during Clinton's second term were made possible by a strong economy projected to remain strong. Given the bitter ideological divisions between Conservative Republicans, on one hand, and Liberals and Centrists on the other, they did not emerge from thoughtful revisions in plans for public spending. Consequently, despite Clinton's end-of-term optimism about budget surpluses as far into the future as the eye can see, with most spending priorities still in place, some economists project deficit spending will recur, perhaps as early as the year 2002.

Obviously, future budget discussions must mitigate extreme partisan conflict, whether or not the Clinton administration's projected levels of economic growth are sustained. Difficult choices about spending were set aside in 1997, 1998, and 1999, as better-than-expected earnings masked problems that still must be addressed. As we look ahead, Americans will need to insist that these choices be made, in line with the activist agenda that most have for the government at every level.

In all of the current economic euphoria, there lurks another major question: How will future budgets deal with the huge national debt accumulated over the last twenty years? As David Sanger reported, just before President Clinton signed the *Balanced Budget Bill:* "If [it] did not have to make its annual interest payments on [the national] debt, the Federal Government would have run a surplus in 1997 of $172 billion, or half the cost of paying Social Security benefits. Instead, those interest payments cost the government $247 billion, or only $220 billion less than the entire defense budget for the country" (Sanger, "A Booming Economy Made It All Much Easier," *New York Times*, 1 May 1997). In other words, unless this debt, too, can be eliminated or significantly reduced, a process begun by the Clinton administration, citizens' dollars will be spent to finance it as far into the future as the eye can see.

But on this complex topic, some food for additional thought: Although the national debt is viewed as a problem of almost incomprehensible magnitude by some, not everyone considers its elimination such an important priority. Why?

Some Americans, usually Liberals, point out that the national debt is a form of government investment in the nation and in the people. Well directed, such investment is much needed. In this view, the national debt may even resemble the kind of investment Adam Smith deemed essential for the economy. The economist Robert Heilbroner, for example, believes that we are led badly astray in our thinking about the national debt by the distinction we make between corporate debt, understood as an asset to leave to our children as bonds in a safety deposit box, and government debt, considered a burden to our children and a drag on economic growth potential.

Heilbroner and like-minded economists and policy analysts contend that *wisely acquired* government debt, like corporate debt, represents investment in people and in the economy. Such investment builds social capital, thereby fostering continuing individual and national prosperity. It is, indeed, money owed, but in this context, writes Heilbroner: "A zero national debt would constitute cause for national, perhaps international, alarm, rather than national celebration" (Silk and Silk 1996, 194).

What is certain amid the array of perspectives with regard to controlling inflation, balancing the budget, and reducing the national debt requires several "musts" and some "must nots" in the telling: The processes by which the federal government, including the Federal Reserve Bank, manages the economy must be credible so as to assure further credible public and private investment, sustaining progress and growth. Inflation must not erode assets. Debt must not grow beyond the value of assets that provide its collateral, or beyond Americans' ability to meet debt payments. But all issues must be evaluated in relation to government's purposes, which, as Adam Smith said in 1776 must assure "the well-being of the people."

Chapter 11

Government and the Global Economy: New Questions

Supported by the Conservative Republican-led Congress, the Clinton administration saw a responsibility of government in the '90s to propound the virtues of a global economy at home and abroad. The global economy Clintonites envisioned would be characterized eventually by open markets and unregulated currency exchange, worldwide. It would include all other nations, whatever their political organization, philosophies, or, it would seem, readiness to introduce capitalism.

What many Americans may not know is that, despite the opportunities that government, multinational corporations, and an increasing number of American investors see for dramatic growth in this vastly expanded marketplace, no one can predict with certainty how a global economy will actually work. The global market drop in August 1998 and the market volatility that persisted after the recovery demonstrated the complex interdependency of the international economy, the difficulty of predicting or controlling its instantaneous, unreflective behaviors, and the limited abilities of any government to respond to global economic crises in a timely fashion.

Unanswered questions abound. In *Making Capitalism Work*, Leonard and Mark Silk warned us, as though speaking only yesterday:

With the end of the Cold War, [people everywhere] confronted . . . the historically unprecedented challenge of a world of nation-states subject to a virtually all-encompassing capitalist order. How will capitalism play itself out on national, regional, and global stages? . . . A full spectrum of possibilities can be discerned: at one extreme, a world that falls back into hostile fears of nationalism and protectionism that cause the global economy to collapse; at the other, a world of increasingly close integration, vigorous economic development, cooperation for building and maintaining peace, and international cooperation to protect the natural environment. Intermediate outcomes between those extremes are more probable, with nationalism and internationalism varying according to pressures on the system and the kind of leadership nations get or fail to get. (Silk and Silk 1996, 183)

Even more pointedly, the economist Robert Heilbroner admits he is "unable to come to any trustworthy conclusion" about the nature or impact of the global economy, which he envisions as "a geographic entity without definite shape, with many economic centers but no political center, composed of national entities whose economic independence is increasingly exposed to erosion of transnational market forces." He wonders whether "world-straddling capitalism" will weaken participants' ability to deal with serious problems, such as global warming or immigration pressures, which affect many countries, regardless of a dilemma's point of origin (218 n.7). These kinds of problems, Heilbroner writes, extend beyond the merely economic and will require unprecedented participative decision making: a level of international cooperation for which nothing in the past has prepared the nations of the world. In its insistence that other nations of the world follow precisely its economic directives, the Clinton administration showed little readiness to foster the levels of cooperation needed.

In recent months, the difficulties of working through interdependent economies have emerged in U.S. dissatisfaction with essential business infrastructures, especially banking, throughout much of the world. With the introduction of the Euro dollar and a European Central Bank, some observers fear costly economic rivalries and disputes about economic policy domination among old friends. Even long-time economic allies have not escaped U.S. blame for the erratic development of the global economy (nor has the United States escaped their charges of our intent to dominate it). But banking practices in large economies such as Brazil and Japan, as well as in smaller or otherwise more fragile nations, such as Russia, have been most problematic to federal government trade and Treasury officials. They've charged that, in many nations, lending practices are erratic; unsecured loans are made excessively, sometimes at a government's behest; and banks or governments unused to being publicly accountable are reluctant to be exposed in all their fragility, error, secretiveness, and sometimes, corruption.

The result is that, when these conditions apply, economically or politically fragile nations may suddenly lose the confidence of investors around the world. Additional problems lie in the speed with which this occurs. Businesses fail. Banks fail. Currencies fail. And, where an affected nation is home to trading partners that U.S. companies had projected and profits that U.S. companies had foreseen, as for example, Thailand or Indonesia, Brazil or even Japan, the American economy is also at loss. Such financial instabilities in emerging or otherwise fragile nations produce predictable social and political turmoil. Think of Malaysia, Indonesia, and Russia, to cite only three of the most problematic at present. China, too, is increasingly vulnerable to international economic turmoil. Suddenly, national and international insecurity abound in both political and economic relationships.

Many people trying to survive unexpected economic devastation appear ready to blame their devastation upon the United States and upon its alleged or actual attempts to force them into cultural patterns and economic disciplines that nothing has prepared them to understand, cope with, or desire. At the very least, we may say that the pace of change that U.S. businesses and the government have assumed the global economy can meet, is not likely to be achievable. One has only to recall the demonstrations at the 1999 meeting of the World Trade Organization in Seattle and since then, to see that this is so. Results in the U.S.-led move toward globalization thus far indicate that Americans will need to respond more realistically to conditions beyond our or anyone else's ability to change overnight.[1]

Nevertheless, global economy enthusiasts, most Conservatives and an ever larger proportion of concerned Liberals, see increasing interdependence as inevitable, desirable, and at hand. They argue that sophisticated technologies already support worldwide management flexibility and markets, and that American business will persist in seeking the ever-greater profits that only these global markets can now deliver. Throughout much of the '90s exports accounted for about a third of U.S. economic growth (Cutter et al. 1997). As early as 1996, several major American corporations had placed more than half of their assets overseas. Indeed, even with economic instability in several of the world's leading economies today, it is in so-called emerging markets that American investors are being advised to look for greatest profit in the decade ahead.

Despite obvious problems, most observers see extraordinary promise for American business in the global economy. The economist and Yale University Business School dean Jeffrey E. Garten predicted that more than sixteen million jobs would be supported by overseas sales by the end of the year 2000 (Garten 1997, 68). Profits generated by sales abroad in the first half of 1997 vastly exceeded expectations, despite a strong dollar that drove up the price of American products purchased abroad. In 1998, profits were curtailed by economic hardship in Asia in industries such as oil and oil services, computer hardware, and financial services. But jobs producing sales abroad, especially those supported by American technology, are and are likely to be among the most lucrative being developed in the U.S. economy.

Other global market proponents doubt the value of export or foreign sales as the primary source of increased American profits over the long term. They see greater promise in our use of overseas production sites for goods to be sold in the United States and in other industrialized nations. Apparently ignoring the threat that American workers see in this development, they cite domestic problems in emerging world economies that will prevent these countries from becoming dramatically larger purchasers of American goods.

In all of this, however, the speed of change and surprise may be the most reliable constant in the developing global economy. For example, in the early '90s, Chinese officials declared their intention not to let their nation become a major importer. China would focus upon meeting most of her own needs and developing exports more fully. This strategy would enable closer government control of China's economy. By 1999, however, the Chinese worldview had changed markedly: in a development engineered by U.S. trade negotiators, China had formally begun the multiyear process of entry into the World Trade Organization. Only a few years earlier, no one would have thought a change of such magnitude possible. It is evidence of the power and speed with which the global economy is developing and further proof of Chinese leaders' changing strategies for developing their economy, including an embrace of increasingly open markets.

For some Americans, the Clinton administration's controversial negotiations with China illustrated further important progress along the road to the global economy that had been one of its objectives from the beginning. However, the agreement will be the subject of hard fought battles in the United States and within World Trade Organization member nations throughout the world. In the United States, Conservative Republicans and many Centrists are likely to support it. As in previous instances of national debate about international trade agreements, Liberals and moderates of both parties will voice concern about its effects upon American workers, and about whether it includes assurances to protect the environment and advance human rights.

The debate will illustrate again the complex, interdependence of global markets. China's huge and developing economy will increasingly be affected by uncertainties in the global marketplace, and the rest of the world by economic and political developments within China. At some point, for example, China could join other Asian nations that have devalued their currency to enhance the competitiveness of exports, a move that would give rise to economic instability in Asia and throughout the world.

Although we and all other nations are moving through uncharted economic territory, proponents of global markets insist that a rising tide of world economic productivity and exchange will result in material and social advancement for people everywhere. They do not fear global "glut," that is, that global production may exceed demand. They cite the clearly deleterious effects of protectionist policies, as in the years after World War I that led to economic depression worldwide, and conclude that the risks of open markets, allowing capital as well as goods to move freely around the world, can be reduced, if not altogether eliminated. They argue that reducing risk can be achieved by systematic international cooperation, including disclosure of economic conditions, lending practices, and debt. Perhaps. But achieving the kinds of cooperation needed will require a stronger and wiser leadership than we and the other developed nations of the world have thus far been able to bring to the issues that confront us all.

NEW DEBATE ABOUT CURRENCY QUESTIONS

The government's responsibility to manage the value of the American dollar abroad without destroying currencies or markets (ours or "theirs") is a good example of the complexities we face. And there can be no doubt that this is a matter for government, not for the private sector only.[2] For example, as chaotic global markets threatened world economies in 1998, there were calls for the Federal Reserve Bank to reduce U.S. interest rates, thereby easing financial pressures on business borrowers at home and abroad, assuring the availability of liquidity. This, of course, it did. Given problems in the economies of other nations, it set aside for the moment fears that inflation would result in the United States. Investors and businesses responded positively, worldwide, initating other measures such as loans and debt restructuring, as well. But the economic chaos of 1998 had developed principally from huge, erratic currency flows into and out of fragile, insufficiently structured economies and from widespread mistrust of banking practices among nations with very different laws, traditions, and expectations.

How to restore sustainable order in global markets at moments of such crisis remains an open and highly controversial question. The possibility of international agreements regulating currency flows, part of a "new financial architecture" being proposed in some quarters, is the subject of debate among international economists. The U.S. position is, predictably, a conservative one, perhaps best described this time as "Right of Centrist." The Clinton administration held that currency flows should not be regulated, but remain subject to the values assigned them in the open market, whatever the result in the near term for fragile currencies and nations.

Preferring to "let the market work," the United States has steadily resisted the regulation of currency flows since it was proposed during World War II at the Bretton Woods Conference in New Hampshire, during Franklin Roosevelt's term, by the brilliant British economist and finance minister John Maynard Keynes. At Bretton Woods, world leaders gathered at Roosevelt's behest to consider economic strategies that would protect recovering nations and enable them to re-create sustainable economies after the war. Keynes believed that some form of currency regulation would be necessary to protect fragile economies and encourage investment in their enterprises.

Since 1972, when the Nixon administration and Congress agreed to separate America's currency formally from the "gold standard" and from fixed exchange rates, the value of the dollar has been exclusively a matter of market perception: relative not absolute, and changing hourly in the increasingly speculative world of currency markets. In the late 1990s, the dollar was the strongest currency in the world (with the value of many other major currencies "pegged" to it), because the U.S. economy was perceived as strongest and our asset base and economic prospects as greatest. Whereas corporate executives and Conservative Republicans usually attribute the dollar's strength primarily to business leadership, Liberals are inclined to see it more broadly, as resulting in large measure from the government's coordinated economic policies just discussed. In any case, the dollar's value is subject to constant change abroad, as are all other currencies.

Under President Clinton and Treasury Secretary Robert Rubin, the U.S. government worked actively to bring about our strong position in the global currency markets. In addition, the Clinton administration tried to make sure that other nations' currency also remained strong, both to sustain their own economies and growth and to enable them to function well as U.S. trading partners and investors in our economy. In this controversial effort, usually waged through the International Monetary Fund and the World Bank, the United States was not, of course always successful, as in Southeast Asia or in Russia, for example.

The strength of any currency is primarily a result of other nations' confidence in the economy that supports it, and that confidence is usually indicated by the willingness of investors to put money into that economy. But in reality problems in nations' maintaining currency valuations that are related to economic fundamentals are even more complex. Currency speculators, those who bet for or against the rise or fall of value in particular currencies, may so influence perceptions of value that, especially in fragile economies, they actually precipitate rises or falls that have little to do with economic reality or prospects.

Just as important, because the value of many currencies in the world is now pegged to the U.S. dollar, when the value of the dollar rises in the international currency markets, the value of these currencies also rises. These values may therefore come to be seen as dangerously, unsustainably high, based upon the economies that support them. In response to this situation, and to other events that place a strain upon a currency pegged to the dollar, the Federal Reserve may add dollars to the world's money supply, usually by lowering interest rates.

This action, in turn, lowers the dollar's value against other currencies and eases financial pressures in their economies, as was done in fall 1998. Such moves will not repair a failed currency, but they may help provide the opportunity for it to regain actual and perceived strength. Obviously, though valuable in an emergency, such actions by the Federal Reserve Bank are not the answer to the world's problem of how to prevent unstable currency markets from jeopardizing the global economy. No one is sure, right now, how the global economy will affect our own or other nations' abilities to manage the flow and value of national currency.

Apart from problems related to instability, why is currency valuation important to Americans? When our currency is the world's strongest, the United States is in the extraordinarily powerful position of virtually setting borrowing and lending rates around the world. Secondly, for American business, as for American citizens, a strong currency expands the purchasing power of the dollar for foreign-produced goods and services, wherever these are actually acquired. U.S. business can establish foreign manufacturing or service sites more economically; a new Toyota or a trip abroad is more accessible for more Americans. The vulnerability of this strength and a matter for Americans to understand is, of course, that a strong dollar may cause exports to be too expensive for many in the world to buy. Largely for this reason, our "balance of payments," the ratio of value between our exports and imports, may tilt seriously out of balance in favor of imports, as we saw during the Clinton administration.

In the vastly complex, mutually interrelated, promising but uncertain context of global markets, the leadership and stabilizing processes of government will be ever more important. The antigovernmentalism propounded by Conservative Republicans simply will not suffice. It's also clear that democracies such as ours will be unable to lead in a global economy without commitments to engage both citizens and business in full and fair discussions of many difficult questions with implications for all. And such discussions must envision a truly national government, that is, they must be coordinated to include policymakers at state and local levels, as well as those in Washington. Achieving the breadth of understanding needed also requires political bipartisanship in defining the responsibilities of government in the economy: government must attend both to citizens' concerns and to business interests.

The complexity of these issues highlights the need for informed citizen vigilance. One now broadly prevalent line of argument assumes that the federal government no longer has the strength or resources to provide leadership in international affairs. Therefore, the argument runs, business, powerful and vital, must assume this role. (We saw this phenomenon at work in the loss of governmental authority in Russia in the late 1990s: as the powers of government weakened under Boris Yeltsin, business tycoons quickly emerged to fill the vacuum. Economic and political chaos has ensued.) Eliminating such corruption is the stated top priority of Yeltsin's successor, Vladimir Putin. In a problematic essay in 1997 addressing the need for government and business leaders to "get their collective act together," Garten called for

> [a] partnership based on two realities of the changing global marketplace . . . that the federal government's ability to conduct foreign

policy in a world preoccupied with economic stability and progress is dwindling, [that] Washington has neither the people nor
money to exert the influence it once could, [but] . . . that even
though business has the money, technology, and management that
make today's world spin, it needs [the government's] help more
than ever, in a world where . . . companies are becoming ensnared
in issues such as human rights, labor practices, environmental protection, and corruption. (Garten 1997, 68)

For Garten, government, the American people's only voice in the international arena, though still important, now occupies only a helping role,
second to that of "Big Business." In this scenario, government's responsibilities appear limited to smoothing the way, for business, around the in-
conveniences that are people. In this era of public preoccupation with
money, profit-making, and consumer interests, abetted by Conservative
Republicans' persistent antigovernmentalism, such assumptions threaten
to dominate Americans' thinking about the economic future, as they did at
the turn of the twentieth century.

In his emphasis upon lowering trade barriers and accelerating the
world's development as a global economy, President Clinton again tilted
Right of Center. Advocating positions that favored business, he drew support primarily from Conservative Republicans. Fellow Democrats expressed the concerns of Liberals and of many workers, sometimes actively
opposing the president, as in his failed efforts to gain "fast track" negotiating authority for foreign trade agreements that had been held by several of
his predecessors. Democrats blocked this negotiating authority, which
would have entitled the president to bring foreign trade agreements to
Congress to be voted up or down, without amendment. Their opposition
supported the concerns of labor unions and environmentalists, who feared
the president would show insufficient concern for the plight of American
workers or for the environment in a global economy.

As we saw in Seattle in 1999, many Americans, including Liberals,
unionized workers not at the hub of international business expansion, and
those generally mistrustful of "Big Business," still fear a global economy.
Their questions reflect both local and national concerns:

- As the government removes protective tariffs and other trade barriers and encourages American business abroad, will more and more

American jobs be lost to workers whose wage requirements are much lower? What are the implications for workers of an ever-larger wave of immigrants, legal and illegal? What do agreements such as the GATT (General Agreement on Trade and Tariffs) and the NAFTA (North American Free Trade Alliance) really mean? What is the agenda of the World Trade Organization?

- What of small business? As the government supports large, multi-, or transnational corporations, will the opportunity for local business, developed by entrepreneurs with local interests, be lost? Will government protect competition, to assure that new, smaller enterprises can be successful in the early stages, while they establish their markets?

- How can individuals and communities prepare for this new, unpredictable economic world?

As the economist Carolyn Shaw Bell has pointed out, concerns like these tend to call up "the protectionist argument [that] lurks behind every political or economic opposition to increasing trade between firms in this country and elsewhere" (Bell, "International Trade Benefits All," *Boston Globe*, 10 June 1997). But, in fact, no one who might have been expected to respond to workers' concerns—neither Clinton Centrists nor presidential aspirants nor business leaders themselves—has made it clear to workers and to other citizens whether or how the proposed transition to a global economy will be made without serious dislocations for American workers and communities. Clearly, the president, whoever she or he is, working with the business community and elected officials at every level, must develop policies to support displaced workers; if this effort is not made, the cooperation of labor and, indeed, of most Americans will not be forthcoming.

In addition to concerns about job security in a global economy, Americans may well harbor broader anxieties, as well, about what, in a global economy, may happen to the traditional roles and purposes of government. Some, usually Liberals and moderates, worry whether national distinctions and initiatives can be sustained in a world increasingly unified by trade agreements that threaten to limit the independent powers of individuals and governments, yielding power to the private sector. What, in an economically interdependent world must the roles of government be, our own or anyone else's?

Yet, even as these all-encompassing issues are raised, it is abundantly clear that in the real, day-to-day world, Americans have no choice but to rely on our government, conflicted as it is, to look out for our economic interests in the global marketplace. Little has changed from our earliest days as a nation in this respect, with one all-important exception: we cannot avoid recognizing that our interests are now not separable from conditions and concerns in the rest of the world. The Asian financial crisis of 1998 was a vivid reminder of economic interdependencies that are with us to stay.

In reality, it will be the effectiveness with which government works with both citizens and business, to assure broad collaboration in the formulation of government's responsibilities in the global economy, which will shape, perhaps even determine, what happens in many areas critical to national and international economic progress: education reform, racial and cultural conflicts, environmental protection, immigration policies, changing social and political organizations, and the development of capitalism where no infrastructure in law or culture exists to support it.

The Clinton administration saw the global economy, led by the United States, as effecting more than just economic progress. Clintonites asserted that increasing economic interdependence would also help to strengthen peace efforts and to advance humanitarian causes everywhere. In Part III we will see how the U.S. government's economic policies are driving post-Cold War U.S. foreign policy.

Part III

Foreign Policy:
The "Indispensable Nation"?

The great rule of conduct for us in regard to foreign nations is, in extending our commercial relations, to have . . . as little political connection as possible. . . . Taking care always to keep ourselves in a respectable defensive posture, we may safely trust to temporary alliances for extraordinary emergencies.

—George Washington

Wherever the standard of freedom and independence has been unfurled, there will [be America's] heart, her benedictions and her prayers. . . . But she goes not abroad in search of monsters to destroy. She is the well-wisher to the freedom and independence of all. She is the champion and vindicator only of her own.

—John Quincy Adams

Chapter 12

What's at Stake?

At the beginning of his second term, President Clinton adopted a phrase that Secretary of State Madeleine Albright used to broadcast the view that America is now the world's "indispensable nation." This phrase, offensive to many at home and abroad, usually Liberals who recoil at the arrogance it conveys, invited inevitable questions: Indispensable for what? Indispensable to whom? Nevertheless, it reminded all hearers that, in the years since the end of World War II, the United States has become the most powerful nation in the world, economically and militarily. Arguably, it is the most powerful nation ever.

With such power, which Stephen M. Walt persists in calling "unprecedented preponderance" (64), has come the recognition that the United States is and must be involved with the future of other nations. For better or worse, it has the responsibility for helping to shape the evolution of world affairs. Accepting this responsibility has meant reversing irrevocably a U.S. tradition of preferred unilateralism in national and world affairs, last envisioned in 1920–1930 in the tragic aftermath of World War I.

It has also meant recognizing the fact that questions about foreign relations, about how the United States uses its power in the world, for Americans and everyone else, are more complicated than ever before. They're about the limitations and dangers of power, as well as about the responsibilities and opportunities it brings. Wielding our nation's unprecedented strength requires vast sensitivity to the individual cultures and agendas of other nations, as well as courage and wisdom to protect our own security

133

and interests. Moreover, as all nations of the world have become more interdependent both politically and economically, U.S. foreign policy has taken on an importance in the lives of ordinary Americans that used to be reserved for problems much closer to home. All of these developments mean that, like other issues before the nation now, foreign policy is increasingly hostage to the partisan divisiveness everywhere apparent in U.S. national government.

In addition to traditional foreign policy concerns about national and international security, the United States now faces nontraditional dangers that many experts find as threatening as military aggression was thought to be when Germany, Japan, or the former USSR were the enemy: terrorist attacks; disease control; environmental hazards and degradation; unsustainable rates of population growth; and the effects of immigration, legal and illegal. Beyond these threats, Americans worry also about very personal matters, economic uncertainties, which are exacerbated by the nation's activities on the world stage: fears and questions about our jobs in the global economy; the fate of our personal savings and investments in globally interdependent but unstable markets; and the uncertainties of world economies, given disparate banking and accounting standards.

As we saw in Part II, it is virtually impossible to separate political/security concerns from economic concerns. And powerful communications technologies and unprecedented world travel give global problems human faces that we cannot ignore. After decades of relatively little involvement or interest, Americans can no longer distance themselves, or be distanced, from debate about our government's responsibilities in so-called foreign relations.

Argument about these responsibilities is dense and tortuous in the United States today. It is bitterly divided between Liberal political and economic objectives, on the one hand, and Conservative Republican perspectives and intentions, on the other. As we'll see, the Centrist Clinton administration again came under wide criticism from both ends of the political spectrum and from abroad for its alleged lack of political vision during nearly a decade in which nations moved to realign themselves in the wake of the Cold War. Meanwhile, the hostilities of Liberal/Conservative oppositions within Congress, or those between Centrist Clintonites and a Congress led by Conservative Republicans, were particularly dangerous to Americans' safety and prospects, given confusion and conflict about U.S. foreign policy intentions and priorities at home and abroad.[1]

Perhaps at no other time in the Clinton years was partisan divisiveness more dangerous to Americans or more damaging to foreign relations policy than in our government's failures to act responsibly on the Nuclear Test Ban Treaty in October 1999. Of course, the contrived move by Conservative Republican Senate leaders to force a vote they knew by prior arrangement they would carry, achieved the intended result. Emphasizing that "America's most honored foreign policy tradition is bipartisanship," a *New York Times* editorial captured this failure of government in both specific and general terms:

> With its abrupt scheduling, rushed debate, and needless negative vote on the test ban treaty, the Republican Senate majority all but abdicated its constitutional responsibility to play a thoughtful and deliberative role in the shaping of American foreign policy. It also undermined [the nation's] ability to provide diplomatic leadership on one of the most important questions facing the world today: controlling the development and spread of nuclear weapons. (15 October 1999)

Chapter 13

The United States and Globalization

THE POLITICS

The speed of our own and the world's movement into "global" thinking about the future has come as a great and still unfolding surprise to many.

With the collapse of the USSR and the end of the Cold War in 1989, knowledgeable observers began almost immediately to foresee a world in which nations would not be aligned with one superpower or the other in a struggle for the allegiance of everybody else. This would be a world unexpectedly freed from alliances and entanglements, in which millions of people would be suddenly liberated and faced with the necessity of re-creating their visions of the present and future. For many, surprised by the speed of such monumental change, it became necessary to re-create, as well, their understanding of the world that had produced such change.

In the United States, people moved quickly to questions about how to spend the money many thought would no longer be necessary for national defense. With the election of President Clinton in 1992, the administration created intense focus upon the need to eliminate annual deficit spending by the federal government, a problem that had been shunted aside, as long as maintaining vast military readiness to defeat the "evil empire," and planning for Ronald Reagan's star wars could be claimed as top priorities. What's happened since 1989 has surprised even the best informed among us, scholars and observers who seem, even now, to be grasping at all manner of real and imagined phenomena to explain the recent past and to foresee the future.

The fact of an essentially unaligned world quickly freed the pent up desires and hostilities of people everywhere. This new found freedom gave rise to religious, racial, and ethnic conflicts on virtually every continent. Some believe the dissolution of the USSR has exacerbated the political conflict between Liberals, Centrists, and Conservatives we've seen in our own country. Almost overnight, the anticipated peace dividend in the United States became an illusion.

The preoccupations of those in the U.S. foreign policy establishment shifted with embarrassing swiftness: What roles now belonged to developed nations in resolving international conflicts whose origins are sometimes ancient and may have little to do with the geopolitics of modern nation-states? Could they be resolved? What policies could guide international relations, when political relationships had become both more interdependent and more fluid, and the national alignments of the Cold War had disappeared?

The still-in-progress quest for answers to these questions quickly gave rise to another: What are the purposes of former political/security alliances in this new world? For Americans, the most important of these political alliances have been the United Nations and NATO, created after World War II at what some call the moment of triumph in U.S. internationalism. In these alliances, as well as in the Marshall Plan to help rebuild ravaged countries of the world after the war, Western nations committed to each other to oppose Soviet communism. We'll have more to say about these and other alliances in the next section. For the moment, let us simply note that both the UN and NATO are at the heart of current controversy about how U.S. foreign relations should proceed.

Questions about U.S. responsibility for conflict around the world and about the nature and responsibilities of its alliances with other governments have elicited several important studies in the '90s, all in response to the same set of political developments.

The comparatively optimistic *End of History and the Last Man* (1992) by Francis Fukuyama, described the possibility of international harmony in a world that had abandoned the poverty and oppression of the former Soviet Union's model of government, clearly preferring American-style democracy and open markets. Of course that naive optimism was quickly lost. In *The Clash of Civilizations and the Re-making of World Order*, Samuel P. Huntington predicted the rise of warring transnational cultures. He concluded this controversial study by predicting that "In the emerging era, clashes of civilizations are the greatest threat to world peace, and an international order based on civilizations is the surest safeguard against world war" (Huntington 1996, 321).

Others foresaw periodic eruptions from long-standing political, cultural, or geographic enmities, such as those in the former Congo and the former Yugoslavia. In *The Ends of the Earth: A Journey at the Dawn of the Twenty-first Century* (1996), Robert Kaplan concluded that conflicts would result from unmet social and human needs that have less to do with nationality or culture, than with whether people can survive extreme hardship brought on by drought, environmental collapse, failed economies, disease, or overpopulation because of mass migration, to name only some of the contending causes of disaster in Third-World countries. These problems, wrote Kaplan and others, will be intensified by corrupt or incompetent governments and by new and poorly structured democratic processes, some of which the United States will have helped to spawn.

In response to what had become widespread dissatisfaction with allegedly murky U.S. foreign policy objectives in the unaligned international community, internationalists at Yale University issued *The Pivotal States: A New Framework for U.S. Policy in the Developing World* (Chase, Hill, and Kennedy, eds. 1999). Former Defense Secretary William Perry and his colleague, Ashton Carter, focused more pragmatically upon creating priorities and strategies in a specialized study, *Preventive Defense: A New Security Strategy for America* (1999).

Pivotal States called for the United States to identify nations on the brink of emergence as international leaders whose futures are nevertheless in question at the moment. These are nations the United States might assist politically and economically, so that they can become regional leaders in the drive for democracy and open economies, worldwide. Kennedy and his colleagues make the cases for Indonesia, India, Pakistan, Turkey, Egypt, South Africa, Brazil, Algeria, and Mexico. Perry and Carter argue for classifying other nations in terms of their capacity to represent danger to the United States and then to focus upon efforts to prevent the rise of tensions or the necessity of military conflict. A review of issues dominating these two studies alone illustrates the complexities in establishing priorities for U.S. foreign relations. It also reminds us that guiding foreign policy decisions requires more expertise than most Americans, including most members of Congress, now bring to the table.

Moreover, the speed and intimacy enabled by new communications technology have changed the nature of successful political action, which must now be convincingly explained. Declaring war, even a highly localized war, is not the autonomous action of one nation against another that it was before worldwide, real time television enabled world opinion to insist that perpetrators explain and end their conflicts as soon as possible, no matter what their causes. Military conflicts among peoples within a current or former sovereign state are often the most complicated to address, as seen in the struggle between Russia and the Chechnyans, or Serbs and Albanians in the former Yugoslavia, or Protestants and Catholics in Northern Ireland. Yet even these so-called domestic problems are fought out or resolved under the scrutiny of a worldwide television audience: other nations take sides, and the political effects are thus more far-reaching than anyone could have imagined only a decade or so ago.

Besides a worldwide television audience for such events (in creating CNN Ted Turner forbade use of the word *foreign* in newscasts), there are many other players in the groves of world opinion, members of values-based, nongovernmental organizations (NGOs) who wield great influence upon people and governments and further complicate problem solving. Yet Americans have long believed that a society that includes effective NGOs, rather like the many associations that Alexis de Tocqueville observed in 1840s America, creates a vital element of democratic infrastructure that may help to focus and discharge political debate and maintain national stability in periods of conflict. (For example, in South Africa the fight for freedom from apartheid was enabled as surely by the network of thriving NGOs that marshaled world opinion against the government as by the insurgents' desperate straits.) International agencies such as Greenpeace and Amnesty International are examples of powerful, citizen-generated international NGOs.

Religious organizations, educational groups, scholarly societies, and organized labor are only a few of the many other individual or institutional participants in the creation and maintenance of global community, or disunity, and of foreign relations. Representing the views of individuals or the interests of particular groups, these institutions often work to greater effect than do governments, and succeed in moving both citizens and governments to action.

If, in a world of such complexity, the United States is the indispensable nation, as President Clinton claimed, perhaps that is so because sheer power gives us unprecedented opportunity, first to command others' attention, and then, to demonstrate for all to see forms of government and kinds of freedoms that may best serve an interdependent world. But we will not succeed in keeping our position of relative influence in the world because of our military and economic strength only, nor because we have devised workable short-term strategies to deal with problems on an ad hoc basis. We will succeed, if we do, because we've created a pragmatic but humane and coherent worldview that political opponents at home will join to support and because that view is supported also by people around the world, for the political convictions and economic opportunities that inform our work with each other and with them.

Unfortunately, this worldview has not yet emerged. Clinton's Centrism engendered confusion at home and abroad; the Conservative Republican-led Congress usually withheld support; communication of a coherent U.S. foreign policy did not develop. The United States does not have a clear and widely accepted framework for a post-Cold War foreign policy. Critics of the Clinton administration claimed lack of a sustaining vision, a view that Secretary Albright refuted: "Boiled down, the goals of American foreign policy have not changed in more than 200 years. They are to ensure the continued security, prosperity, and freedom of our people" (Albright, *Foreign Affairs*, December 1998, 51).

Citing former Secretary of State Dean Acheson, Albright insisted upon foreign policy as a permanent process, arguing as Acheson had, that "all our lives the danger, the uncertainty, the need for alertness, for effort, for discipline will be upon us" (50). She also admonished critics of the administration's Centrist policies by reminding them that Americans should not "claim too much" for that "much abused term, vision," because "implementing a framework is far tougher than designing one" (54). Meanwhile, in the fiscal year 2000 budget request, the Clinton administration included the most dramatic budgetary increase for weapons since the end of the Cold War.

As we shall see, there are many important differences of opinion in the debate about the right direction for U.S. foreign relations. Usually, they are part and parcel of the partisan conflict between Liberals' ideas, on the one hand, and Conservative Republicans' aims on the other. But there can be no mistake about what's at stake for Americans in this debate: nothing less than the prevention of chaos and anarchy that will result if the United States fails to discover and clarify, with others around the world, a principled and consistent political rationale and method for the uses of our nation's leadership and of its unprecedented wealth and power.

THE ECONOMICS

The economic sphere of international relations, which developed apace during the economic boom years of the Clinton presidency, has also produced a rich mix of not necessarily reconcilable predictions about the years ahead. Here are several of the most prominent:

- Although the nations of the world will manage to avoid cataclysmical wars, at least in the short term, they will be generally unstable, unpredictable, and uncentered because economic tension will generate new conflicts. These will come from further development of a global economy based on Western-style free markets and currency exchanges, though not in Western-style democracies or cultures.

- Economic alliances and conflicts will be even more important than political ones in the coming century. Corporate chieftains and central bankers, who have an enormous impact on the development of world opinion and thus of foreign policy, will challenge the roles and purposes of all governments in nations that are increasingly less autonomous. For example, speaking in Tokyo on the day after Japanese prime minister Hashimoto resigned from office in July 1998, U.S. Federal Reserve Board chairperson Alan Greenspan advised the new Japanese government-in-the-making to move immediately to address internal banking problems in the interest of its own and the world's economic stability and opportunity for further progress. (Meanwhile, it was widely believed in Japan that the prime minister's political party had suffered defeat because of U.S. condemnation of its economic policies.)

- Although transnational businesses will change international relations as we know them, sovereign governments and political organizations will continue to prevail because governments and law must represent the common weal and control market forces, no matter how powerful transnational business becomes. Adam Smith knew this, and so must we.

- The world of the future will require unprecedented cooperation between political and business/economic interests. They are inextricably merged now because, more than ever before, people everywhere recognize economic stability as the basis of political stability and world peace. (Awareness of this reality explains the success of U.S.

business lobbies in prevailing upon a Conservative Congress in July 1998 largely to abandon economic sanctions as a means of punishing nations for U.S.-diagnosed political transgressions. In recent years our government had imposed unilateral economic sanctions against twenty-six countries, or half the world's population. Members of Congress appear persuaded now that economic sanctions are not, in general, a satisfactory way to conduct foreign policy. Cuba, of course, still lies beyond the pale of these constructive changes.)

Contradictory emphases in debate about the place of economics in the conduct of U.S. foreign relations or about the purposes of government in foreign policy are certainly not new. In 1998, even as revised thinking about economic sanctions was developing in Washington, Conservative Sen. Jesse Helms (R-NC), who headed the Senate Foreign Relations Committee in the Clinton years, argued that economic sanctions are an effective and principled foreign policy tool, "older than this Republic itself."

True, the bases of U.S. foreign policy, except in periods of military conflict, have from the very beginning been primarily economic, an effort to gain and maintain economic advantage, usually through export/import agreements. In far simpler days, this foreign policy priority was first enunciated for the United States by George Washington who, of course, had warned in his "Farewell Address" against long-term political entanglements with other nations. Americans of all political persuasions have generally approved of this approach to international economic relationships over the years, as part and parcel of the responsibility of our government to protect "life, liberty and the pursuit of happiness" at home.

At present, in positions widely thought to reflect Republican Conservative values more fully than those of Liberals, usually Democrats, the government unabashedly supports an economic focus in foreign policy as most likely to sustain both peace and prosperity. While Liberals insist upon a more serious consideration of issues we may broadly categorize for the moment as human rights or social problems, the Centrist Clinton administration received full and consistent support from a Republican Conservative-led Congress for policies designed primarily to link nations of the world more fully in economic relationships.

Immediately after his election in 1992, President Clinton introduced a fully merged political and economic foreign policy agenda for the United States, characterized as a softening of boundaries between domestic and international relations.[1] This merged agenda, though more comprehensive than any before it, found specific twentieth-century antecedents before and just after the two world wars.

These antecedents included Woodrow Wilson's beliefs about the relationship of economic stability to political stability and the architecture of Franklin Roosevelt's administration. A key Roosevelt adviser, Henry Stimson, led a group of so-called wise men, many of them Republican Conservative corporate titans, who guided a U.S. foreign policy establishment during the FDR years, men who sustained influence well into the Reagan administration. They believed that U.S. political and economic interests require economic stability and the development of open markets worldwide; that economic stability and open markets are allies of democracy and vice versa; that democracy is desirable wherever it can be achieved; and that, because our own economy requires stable, prosperous trading partners, Americans must recognize the unprecedented prospects, not only for Americans, but for people everywhere in a barrier free, international economy.

Despite these noble antecedents, not everyone agrees that President Clinton's approach to foreign policy was sufficient to the political and social requirements of the 1990s. In any case, what's at stake for the nation in the economy-driven, now thoroughly entangled, international politics of today is virtually the same economic opportunities that have always been at stake. But now, in a bitterly partisan U.S. government whose congressional leadership is antigovernment in any case, and in a world still trying to adjust to the loss of political alignment that had guided so much of international relations in the Cold War, the stakes are higher than ever before.

The U.S. economic agenda abroad now touches all Americans in its impact upon the domestic economy and extends boldly throughout the world to include nations everywhere as trading partners. We have come to realize that capturing advantages of the global economy for the United States means capturing them for everyone else, as well. Economic failures elsewhere, in the Far East or Latin America, affect economic performance in the United States. And success in international trade requires, as it always has, imaginative strategies not yet in evidence to support globalization and to assist those Americans who are caught in the waves of disruptive economic change. The strike against General Motors in summer 1998 illustrated the serious domestic dislocations U.S. workers and unions fear: that American jobs will be lost to foreign workers. Disruption of the Seattle World Trade Organization meetings in 1999 (toward which President Clinton was sympathetic) and efforts to repeat such disruption in Washington, D.C., in April 2000 renewed the concerns of many Americans. Organized labor, human rights groups, and environmentalists all sought greater openness in discussions of world economies and their interdependence.

Secretary of State Albright often reaffirmed the centrality of developing a global economy to U.S. foreign policy, insisting that Americans "must recognize and capitalize on the linkages between democracy, stability, and economic growth" (Albright, *Foreign Affairs*, December 1998, 53). In fact, as her Liberal critics have asserted, it has become difficult to discern any other consistent, persuasive rationale for U.S. foreign policy as we have it today.

Chapter 14

Current Debates

THE POLITICS

Recent events illustrate U.S. vulnerabilities to failure in achieving foreign policy objectives and dramatize our need for both a clear agenda and effective strategies to build international partnerships. Such events have included a lack of international support to U.S. positions in resolving conflicts in the former Yugoslavia (where Conservative Republican partisanship at home also interfered with administration efforts); in establishing a UN-sponsored plan for a World Court; and in U.S. efforts to gain economic reforms in the Far East. Meanwhile, other divisions on foreign policy abound in our own government, based in conflicting ideologies about U.S. political and economic responsibilities at home and abroad.

In its broadest terms, political debate about how the United States should proceed in foreign policy is divided between two camps: on one side, those who believe that the United States should claim "benevolent hegemony," a phrase coined by the Conservative Republican editor William Kristol. A philosophy of benevolent hegemony takes for granted the U.S. position as the world's most powerful nation, and proceeds unabashedly to argue that global politics and the world economy should be shaped according to Americans' politically and economically enlightened and generally humanitarian vision for other nations and peoples of the world. On the other side, opponents of this so-called hegemonic strategy, aware of the fateful history of nations that have sought world dominance, push for realistic "multipolarity," a distribution of power among nations responsible for working out a system of international relationships and of the strategies for globalization. They foresee that, as stakeholders in the results, these nations would more willingly assume the costs of their responsibilities.

Republican Conservative hegemonists make the following case: more than any nation ever, the United States has recognized that its own well-being depends upon that of others; despite the power to have claimed territory or other forms of control over nations less powerful, it has not done so (except for a spate of minor colonialization at the turn of the century, later abandoned or justified mainly in security terms); and there are really no alternatives to U.S. leadership in the world and are unlikely to be, since no other nation is willing to bear the material or political costs of responsibility that comes with the power to lead.

Their opponents speak from various political emphases that divide policy choices in more ways than the usual Conservative/Liberal/Centrist debate. Liberals recoil at the arrogance of the United States in assuming that it knows best for everyone, politically and economically, and in dismissing, through ignorance or intentionally, deeply seated cultural realities embedded in the values and strategies of other nations. So-called realists take a more Conservative worldview: Unlike the hegemonists, they worry about the danger of alliances against U.S. interests, born of international backlash to perceived U.S. domination. They believe that a balance of power in world affairs is generally safer for all parties and that, in reality, every responsible government conducts its affairs within a balance of power context, protecting its own advantage. The realist camp includes Republicans Henry Kissinger and former UN ambassador Jeanne Kirkpatrick.

Yet other observers point to the costs of maintaining hegemony: tax dollars spent on a far-flung foreign policy bureaucracy and for the world's most powerful military establishment would be better used for other purposes, such as improving the quality of life for many disadvantaged Americans. Still others, Conservatives and Liberals alike, worry about the impact of power upon "the American character"; they warn against the loss of opportunities to work in new and different ways with those governments throughout the world that are less concerned with power and the creation of wealth than with realizing humanitarian purposes. They see the potential for great danger in a world where disparities in income and quality of life are rapidly increasing among developed nations and among all others.

In this as in so many other aspects of government, the Clinton administration frustrated ideologues on all sides and bore the brunt of criticism from all. In foreign relations their pragmatic, politically Centrist aims (again described as the "third way," by some) meant that the federal government was to proceed along all practical fronts, however idiosyncratically: The government was hegemonist, but humanitarian; it sponsored open markets and democracy, worldwide; it was arrogant in its claims for the "indispensable nation," but also claimed that it desired and depended upon multilateral decision making and respected multipolar leadership, while often waiting until the eleventh hour to take political or military action deemed necessary by all of its allies. (But journalist Craig Whitney has pointed out that, after the war in Kosovo, our allies were unhappy because of alleged American "highhandedness" [Whitney, "NATO at 50: Is It a Misalliance?" *New York Times*, 15 February 1999].)

Through intensive lobbying of other nations to accept U.S. strategies, the third way sought to satisfy Liberals' devotion to democratic ideals and to assuage Republican Conservatives' fears that the government would yield national autonomy or military supremacy. Yet, the federal government under Clinton did more to fuel the debate about the nation's responsibilities in foreign relations policy than to resolve it. Nevertheless, Americans are still in a strong political and economic position from which to determine what intentions the nation might claim as the bases for U.S. actions in the future.

International Alliances

Nowhere are the contradictions and problems of U.S. foreign relations policy more obvious than in the nation's relationships to the largest and most complex of international alliances: the United Nations.

In the formally unaligned world of the 1990s, the UN is challenged as never before to define roles for an expanded membership divided by vast cultural and political differences. Its activities involve around one hundred ninety member nations to address complex security concerns: peacekeeping efforts, as in the Balkans and East Timor; response to new nuclear testing, as in India and Pakistan; and specific efforts to encourage progress in the multifaceted peace negotiations among Israel, the Palestinians, and Syria. In addition, the UN coordinates discussions of global problems such as population growth, the care of women and children, disease control, the prosecution of crimes against humanity, and environmental protection.

As the world's only military and economic superpower, at least for now, how does the United States relate to the political processes of the world's most comprehensive political organization, an organization that the United States was chiefly responsible for creating? How does the UN relate to it? A short answer to both questions is, With great difficulty.

The world acknowledges that the United States was primarily responsible for the creation of the UN. In 1941, even before the United States entered World War II, its organization and purposes had already begun to form in the imagination of President Franklin Roosevelt. Although the president died before it was actually formed and chartered, the UN is a major part of his legacy, built on the nation's failed efforts under Woodrow Wilson to create an international forum, the so-called League of Nations, to promote understanding and, ultimately, world peace.

It is important to realize why the UN has never lived up to the hopes that both Franklin and Eleanor Roosevelt worked so relentlessly to create for it, and how it has fallen so far from grace in the halls of Congress. In brief, the idealism of UN participants in the early years, beginning in 1945, was almost at once killed by the aggressor motives of Stalin's USSR, one of its leading members. No one quite anticipated the development of the Cold War, with all that it brought to world politics for more than forty years. Yet, as early as 1946, the first problem to come to the permanent members of the UN Security Council was the former Soviet Union's threat, a threat by one of the founding members of the Security Council, not to evacuate its troops from postwar Iran.

Roosevelt's dream of a supreme council of peace keepers was quickly dashed. Nevertheless, the UN became the locus of other valuable activities: it was and is an emergency forum where incipient conflict may be discharged; a screen behind which powerful nations may save face when they wish to avoid taking political positions difficult to defend at home or abroad. Almost from the beginning, it was a convenient scapegoat for failed policies: group failure is easier to communicate to voters than is the failure of one's own diplomacy or military action.

Perhaps these various roles were to some extent inevitable, given human nature and politics, but they resulted in congressional perception of the UN as little more than a political sideshow and battleground, unlikely to be the source of forthright discussion or honest debate that can lead to joint problem solving. This has been especially so when the stakes were high. Ballooning UN membership in the wake of rapid decolonization after India gained her independence from Great Britain in 1947 also complicated discussion and decision making in unforeseen ways, almost from the start.

By the 1970's, so-called Third World countries had gained a voting majority in the General Assembly and used it often as a political bloc to oppose the proposals of Western democracies. Many of these actions were stimulated by the former Soviet Union, seeking to win the fledgling nations to the Communist bloc. Many of the new nations also took positions against the State of Israel, further alienating Congress by eroding the strong, bipartisan UN support for Israel that had been so vital in the early years.[1]

Today, opinion about U.S. relations to the UN largely follows the lines of partisan conflict about the purposes and strategies of U.S. foreign policy. And this conflict itself is but an extension of partisan divisiveness about the purposes of our government. In general, Conservative Republicans have withdrawn their support from the UN. Some, demonstrably ill-informed about foreign policy questions, insist on national autonomy, a clear capacity to act unilaterally as needed, and comparatively little responsibility for the development of other nations. For most of the 1990s they were unwilling to pay dues owed the UN (arguing that the United States more than meets its share of costs in keeping world peace) or, in the main, to support UN initiatives if doing so might suggest that the United States is somehow constrained from independent action.

The U.S. debt to the UN was more than $1.5 billion by the time the Clinton administration in 1999 brokered a controversial compromise with congressional Conservatives. In its failure to grant funding for this debt, the Conservative Republican-led Congress had earlier seriously undermined our ability to work successfully with other member nations and called into question U.S. entitlement to offer leadership in resolving questions before the UN. U.S. ambassador Richard Holbrooke, finally confirmed by Conservative Republicans in Congress after more than a year's delay, spent the first months of his assignment literally buttonholing members in elevators to lobby for payment of the debt. U.S./UN relations remain strained, essentially because U.S. "policy" communicates to all the world our apparent intention to both dominate UN decisions and to accept little responsibility to act within the organization, except when it is to our advantage.

Conservatives' loss of commitment to the UN began in earnest under Ronald Reagan. Since then, they have continued to cite poor administrative and political leadership, excessive costs, and a generally disadvantageous climate for debates likely to advance our agenda in the world. They note the vulnerability of U.S. interests in a forum numerically dominated by Third-World representatives whose cultural and political interests are typically different from those of the United States. Perhaps most important, they cite UN failures in several peace keeping missions of the '80s and '90s: in Bosnia, in Somalia, and in Rwanda. They conclude noisily that no vestige of U.S. autonomy should be granted to the administration of such ill-conceived and poorly led actions (Urquhart 1998, 1999).

But proponents of the UN, usually Liberal Democrats, have produced dozens of studies proposing ways to fix it. They reject the arrogance of Conservatives who prefer to go it alone in foreign policy-making. They assert that if the UN didn't exist, it would have to be invented and claim several UN successes in the last decade or so, among them, at least the following:

- UN-sponsored human rights conventions that set standards for governments not now easily ignored;

- The use of UN-sponsored troops in international peace-keeping actions;

- The Law of the Sea Treaty, which regulates national conduct on the seas and works to protect maritime ecology—only one instance of success, supporters claim, through UN programs designed to help protect the global environment;

- UN-sponsored monitoring of national elections around the world;

- A series of widely attended world conferences that have resulted in action plans for such problems as environmental preservation, population growth, and women's rights.

Liberals typically see political danger in the U.S. government's failures to work with and support the UN. They welcome UN successes as opportunities to explain its alleged failures. They point to recent studies that show how, especially in the first Clinton administration, the United States abused its power, pushing the UN into several peace-keeping missions which, in retrospect, were doomed to failure by inadequate support from all participating countries. They argue, for instance, that in the waning days of the Bush years, the United States forced a reluctant UN administration into nothing less than a nation-building exercise in Somalia, though the UN leadership itself believed all along it would fail. They charge that the United States used the imminent arrival of UN forces as a pretext for the premature withdrawal of its own forces before all efforts to bring political and economic order to Somalia had publicly failed.

Brian Urquhart agrees, arguing further that the United States blamed the UN for the failure of the mission in Somalia, when it had clearly resulted from failures by the U.S. military. In any case, he writes, Somalia marked "the end of the brief period of [U.S.] enthusiasm for United Nations efforts to salvage nations or peoples in desperate straits" (Urquhart 1999, 28–29) and has resulted in paralyzing any quick response the UN might mount in crises such as that in East Timor in 1999.

Other Liberals have seen political danger and arrogance in U.S. failure to participate in worldwide efforts to ban land mines from future military conflict. Still others note that in July 1998 the United States unwisely failed to join with other UN member countries supporting in a vote of 120 to 7, a plan to create a new World Court along lines broadly agreed to by most members, including many of our staunchest allies. Twenty-one nations abstained from the final vote, also declining to support the U.S. position.

This result followed weeks of effort by other nations to accommodate U.S. demands that our military and diplomatic personnel stationed abroad be excluded from prosecution. U.S. representatives claimed exceptionalism and expressed fear of unfair treatment for American soldiers and diplomats, a possibility that most other nations of the world are prepared to risk for their citizens. In so doing, the United States significantly undermined a vital international effort to establish agreed upon elements of international law and frustrated most other nations, including many close allies. Their frustration and anger deepened further in early 1999, after a U.S. marine pilot whose plane had brought down a ski lift in Italy killing more than twenty civilians, was brought back to the United States for trial and subsequently acquitted by a military court.

An equally dramatic UN/U.S. confrontation occurred in October 1998 in response to U.S. policies on Cuba. Only Israel stood with the United States in insisting upon the legitimacy of the *Helms-Burton Act* sustaining economic sanctions against Cuba and her international business partners for U.S.-alleged human rights violations. Seeking strategies to soften U.S. relations with the Cuban people (short of an unachievable congressional repeal of the *Helms-Burton Act* that Republican Conservatives support), the Clinton administration in 1999 proposed various efforts to improve relations. These ranged from playing baseball to permitting the flow of more American dollars into Cuba, as long as they would not support actions of the government.

These U.S. initiatives, which did not require congressional approval and did not anticipate interaction with the government of Cuba, looked ill-advised from a diplomatic perspective and not a little ridiculous. Most important, they illustrated the fragmented state of U.S. foreign policy and the cost of bitter ideological and political partisanship in Washington, a divisiveness that has usually brooked no possibility of compromise, no matter what the cost to the nation.

In all of these instances, many Liberals have supported UN positions against the policies of the U.S. government. They find U.S. foreign policy, as reflected in current U.S./UN relations, proof that Conservative Republicans since 1994 (as earlier, in the Reagan and Bush administrations) have lost sight of our government's responsibilities in foreign relations. They look with dismay at the erosion of political support for U.S. positions throughout the world.

Liberal critics are also concerned about the administration's recent decisions in our other most important international alliance, the North Atlantic Treaty Organization (NATO). They cite especially strategies that the second Clinton administration employed to expand the NATO alliance, which in the Cold War had served primarily to present a unified front against a belligerent Soviet Union. The United States insisted on the expansion, even though policies to support it were far from clear, and the political fallout around the world was damaging to both the United States and the alliance. Russia, in particular, objected to it as an expansion of strategies intended from the outset for use against the former USSR.

All such considerations to the contrary, the Clinton administration persisted, arguing that an expanded NATO somehow finalized an historic end to earlier divisions in Europe and promised fruitful interdependence through American-led protection for all. Later, the wisdom of the NATO expansion was bitterly questioned as the NATO military attack in Kosovo gave rise to troubled relationships with a Russia already bruised and alienated because of her traditional alliance with the Serbs.

Even more important, however, was the Kosovo action itself. Taken without the UN authorization that the member nations expect in any military intervention by one or several nations, the NATO action suggested that, under U.S. leadership, the organization felt free to disregard international norms for reasons it deemed justifiable. NATO explained its action as protection of human rights. Nevertheless, its invasion of Kosovo without the support of the UN understandably caused concern among all nations not in NATO, who wonder when a U.S.-led coalition might next interfere within the borders of a sovereign state. Among the nations expressing such concern are Russia and China.

Open Questions

As always, issues such as these elicit often unsatisfactory recommendations for current and future U.S. foreign policy priorities and alliances from foreign policy experts. Several of the most influential illustrate how government officers and the pundits who advised them in the '90s failed to represent the coherent, principled statements so desperately needed in U.S. foreign policy today.

In his book, *The Reluctant Sheriff: The United States After the Cold War* (1997), Richard N. Haass, director of Foreign Policy Studies at the Brookings Institution, suggests that for the foreseeable future the United States should steer clear of complicating alliances and simply play "sheriff" to the world, gathering international "posses" to help us deal, on short-term bases only, with problems as they arise. Haass distinguishes this approach from our attempt to play "policeman" around the globe, because the latter would mean acting in concert with principles of international law—which he considers nonexistent—over a longer period of time. Haass appears to find it unobjectionable for the United States to act in its own interests (or those of our allies) pro tem and without principles of international law, as long as we are quick and our actions are short-lived. It is hard to justify Haass's proposed conduct of U.S. foreign relations on any grounds except those of grossest expediency. Such an approach could be contemplated only by the nation that is, for the moment, the most powerful in the world, and then only with considerable risk to long-term relationships.

In a phrase taken directly from the language of economics, Haass also suggests that most political/military alliances will not be useful in what he calls the "deregulated world" of the present and future. Drawing unflinchingly upon market rhetoric he assumes all Americans understand, he proposes that the United States adopt a foreign policy based on the notion of regulation. The United States should act, whenever possible with others, but alone when necessary and feasible, "to shape the behavior and, in some cases, capabilities of governments and other actors so that they are less likely or able to act aggressively either beyond their borders or toward their own citizens and more likely to enter into trade and other mutually beneficial economic relations. . . . Bringing about such a world, one in which countries settle economic and political disputes peacefully and governments act responsibly toward their own citizens and their neighbors, is the aim of regulation" (Haass 1997, 4).

These views resemble those of another foreign relations specialist, David Abshire, longtime president of the Center for Strategic and International Studies, who in 1996 proposed an "agile" strategy for U.S. foreign policy. Recognizing that the United States had not yet created a foreign policy for the post-Cold War world, Abshire argued that our point of view should be linked to certain "unswervable aims," such as support for Israel and Europe. Decisions about other problems in the world would be inextricably linked to causes we know we want to support. "Innovation, freedom of action, and new priorities" should be our foreign policy aims. In deciding when to use power and where to try to achieve peace our "approach should be characterized by agility" (Abshire 1996, 41). Here, as in the pronouncements of Haass, the reader looks in vain for coherent principles to guide decision making or the creation of policy priorities.

Somewhat similarly, when Madeleine Albright became secretary of state in 1996, she frequently described the approach to foreign relations she would take in Clinton's second term as pursuing "assertive multilateralism." The United States would seek relationships with many other governments and institutions, including but by no means limited to the UN and to an expanded NATO, since these would help to ensure support to the United States's foreign policy agenda, whatever its needs and priorities became. Although she stated her intention to help Americans broaden their knowledge of, and interest in, foreign relations problems, Secretary Albright did not explain what rationale she would apply to guide U.S. relationships abroad. Later, in 1998, she stated simply: "Freedom is America's purpose. . . . In opposing injustice, Americans have responded not in accordance with any single foreign policy theory but in a way that reflects . . . the American character" (Albright 1998, 64).

More substantive visions have, however, been advanced. For example, in *The Pivotal States: A New Framework for U.S. Policy in the Developing World* (1999), the editors respond to the absence of coherence that results from the lack of overarching aims for U.S. foreign policy today. Noting that, in the long term, it seems unlikely that the balance of power will tilt in favor of either the United States or Europe, they argue for U.S. engagement with developing nations whose rise to prominence in the future will determine the prospects for our own security and prosperity.

Old approaches to foreign policy that stress the "importance of military security [will] not adequately attend to the newer threats to American national interests," the editors assert. Since governmental instabilities will be caused by many factors in the future, the United States will need new conceptions of security that take a "global or holistic approach . . . through UN conferences, NGO's, and civil society actors." All of this must recognize the necessity of "working with national governments" to achieve solutions (Kennedy *et al* 1999, 5). To these remarks, which entail thoughtful, deliberative approaches to the creation of U.S. foreign policy so long missing from our ideologically divided government, we say a resounding "yes."

A perhaps more philosophical approach to U.S. foreign policy dilemmas is taken by the Conservative historian Walter A. McDougall in his study, *Promised Land, Crusader State.* He writes: "Confusion and discord have been the norm in American foreign relations, not because we lack principles to guide us, but because we have canonized so many since 1776 that we are pulled every which way at once" (McDougall 1997, 4).

McDougall attributes our history of confusion to the nation's gradual evolution away from the Founders' clear-headed, principled thinking about human nature in their plans for a democratic promised land that would focus upon protecting the freedoms of its own citizens. Our twentieth-century political and economic "messianism," that is, U.S. efforts to change the rest of the world to make it more like us, is responsible for many of our foreign policy errors, he charges. McDougall warns against U.S. arrogance in all its forms, including efforts to impose democracy where nations have no infrastructure to support it, or open markets where modern accounting standards, or, indeed, any standards of accountability, are all but unknown. He also warns against U.S. failures to accept deeply seated cultural, social, and religious differences in the "national character" of other sovereign states.[2]

For him, the first principle for U.S. foreign policy should be to secure the perpetuation of our own "national character" and ideals, as well as the military and economic strength to protect them. He insists that "the only workable internationalism is one rooted in the same 'healthy nationalism' defined and nurtured for America by Washington, Jefferson, and the Adamses, and espoused by Theodore Roosevelt and Henry Cabot Lodge," adding persuasively, "No international bureaucracy, much less a single nation, however powerful and idealistic, can substitute itself for the healthy nationalism of [any other] people" (McDougall 1997, 220).

We might call these arguments "an approach to international federalism." They offer for Americans a lesson in genuine regard for the validity of distinct cultural and political traditions and objectives among all nations. We'll return to this idea in the next section.

What is really needed in U.S. political relationships abroad? Coherent, long-term goals and strategies and a commitment to working with other nations as partners in the eternal quest for success. Efforts to dominate, whether military, political, or economic will not achieve any of the aims Americans must now seek. Rather, as the Harvard internationalist Samuel P. Huntington put it, Americans must recognize that even if there was a moment when the United States could command the future of international relationships, as the USSR dissolved in 1989 and the Cold War ended, it has now passed. American policymakers and policies must now reflect Liberal awareness that, in the future, international relations will have many leaders, not one leader only (Huntington 1999, 47–49).

In the view of people in other countries of the world, the United States will not be, as Albright and Clinton insisted, the "indispensable" nation, or not the only one, as they declared in 1996. At this juncture, Americans must realize that U.S. Centrist political pragmatism and braggadoccio will not serve the nation and the world. They are unworkable approaches, and the moment to understand that fact is upon us.

THE ECONOMICS

Questions about international political alliances and relationships are inextricable from questions about economic partnerships. And nowhere are U.S. claims to have the model that all other countries of the world must follow more dangerous to the future of U.S. relations with other nations than in economic policy.

President Clinton's political Centrism both embraced the Conservative Republican agenda to develop the global economy as a way of assuring the continuing expansion of American prosperity and responded to all Americans' hopes that an interdependent global economy offers the best chance to sustain world peace. But political problems lurked and lurk in the reality that, as in efforts to dominate other nations politically and militarily, an unabashed intention to economic dominance is antithetical to Liberals' ideals of true alliance or shared advantage through partnership.

The United States leads the drive toward a global economy at least ostensibly characterized by open markets and free trade. Most economists believe that the case for such a drive is ironclad, not only for building strength in our own economy, but for enabling other countries to achieve progress, in the economic, political, and social spheres. With trade, any country grows richer than it would otherwise be, because it gains access to more goods, at lower prices. Thus, under Clinton, the U.S. government sustained a primary objective to gain open markets and free trade. It maintained a Centrist position in the ongoing debate between Conservative Republicans and Liberals about the roles government should take in bringing our own and other nations into participation in the global economy.

What is this debate really about? Consistent with their ideas about government's roles and purposes in other aspects of U.S. government, Conservative Republicans advocate very limited government involvement in the development of global business. If there is the opportunity for government to facilitate international commercial opportunity through political diplomacy, as, for example, in negotiating to lower or eliminate trade barriers in China, it should, of course, be taken. In general, however, both Conservative Republicans and Clinton Centrists believe that multinational corporations should be largely free to extend their private-sector efficiencies into the markets, natural resources, and labor pools of the world with little regulation by government. Even opportunities to stabilize fragile currencies (through the World Bank or the International Monetary Fund) are anathema to many.

Perhaps most important for our purposes here, proponents of unalloyed freedoms in the U.S.-led global economy are likely to believe that the power of open markets should also be given relatively free rein to challenge the politics and cultures of other nations, whether or not these nations are prepared or wish to prepare for such change. Typically, they see a private sector or individual responsibility, not a role for government, in coping with the economic and cultural dislocations people experience in a highly technologized, global manufacturing and business world.

For their part, Liberals also recognize the opportunities, indeed, the inevitability, of a global economy, but they are likely to express such concerns as how to provide new opportunities for displaced workers; how to protect the global environment from the ravages of profiteering; how to assure the relationship of global business to acceptable labor practices; and, in fact, how to assure the continuing powers of government in a world that seems likely to be dominated by multinational corporations. Leading Liberal economists call for partnerships between government and business that are closer than ever before to assure that government maintains essential controls and direction while fostering the development of global business. It is

Liberals who remind us that Adam Smith advocated such mutually reinforcing roles for any capitalistic society in 1776 in *The Wealth of Nations.*

Virtually everyone agrees that there is a lack of connection between
what many economists assert about U.S. prospects in the global economy
and the beliefs of many workers, in the United States and abroad. In the
United States, workers are likely to believe that exports are good, but imports, because they threaten American jobs, are bad, and that imports are
especially bad if they come from a country to which an American company
has moved its manufacturing facility in order to capture lower labor costs.
As Clinton reaffirmed at the November 1999 meeting of the World Trade
Organization, it will be essential for government and business leaders
everywhere to hear workers' concerns and to foster their understanding and
involvement in the ongoing development of economic globalism.

This requirement makes it useful to review some of the leading arguments for U.S. support to globalization, arguments which, as Liberals realize, many Americans have not yet fully understood. In developing this
summary, we are indebted to Gary Burtless and his colleagues, in *Globaphobia* (1998) and to Thomas L. Friedman in *The Lexus and the Olive Tree*
(1999). They make the case for both an integrated global economy and
government assistance to those whom the new economy will disadvantage:

- In the prosperous years before 1973, when the United States globalized rapidly, workers' productivity and wages increased and income inequalities were reduced. The U.S. economy is no more
  globalized today than before World War I.

- When taken by the U.S. government, protectionist measures, such
  as high import taxes, are harmful to the very workers they are
  thought to help. Competition and innovation suffer, thus lowering
  workers' long-term prospects. Import taxes cause other nations to
  retaliate with import taxes of their own, making U.S. goods harder
  to trade overseas. Eventually, they may actually depress the U.S.
  economy.

- The most serious problem faced by workers in the United States is
  not foreign competition; it is the mismatch between the skills employers need and the skills that many workers bring to the market.

- Trade barriers are likely to harm the very industries in which America leads the world: agriculture, financial services, pharmaceuticals,
  aircraft, and telecommunications. Open trade benefits everyone by

giving people access to more goods at competitive prices, thus helping to contain inflation.

- Progress always requires temporary though important dislocations, since the whole point of trade is to shift resources such as investment and worker energies toward their most productive uses. This process is always painful to those required to shift.

- National debate in the United States about effects of the global economy can only be resolved through concerted efforts by activist government and business to help U.S. citizens, first, to recognize the kinds of economic and social progress a global economy may bring worldwide, over time; and, second, to gain the skills American workers need to retain their jobs and advance in a workplace that is being radically changed in all respects, day by day.

These responsibilities of government are most likely to be met in a Liberal or moderate political agenda. They are also an important part of an activist government's roles in the larger context of U.S. foreign relations: if humane foreign policy aims are to be envisioned and met, workers at home and abroad must be helped to find their places in the larger conceptual scheme of things, that is, in a vision of international relations that relies upon economic advancement for everyone. But a further question looms: Even if U.S. government and corporate leaders do understand better than any of their counterparts around the world what economic policies should prevail at home and abroad and persuade other Americans to agree, is the United States entitled to force its ideas upon other nations and their cultures, as we see in the Clinton years? Can such an effort succeed?

Here, we are at the heart of current argument and recent crisis. Arguably, one reason for the global economic meltdown in 1998 (when several of the world's major economies experienced devaluation of currencies and loss of international confidence that caused investors to remove capital needed for further development) was resistance to change the United States imposed upon vulnerable countries. In a perhaps unprecedented form of government activism in the international economy, the Centrist Clinton government, propelled by a tail wind of Conservative Republican capitalist practice, had force-fed several countries U.S. standards and practices for managing their economies.

Predictably, these measures failed in the short term and are now thought by many to have been erroneously austere and unrealistic. The countries involved thus became victims of what some U.S. economists, including those in government, blithely called "creative destruction." They would need to suffer economically in the short run, said these Conservative Republicans and Clinton Centrists, but, in the end, everyone would be better off: they would have instituted reforms, especially in their banking systems, which the United States and its capitalist partners believed necessary for reliable investment in their countries. By late 1999, most of the economies affected by these U.S.-led policies of austerity and externally imposed disciplines were recovering, but their recoveries were preceded by periods of major loss and dislocation by millions of people throughout the world.

Chapter 15

Reaching the Present: Foreign Policy Through the World Wars

What foreign policies guided the United States in the twentieth century? Why does it matter now? Answers to these vital questions must necessarily be abbreviated here, but they should encourage further investigation.

In brief: Having been led reluctantly into World War I by a crusading Democrat Woodrow Wilson, the nation's responses both to that experience and to World War II prefigure the still prevalent conflict about the extent to which the United States should involve itself in conflicts abroad. Following World War I, Wilson's attempt to extend U.S. involvement through participation in the international politics of the League of Nations met with Conservative Republican partisan resistance and ultimate failure in a Congress determined to withdraw again from the conflicts of Europe. Though it quickly proved to have tragic consequences, that decision can be understood as a near-final manifestation of the U.S. tradition of unilateralism in foreign policy.

U.S. withdrawal from involvement in Europe's political problems after the devastating "War to End All Wars," left a vacuum in leadership and destroyed such confidence as Europeans had begun to develop in U.S. capacity or will to help assure a sustainable peace. The decision also resulted in our last but perhaps most far-reaching economic withdrawal. That the ravaged nations of Europe could not recover quickly from World War I was in part due to the excessive economic penalties the victors, led by the United States, placed upon Germany, thereby preventing her participation in efforts to restore the continent's economies.

Meanwhile, the U.S. economy also fell into an intractable depression that culminated in the great market crash of 1929. Much has been written about the causes of this Great Depression, as well as about mistakes made in trying to reverse it, one of the most serious of which was the imposition of protective tariffs, especially the *Smoot-Hawley Act*, enacted under Republican President Herbert Hoover in 1930. Designed to protect manufacturers by taxing imports from abroad, this strategy only made things worse. It deprived the consumers of the benefits of competition and reduced the opportunity for economic growth and stability, not only in the United States, but throughout the world. In Europe, it fueled the economic hardships that helped Hitler to assume leadership in a war-ravaged and demoralized Germany.

As a result of Democrat Franklin D. Roosevelt and the New Deal that became government policy in 1932, the years of struggle to end economic depression and to restore U.S. financial stability and economic prospects with the direct involvement of government in the formulation and enactment of economic recovery measures began immediately. Significantly, in 1934, Congress gave FDR the authority to negotiate reciprocal tariff reductions of up to 50 percent with other countries, without having to obtain further congressional approval. FDR had completed thirty-two such bilateral agreements by 1945.

Only with the greatest reluctance and out of almost total unpreparedness was the United States drawn into military conflict again, in World War II, almost simultaneously on both sides of the world. The economic depression at home came to an end. After the war, it was clear to all that the United States could not again withdraw into splendid unilateralism, politically or economically: it would need to accept broad responsibility for determining how the international community might function for the future and for helping to rebuild the countries devastated by the war. Out of this need, of course, came the Marshall Plan, discussed in Part II.

U.S.-led political and military alliances that marked the end of World War II brought the world eventually both to economic recovery and to the Cold War, that is, to both positive and deeply controversial outcomes in the postwar period. Certain generous U.S. foreign aid programs, part and parcel of our political agenda then, continue into the present. In the postwar years, we set a course to assure political and economic advantage from which we have never departed. The intent was to make of nations we have assisted capitalist democracies that resemble the United States as fully as possible.

To be sure, in the rebuilding process, the United States was motivated by both humanitarian and intensely practical motives. The government saw not just an opportunity but a necessity to merge its political and economic agendas in foreign policy more fully than ever before. In politics, FDR's dream of a workable international alliance, the UN, was realized after the war, though it was quickly subverted to uses he had not foreseen. And his successor, Harry Truman, led Western Europe into the North Atlantic Treaty Organization (NATO) to oppose the developing political and military threat posed by the former USSR.

These political advancements were balanced by equally important U.S.-led economic recovery strategies for defeated nations: stabilizing international currencies and providing finance for recovering nations through the Bretton Woods agreements; creating the International Monetary Fund (IMF) and the World Bank; implementing the Marshall Plan, with its particular sensitivity to the leadership that recovering nations would themselves need to produce for rebuilding Europe (and, later, Japan through somewhat similar strategies) and re-creating trading partners for a bourgeoning postwar U.S. economy in the process.

In addition, these years also saw the enactment of another element of U.S. foreign policy many still consider the most successful international political strategy in our history, the concept of "containment." This strategy was conceived, apparently inadvertently, by a distinguished career officer in the Foreign Service, George Kennan, who had also been a primary architect of the Marshall Plan. It enabled the United States and its allies to enact political, military, and economic measures to contain Stalinist aggression and Soviet communism within the borders of the former USSR and within the territories awarded to its control in the post-World War II settlements.

These Cold War containment measures were applied by the United States and its allies, led first by President Truman (whose administration included many of the same foreign policy advisors who had served during FDR's terms) and then by every other president up to and including Ronald Reagan, until the collapse of the USSR in 1989. Although the process required nearly forty years to meet its aims, it ended as Kennan had foreseen, with the USSR's crumbling from within, its people starved in every conceivable way by their isolation from each other under despotic regimes and, by the Cold War, from the rest of the world.

Inevitably, the policy of containment has had its critics. And the Cold War may, indeed, have been more responsible for the Korean conflict and

for the tragedy of Vietnam than any other concept. Kennan himself has denied that the outcomes of containment were what he envisioned. Other
forms of interaction with leaders of the USSR after Stalin might have enabled different and less costly relations among the nations of Europe, fos-
tered broader international progress, and prevented what can only be called
the tragedy of contemporary Russia and the other nations of the former
USSR. There was opportunity to apply in Russia a version of the jointly
developed rebuilding strategies so successful in Europe and Japan in the
post World War II period (and the availability of resources through the
IMF and the World Bank to do so). In the failed strategies brought to bear,
many still intensely controversial, Americans must recognize that this U.S.-
led process has brought Russia into desperate conditions that pose great
dangers both inside the country and elsewhere.

U.S. policies of containment resurfaced in the late 1990s in announced strategies to unseat Iraq's president Saddam Hussein. We must
observe the effects of this policy closely, trying to assure that any success
does not again leave behind an all but irrecoverable society or one that har-
bors only fear and suspicion of the United States, its policies and allies.
Possibly such undesirable consequences can be prevented by current efforts
to strengthen U.S. relations with other Arab or Islamic states and with the
people of Iraq.

In any case, our point is this: Containment of perceived enemies has
been a policy that brought very costly, highly questionable success to the
United States and the world. Specifically, Americans must acknowledge
what has happened to the Russian people: Where are their opportunities?
Are they or the world safer from Russian political corruption or weapons
of mass destruction than before? What has happened to their traditional
culture? Or, to raise the most urgent question for U.S. foreign policy as we
knew it in the '90s: Can we foresee that Russia and her sister states can participate in the growth of a global economy in the foreseeable future?

These questions illustrate fundamental short-sightedness in U.S. foreign policy over several generations of leadership, to the present. Among
other lessons, they teach us that Western democracy cannot be expected to
take hold overnight where there is no experience of democratic practice or
institutions; that a nation unfamiliar with the characteristics of capitalism
cannot successfully become capitalist without patient assistance, over time,
as accountability is built and infrastructure put into place; that capitalism
may not meet all of the needs of people who have known only oppression
and planned economies for several generations; that policies limiting con-

tact and fostering separation from other nations breed uncertainty and fear, not confidence.

Formulating coherent U.S. foreign policy for the future is one of the nation's most critical challenges. Formidable in any case, it is the more so because of the partisan extremism that easily converts complex international political and economic relationships into vicious internal wrangling, preventing sober reflection, and consideration of alternative actions. The failures of the Republication Conservative-led Congress to support virtually any form of international political engagement in the '90s except economic advancement do not bode well for the future. Its rejection of the Nuclear Test Ban Treaty in 1999 was but the most glaring expression of its unworkable unilateralism. In the confusion that currently abounds at home and abroad, Americans are compelled to ask, What is the road ahead? How can we reach it?

Chapter 16

What Next?

AMERICA: "INDISPENSABLE" FOR WHAT?

Questions about why and how the United States should use its resources abroad are enormously complex. But the rich mix of American intellectual traditions regarding foreign entanglements may yet guide us as we look ahead. Consider the following:

- Historically, we've accepted responsibility to participate in the conflicts of other nations reluctantly and only when prevailed upon by those involved, or to ally ourselves against crimes against humanity or perceived aggression. In recent decades, we've been criticized abroad as much or more for failing to be involved as for our involvement.

- We've recognized, perhaps more fully than any other country, that prospects for our own peace and prosperity depend upon others' enjoying opportunities similar to ours, and at least some of the time, we've tried to help create those opportunities.

- We've retained military strength sufficient to defend our own nation and to aid the defense of others. When we have erred, as indeed we have, in Vietnam, for example, we've openly admitted, eventually, tragedies associated with our errors.

These are, indeed, important strengths. But our vulnerability in foreign policy now is the lack of a well-established, broadly communicated, and thoughtfully evolving rationale to guide our decisions. This is true, whether one thinks of U.S. relations with old, well-established allies or with developing nations.

The absence of such a clearly articulated rationale is but one result of intractably divided, partisan ideologies in the federal government. As we've seen, Republican Conservatives generally favor U.S. hegemony, international dominance, and resist alliances they believe prevent the United States from taking unilateral action in any matter considered important to U.S. interests. They favor minimal government intrusion in the development of markets and in the lives and prospects of those affected by them. Since gaining control of Congress in 1994, Conservative Republicans have brought to bear a characteristically uncompromising moral and social agenda dominated by Fundamentalist Christian points of view. This, of course, has further complicated the development of a necessarily ecumenical, broadly humanistic foreign affairs agenda. Its effects were seen in 1998, for example, in former house speaker Gingrich's unilateral efforts to ally American political Conservatism and religious fundamentalism with those of Israel, actions that complicated and interfered with policies of the Clinton administration.

By contrast, Liberals are likely to seek mutually reinforcing alliances, the development of democratic institutions, and recognition of national, cultural, and religious differences in any vision of the international future. They usually resist U.S. domination of other nations and cultures; are likely to value cultural, religious, and political ecumenism; and recognize that, for the future, U.S. strength depends upon Americans' leadership in developing collaborative decision-making processes and international norms that protect human rights and the opportunities of everyone to prosper.

As we've seen, Centrists such as President Clinton attract the criticism of ideologues at either end of this continuum. Even when their rationale is clear and compelling, as it so often was not under Clinton, Centrists have found it difficult to act convincingly. Successful action in U.S. foreign affairs today and in the future will have to entail broader efforts to inform and engage the electorate in problems to be addressed and strategies for their solution. It also will require effecting political compromise both at home and abroad, an achievement that partisan extremism rendered virtually impossible in the United States in the '90s. As President Clinton announced military action against Iraq in late 1998, his policies were overtly challenged by Conservative Republican leaders in Congress, intent then upon political action leading to the president's removal from office. This breach between president and Congress at a moment of U.S. military conflict abroad was unprecedented. Similar failures of congressional support greeted his policies in Kosovo a few months later.

Whatever the dangers of excessive pragmatism in Centrist politics, especially as practiced in the Clinton administration, the wisest directions in foreign policy, as in most other problems of government, are more likely to be fashioned through Centrist, ideologically moderate thinking than through partisan extremism, a fact historians recognize in reminding us that American government was built upon the requirement of compromise. As we saw in Part I, the Founders' brilliance lay in their reliance, not upon anyone, or any group, but upon everyone, upon the American people. American democracy would require collective political action, across innumerable differences. Indeed, the presence of a loyal opposition in any argument would protect the nation against extremes. In these realities lives our argument for increasing efforts by government to engage an informed electorate in the development of foreign policy rationale.

A FINAL NOTE

Writing in *Democracy in America* (1834) about his visit to America a few years earlier, the French political philosopher Alexis de Toqueville described the likelihood that foreign policy in democracies will be decided on purely domestic grounds. De Toqueville was correct in applying this observation to nineteenth-century America, and, given the intractable political divisiveness that paralyzes federal government today, very little has changed since then. But the excessively partisan conflicts that have so crippled the nation's abilities to think coherently about crucial matters in foreign relations must be reined in and the energy being wasted in domestic political hostilities redirected to national advantage.

Part IV

Can the Center Hold?
A Case in Point:
Immigration and Immigrants

Immigration and immigrant policy is about immigrants, their families and the rest of us. It is about the meaning of American nationality and the foundations of national unity. It is about uniting persons from all over the world in a common civic culture.

—U.S. Commission on Immigration Reform

Chapter 17

What's at Stake?

Erosion of Madisonian federalism, extreme political partisanship, antigovernmentalism, and single issue politics in our national government, especially throughout the '80s and '90s, have brought only Band-Aid solutions to complex problems that require broadly deliberated, principled, long-range remedies. These dangers, themes we've seen in Parts I–III of this book, are rapidly diminishing Americans' capacities to direct our future as a nation. Perhaps, as W. B. Yeats put it: "the center" will, in fact, not retain strength to "hold."

The sorry state of our immigration and immigrant policies is a dramatic instance of this vulnerability. Fragmenting forces inherent in these issues are in any case powerful, and they are being exacerbated by the short-term, politically expedient approaches an increasingly fragmented government is taking to address them. In the absence of courageous and thoughtful leadership, these failures of government—*national* government—threaten both our understanding of ourselves as Americans and the world's faith in American democracy.

In the eighteenth century, the Founders envisioned a nation in which a great variety of people, ideas, and interests would, for all their diversity, be held together by their commitment to a common future and to certain fundamental principles, most of which are embodied in the Declaration of Independence and in the United States Constitution (Wood 1992). It is the future of that vision that is gravely imperiled today.

We should note that, following the lead of the Urban Institute, scholarship now usually distinguishes between *immigrant* and *immigration* policies (Fix and Passel 1994). Consideration of *immigration* policy raises such questions as: Who shall be an American? and Who shall be welcomed as a legal resident, long term or temporary, and for how long? Questions about how to control illegal immigration also fall under this rubric. Issues concerned with *immigrant* policy lead to such questions as: What steps could facilitate the integration of immigrants into our society? and What, if any, distinctions, should be made between noncitizens and citizens, whether native or foreign-born? Inevitably, the ultimate question in both contexts, of central importance to our study, is: Who is to make these kinds of decisions?

These are straightforward questions, but they force us to confront issues that are extraordinarily divisive, complex, and far-reaching in their potential to affect virtually all aspects of national life: political, economic, social, and moral. They evoke a range of responses which, at their most extreme, are capable of pitting neighbor against neighbor, undermining hope for national coherence, and obscuring any vision of the open, democratic society we seek so eagerly to project to the world.

In the world of politics, partisan difference about immigration policies tends to cluster not only around whether decisions will be made at the state or federal level, but also around unresolved questions about immigrants' importance to the work force; their role as boon or burden in the economy; and their impact upon a recognizable American culture and society. In addition, there are very different points of view about the impact of immigration policy upon U.S. relations with other nations in an increasingly interdependent world.

In relation to immigrant policy, Republican Conservatives and Liberals are divided over whether and to what extent noncitizens, including legal immigrants, are entitled to public support and services: welfare, health care, job-training programs, and special educational programs such as language training. Some of these elements of debate seem poised to divide Republicans, also separating social moderates from the Far Right.

At first sight, the intensity of clashes on these matters seems strange, almost paradoxical. After all, America has always been a nation of immigrants. A nation proudly different from all others just because everyone here—except, of course, for Native Americans—has ultimately, in this or past generations, been a "foreigner" from elsewhere. The sole instance in which the Constitution distinguishes absolutely between the rights of native-born and naturalized citizens is in restricting eligibility for the presidency to those born in the United States.

Yet, some Americans opposed immigrant expansion almost from the first, citing virtually the same arguments advanced by opponents today: immigrants were a threat to the economic prospects of American citizens; they were costly to taxpayers; and they brought cultural disruption to the society Americans knew. These voices, however, seldom prevailed. On the whole, the United States favored such expansion through most of the nineteenth century and, intermittently, thereafter. Restrictionism dominated for relatively brief periods, typically in response to serious faltering of the economy, as in the depression of the 1930s. In more prosperous times, our welcoming shores symbolized the noblest ideals of a land of opportunity for all, as streams of newcomers provided essential workers, and ultimately settlers and consumers, to fuel U.S. prosperity.

In our early years, the widely agreed upon purpose of planned or expansionist immigration was to strengthen the labor force. In his *Report on Manufactures* (1791), commissioned by the first Congress under the Constitution, Alexander Hamilton declared it in the national interest "to open every possible avenue to emigration from abroad." Consistent with his vision of a commercial empire and a strong central government, Hamilton saw aliens as "an important resource, not only for extending the population, and with it the useful and productive labor of the country, but likewise for the prosecution of manufactures" (Jacobson, 405).

Others advanced more lofty rationales for expansionism. In 1817 Thomas Jefferson, Hamilton's nemesis and the Founder perhaps best able to express American idealism, envisioned the United States as a "new Canaan," where immigrants would be "received as brothers and secured against . . . oppression by participation in . . . self-government" (ibid.). This idealism, too, like Hamilton's economic pragmatism, continues to echo in today's debates about immigration and immigrants. The successful immigrant became, across those years, a staple of the American myth. Within a generation or two, sometimes more rapidly, batch after batch of newcomers was more or less fully integrated into the existing culture, making substantial contributions to American life and well-being. In myth, and much of reality, the typical pattern for immigrants then was one of upward movement economically, educationally, and socially.

To be sure, Americans have never been entirely consistent in welcoming newcomers, nor have they necessarily been impartial or generous in dealing with recent arrivals. English-speaking newcomers were the most welcome and those from northern Europe were usually preferred to Italians and other, darker-complexioned arrivals from further south or east. Asians, who differed more obviously from the majority in appearance, culture, and custom, were typically viewed with a particular hostility, especially once their labor was no longer needed to build the railroads and dams so important to the development of the West in the nineteenth century. During the 1870s, many cities, counties, and states passed anti-Chinese legislation, and in 1882 the *Chinese Exclusion Act* totally prohibited immigration from China.

In the twentieth century, following the depression and World War II, America once again opened its doors to a larger immigrant influx as our economy boomed. But the flow of newcomers was strictly regulated by a system of national quotas, giving significant preference to "desirable" immigrants, while sharply limiting opportunities for others, most especially for Latin Americans. In the sixties, the Civil Rights movement highlighted the unfairness of such discrimination. During Democrat Lyndon Johnson's presidency, the *Hart-Cellar Act* (1965) ended the quota system, setting only total numerical ceilings for new admissions. Family unification was now the priority; its consequence was an unprecedented flow, a virtual explosion, of both legal and illegal immigrants. By the mid-1980s, there were signs of a leveling-off, but numbers rose again after the Reagan administration in the *Immigration Reform and Control Act of 1986* gave legal status to more than three million undocumented aliens, mostly Central Americans who had lived in the United States continuously since 1982, or worked in agriculture.

As the '80s drew to a close, many Americans were convinced that immigration had again gotten out of hand. Suddenly there was intense concern on a number of fronts. Weren't there far too many foreigners? Were recent newcomers, so many of them Latinos, too unskilled to function well in our society? Was our social safety net now being disproportionately burdened by an immigrant "underclass"? Perhaps foreign customs, traditions, and languages were undermining the coherence of American values and communities. Did these people even want to become U.S. citizens? So many seemed to have no interest in naturalization. And what, finally, of the manifestly uncontrollable, frightening influx of illegal, that is, undocumented, aliens, especially across our southern borders, bringing with them, it seemed, the triple evils of poverty, drugs, and crime?

Clearly, a quite different immigration myth was shaping itself in the American consciousness. Centered in the states and regions with the largest immigrant populations—California, New York, Florida, Illinois, New Jersey, and Texas—the news media carried its echoes across the nation.

Once again it was time for the government to act, but to what end and with what consequences? How would a world now so tightly interconnected by global communication and business react if the United States became a kind of fortress nation, reversing our long-standing traditions of relative openness? Could we afford to deprive ourselves of a source of creativity and a labor pool essential to our economy's continuing growth? And what of the internal repercussions of any such move, given our already so diverse population? But if, on the other hand, we accepted the growing multipolarity of our society, how could we protect a clear sense of the meaning of American identity? Could we keep our politics from becoming ever more dominated by the factionalism of varied and proliferating minority cohorts? Momentous questions such as these provoked extreme, partisan responses. There was little agreement, even about the accuracy of "facts" related to immigration and to immigrant life that reached the public.

Nonetheless, as this decade began, Congress attempted yet again to reform immigration policy in response to then current needs and perceptions. The *Immigration Act of 1990* reordered priorities and set new ceilings. The number of employment-based visas was increased, with high-skilled workers given preference for admission. This time the effect was to more than double the number of immigrants from Europe. Taking a further, potentially very important step, the *Act* also authorized appointment of a U.S. Commission on Immigration Reform to make recommendations for the future.

The bipartisan commission was finally appointed in 1994 by President Clinton, who chose widely respected congresswoman Barbara Jordan as chairperson; Jordan served in that role until illness forced her retirement in 1996. In its four annual reports to Congress between 1994 and 1997, the commission recommended gradually reducing the total number of new immigrants. Policies to sustain immigrant family reunification established during the 1980s were retained, although priorities were somewhat rearranged, with an emphasis on the nuclear family. No slots were set aside for unskilled immigrants, who were, however, admissible under the reunification category.

As it turned out, however, all this earnest and honorable work achieved relatively little. Throughout the 1990s, Congress, led by Conservative Republicans, failed to follow up on recommendations that might have led the nation a considerable distance toward mature, coherent and consistent immigration and immigrant policies. We will have more to say on this topic in the next section. Although the immigration flow slowed between 1991 and 1995, legal immigration subsequently resumed its unprecedented rates of increase, while the number of illegal aliens also increased dramatically.

Having failed in efforts to control immigration directly, Congress changed its strategy in 1996. The new thinking focused on creating financial disincentives and barriers to immigration, while also considerably expanding the states' decision-making powers. By legislation limiting immigrants' access to social benefits, members hoped to make the United States less of a magnet for potential newcomers, thus simultaneously reducing immigrant numbers and effecting large savings for the government. With these goals in mind, and in the context of their general intent to dismantle much of the country's social safety net, they moved to curtail immigrants' eligibility for such benefits as food stamps, Aid to Dependent Children and Supplemental Social Security Income. At the same time, Congress also raised the financial threshold that potential immigrants and/or their sponsors would have to meet before visas would be granted.

Underlying the specifics of benefit limitation was a policy question with serious long-term implications, not simply for immigrants, but for the very idea of America: is it appropriate, that is, consistent with our traditions and values, to make distinctions in law between legal noncitizen immigrants and citizens? Throughout its reporting life, the Jordan Commission said no. Nonetheless, in 1996, with Newt Gingrich as speaker of the house and Conservatives in the ascendancy, a congressional majority decided differently, a decision that dramatically reoriented American assumptions about the status and role of immigrants in our nation and federal government's responsibility toward them.

Both the Welfare Act and the *Illegal Immigration Reform and Immigrant Responsibility Act* were signed into law by President Clinton in August 1996. Their unprecedented provisions went beyond making all immigrants, including those here legally, ineligible for many forms of government assistance available to citizens. They also vastly expanded the power of states to initiate and implement immigrant policies. Opponents of large-scale immigration trusted that the decisions a Conservative Congress made in the domain of immigrant policies would function as a backdoor way to limit immigration itself.

This harshness did not, however, sit well with many Americans. Under Clinton's leadership and with the support of most citizens, the government moved to partial restoration of some essential benefits, especially for children, the elderly, and the disabled. Eligibility to receive food stamps was restored to many, though by no means all, legal immigrants in 1998. With an eye to the November 2000 elections, both parties, but especially Republicans, engaged in piecemeal restoration of many other benefits, and in a general loosening of earlier restrictions. However, most modifications applied only to immigrants already in the United States as of the target date, August 1996, excluding those legally admitted thereafter. Absent additional changes, future immigrants will continue to face unprecedentedly stringent financial hurdles. Finally, and perhaps in the long run most important, even the now somewhat more generous approach to benefits leaves intact the unprecedented distinction between citizens, other legal residents, and aliens generally.

In March 2000 the Conservative-dominated Supreme Court upheld the distinction between legal immigrants and citizens when it refused, in the words of *New York Times* correspondent Linda Greenhouse, "to hear a challenge . . . to portions of the 1996 welfare law that made legal immigrants ineligible for various kinds of federal welfare assistance" (27 March 2000). The appeal, *City of Chicago v. Shalala* (No. 99-898), challenged lower court rulings that the 1996 distinction does not violate "equal protection" under the Constitution as long as it is "rational." That standard was met, these courts declared, by the rational connection between benefit restrictions and the government's interest in both unburdening the welfare system and fostering self-reliance. Given the Clinton administration's moves to restore various immigrant benefits after 1996, their support for the Justices may surprise. Observers should ponder the wisdom of arguments largely motivated, it would seem, by immediate financial concerns.

Clearly, the politics of immigration have been shifting since 1996. By 1998, Democrats and Republicans tried in their midterm election campaigns to steer clear of policy issues concerned with immigration and immigrants. In particular, Conservative Republicans had realized after the '96 elections that their restrictive postures had resulted in a number of unintended consequences: they had alienated most Hispanics (and other immigrant constituencies) and precipitated both an unusually large turnout of those eligible to vote and a rush to citizenship that would, they feared, significantly swell this voter pool by the next round.

Damage control became the order of the day. Most Liberals, usually Democrats, avoided reopening immigration/immigrant policy issues, fearing a backlash from those native Americans in their constituencies concerned about immigrant competition for jobs. Conservative Republicans initiated aggressive campaigns to woo Hispanic communities and votes around the country. A great deal of money was spent on friendly media messages in Spanish. As the 1998 election results demonstrated, these efforts were largely unsuccessful.

Between 1996 and 1998, Hispanic voters had become a significant political force, helping to decide key races in several states. Prior to the elections, 6.6 million Hispanics were registered to vote, 3.9 million of these in Texas and California. According to 1998 exit polls, they accounted for roughly 5 percent of all U.S. voters, the highest proportion ever, which is expected to continue increasing. A headline in an Hispanic magazine announced with pride and defiance, "The Hispanic Vote: A Sleeping Giant Awakens" (*LatinoLink*, 30 October 1999). And the pre-2000 election slogan of the Spanish television network Univision, headed by former HUD secretary Henry Cisneros, proclaimed simply, Hispanic Voters: A New Force.

Furthermore, there is now also a second generation of immigrants actively involved in state and local politics. A surprising number of Hispanic candidates competed successfully in 1998, and not just in states with large Hispanic populations. In 1999, Michigan had two Latino state legislators, Wisconsin one, and Massachusetts three. The largest gains were made in California, where, in addition to achieving victory for the lieutenant governor, Latinos significantly increased their representation in the state Senate and in the Assembly.

In high-immigrant regions only those moderate Republicans able to display a relatively consistent openness to immigrant concerns, among them most prominently Texas governor George W. Bush, held their seats. Whether Hispanic votes favoring popular individuals like Mr. Bush signified a new acceptance of the Republican Party, however, is an open question. As was reported one day before the election, many Hispanics had trouble reconciling Republicans' "new" and "old" faces (*Wall Street Journal*, 2 November 1998). Looking ahead, Conservative Republicans understandably feared that more Hispanic legislators, foreign-born voters, and citizens who, even in the second or third generation identify with immigrant causes, would continue to swell Democratic ranks.

Conflict about how to achieve an accurate count of the U.S. population in the year 2000 Census illustrated the tension around this fear.[1] Liberals, usually Democrats, moderates of both parties, and immigrants favored statistical sampling rather than the direct counting that constitutional language had seemed to call for. They contended that this method would correct previous undercounting of immigrant, minority and poor residents. (The 1990 U.S. Census estimated that Latinos were undercounted by 5 percent or 1.5 million people. Asians followed closely at 4.4 percent.) Supporters of sampling were also aware of the fact that it was likely to result in a redrawing of both congressional and intrastate voter districts. States and locales with large immigrant populations, both illegal and legal, would gain political power and government funding at others' expense. California, Texas, and Arizona would probably have the largest gains.

Because such reapportionments would probably benefit Democrats and Liberals, alarmed Republicans challenged sampling on constitutional grounds. In 1999, the Conservative U.S. Supreme Court ruled 5 to 4 in *Department of Commerce v. U.S. House of Representatives* (525 U.S. 316) against use of statistical sampling for redistricting purposes. Nonetheless the Clinton administration at once stated its intention to use both sampling and direct count in order to achieve a more accurate picture of the nation's actual population.

It seems all too evident that each political party will continue to insist upon the approach that will most benefit its future prospects among immigrant populations. Many observers realize that the Census-counting debate was largely about the number six, the number of seats by which Republicans currently hold their majority in the House of Representatives.

Clearly, a whole mass of unresolved issues in the domain of immigration and immigrant policies remains bubbling just below the surface. Many attribute Americans' now somewhat diminished distress about immigrant numbers and the effects of immigration on our immediate lives to our general prosperity. They predict that the old concerns and hostilities will erupt with devastating force should our economy falter and unemployment intensify competition for jobs. In fact, local news coverage in areas with high immigrant populations emphasizes the fact that many native-born Americans are still extremely uneasy with proliferating languages, changing neighborhoods, and the costs of immigrant support. Some workers, especially in the lowest-paid, least-skilled jobs, already fear immigrant competition. Slightly more than half the respondents to nationwide polls published in March 2000 by the public opinion research firm Zogby International favored limited legal immigration and vigorous prosecution of illegals. African-Americans and Hispanics, however, were for immediate curtailment of all immigration (Zogby, 30 March 2000).

The tendency of immigrants to cluster in relatively large numbers in such cities as Los Angeles, Chicago, and New York exacerbates concerns in those locations, even as the virtually unprecedented proliferation of these enclaves in several noncoastal states unaccustomed to such influxes raises new problems. In once remote central Kentucky, for example, communication between officials and newcomers is so greatly impeded by a dramatic increase in the number of Hispanic residents that police officers are now required to take instruction in basic Spanish. As the year 2000 began, Population-Environment Balance, a Washington, D.C.,-based organization, launched a radio spot warning Iowans that unless immigration is curbed, "your town" will turn into a "congested, dirty copy of Los Angeles" (Michael Conlon, Reuters, 20 January, 2000).

Because the explosive potential of immigration and immigrant issues and the consequences of bad policies are still most evident at the regional or local level, the reality that these are in fact national issues with current and future consequences for the commonweal as a whole is still largely overlooked. At the same time, the woeful inadequacy of dealing with such complex, interrelated matters piecemeal and at random is ever clearer. The short-sighted partisanship, whether based on party or regional loyalties, which has largely dominated the debate and allowed, even encouraged, fragmentation to flourish no longer serves.

The new alertness to immigration and immigrant issues evident in party platforms and in questions put to presidential candidates before election 2000 was a promising start. In the pages that follow, we argue that these issues must receive long overdue reasoned deliberation.

Chapter 18

Issues in Immigration Policy

ILLEGAL IMMIGRATION

There is virtually total agreement among Americans and their elected representatives that illegal immigration is radically out of control and must be stopped. However, even a casual perusal of the day's newspapers demonstrates how difficult it is to achieve that goal in a country like ours. Millions of people, foreigners and U.S. citizens alike, enter the country annually. Thousands of miles of our northern and southern borders are geographically unprotected; people are free to move at will within the United States; immigrant enclaves make it difficult to spot illegal residents; and some employers, especially in manufacturing and farming, are not reluctant to hire illegals willing to work below minimum pay in extremely poor working conditions.

How serious is this problem? Best estimates are that between 1990 and 1996 the U.S. population grew by roughly 420,000 undocumented newcomers annually. When the estimated number of foreign nationals leaving the country is subtracted, the net annual increase is thought to be somewhere between 200,000 and 300,000. Current Immigration and Naturalization Service (INS) estimates assume about 5.5 million illegal residents with an annual growth rate of about 275,000. However, there are reasons to belive that the total may be closer to 6 million. Moreover, because of their underground existence, illegals are least likely to climb out of poverty and are most likely to be involved in crime. Especially in the Southwest, the problem of illegals is almost synonymous with drug trafficking. Yet, a high percentage of illegals, perhaps almost half, are not border crossers at all. They are people who initially entered the United States legally but over-stayed their temporary visas; many are students and workers with good jobs.

In addition to excluding illegal aliens from most social services and welfare benefits, provisions of the *Illegal Immigration and Immigrant Responsibility Act* (1996) called for large-scale deportation of the undocu-mented already in the United States and greatly enhanced border control. The INS was held to new, much stricter standards and given substantial additional resources for their work. As of 1998, according to an Associated Press report, the agency's budget exceeded the FBI's and its staff was larger than that of either the State or Labor Department. Even with this extraor-dinary expansion, however, the work load was so huge (deportations, for example, were up 50 percent in fiscal year 1998) that a shortage of funds reportedly limited enforcement operations.

Enforcement has nevertheless been successful up to a point. The num-ber of deportations and incarcerations of those awaiting deportation and/or appealing such decisions increased dramatically after 1996. Wire fences, brightly lit observation towers and patroling guards, often accom-panied by specially trained dogs, reduce, but by no means eliminate, illegal border crossings. Often, numbers decrease dramatically in one closely con-trolled area but very soon show a proportionate increase in other, more open territories. Suspected employers of undocumented aliens are closely watched; there have even been agreements between the INS and some large commercial enterprises, for instance, an eastern shore poultry producer, to cooperate on the apprehension of these workers in order to avoid the costly work stoppages of unannounced raids.

Though government must enforce its laws, many Americans find these measures distasteful. They are reminiscent of police states and raise fears about the extent to which government is able and willing to track down in-dividuals and reach into individual lives, often with no conclusive evidence of wrongdoing. In early 1999, the INS acknowledged these and other dif-ficulties associated with tracking down illegal immigrants by announcing that vigorous efforts to apprehend illegals would be limited to those be-lieved guilty of drug trafficking or accused of other criminal activity. Even so, President Clinton's proposed budget for the year 2001 sought 430 ad-ditional Border Patrol agents, along with several hundred inspectors for land borders and airports. One thousand new detention bed spaces were also requested.

LEGAL IMMIGRATION AND LEGAL RESIDENCE

The challenge of stopping illegal immigration, however formidable, involves the implementation of policies most Americans consider desirable. There is no such clarity with respect to policies to guide legal immigration and residence. Certainly nobody wants to close the country totally to newcomers, nor to open it without restriction to one and all. Between these extremes, however, is a wide range of irritably argued positions separating those who generally favor expansionist immigration policies and those favoring tight numerical controls.

Moreover, decisions about gross numbers are not the only ones to be made. Interacting with potential numerical ceilings are all sorts of "qualitative" variables that receive greater or less emphasis depending on one's point of view: How important is family reunification? Are immigrants from some countries likely to contribute more to the nation's well-being than others? What priority should be given to prospective newcomers with high levels of education and/or documentable skills? Should the needs of American business (including agriculture) for particular categories of workers, current or anticipated, temporary or long term, be taken into consideration? What policies are most likely to prevent immigrants from becoming financial burdens to their communities? How much consideration should be given to consequences in such other areas as foreign policy or international trade? A dawning awareness that it may no longer be wise or even feasible for any nation to establish immigration policies unilaterally further complicates matters.

WHO ARE TODAY'S IMMIGRANTS AND HOW MANY ARE THERE?

As of March 1998, the total U.S. population as determined, however imperfectly, by the Census Bureau stood at 270.3 million. Almost one out of every ten residents was foreign born. Half of these were from Central or South America or the Caribbean, about 28 percent from Mexico alone. About 10.5 million foreign-born noncitizens resided legally in the United States.

Roughly three-quarters of the total foreign-born population, legal and illegal, has been admitted since 1970; close to 30 percent since the start of the current decade. According to the 1999 *World Almanac*, the immigrant population grew four and a half times faster than the native born in the 1990s. In early 1999, the INS estimated the growth of illegal aliens at around 275,000 per year. These counts will probably be higher still when the 2000 Census is complete.

WHERE ARE WE HEADED?

Just a few years ago, projections for the year 2050 had assumed a total U.S. population of 387 million; however, the most recent study released by the Population Reference Bureau has raised this figure to 394 million (Pollard and O'Hare 1999). Immigrants and their families—again, without distinguishing between legal and illegal—will account for about two-thirds of that growth. Hispanics are expected to become the largest minority ethnic group by the year 2005. By the year 2020, non-Hispanic whites will have lost their majority status in four states, and by the year 2050 they will constitute barely half of the nation's total population. "Within the lifetimes of today's teenagers, no one ethnic group—including whites of European descent—will comprise a majority of the nation's population" (William Booth, *Washington Post*, 22 February 1998).

Scholarship in immigration patterns gives us no reason to believe that, absent draconian national and international measures, efforts to emigrate to the United States will abate in coming decades. In "March of Folly: U.S. Immigration Policy after NAFTA," Douglas S. Massey, who has written extensively on immigration's effect on U.S. culture, argues persuasively that the more advanced societies like ours invest in Third-World or developing societies, the more conditions in those societies converge to create pools of emigres (Massey 1998). And no one doubts that the United States is likely to remain the nation of immigrant choice. August Gribbin cited Massey's designation of the United States as "a country of perpetual migration" (Gribbin, *The Washington Times*, 4 October 1999). Only a major war or economic catastrophe could halt the otherwise uncontrollable flow.

CONFLICTS AND CONCERNS

Current numbers and projections make it easy to see why native-born citizens, even those sympathetic to the human dimensions of immigration, may feel swamped by the magnitude of change around them, especially when many Republican Conservatives in Congress and elsewhere represent immigration as a threat to the very integrity of our nation. Regrettably, America's unresolved racial tensions are a major component in attitudes toward immigration/immigrant policies. Many Caucasians are fearful not just of being swamped by foreigners; they fear losing power and ascendancy to foreigners of color. The dramatic rise in the number of Hispanics, partly black and generally darker skinned, is often a particular concern in the West and Southwest.

In addition, there is widespread fear that immigrants in large numbers may increasingly become a new economic underclass, draining resources from their communities and making few, if any, positive contributions to the overall quality of life. Many studies document disproportionate levels of unemployment, low wages, and poverty among at least some immigrant groups, especially those with low skills and education, and Hispanics. These perceptions enter into virtually every debate and significantly influence decision making at every level.

Those favoring major revisions of our immigration policies by reducing overall numbers and shifting admission priorities to skilled workers typically use their findings on immigrant poverty to support these goals. For example, in *Importing Poverty: Immigration's Impact on the Size and Growth of Poor Populations in the U.S.* (1999), Steven Camarota, director of research at the Center for Immigration Studies, finds immigrant poverty increasing at a faster rate over the current decade, despite an improving economy with higher incomes for most people. In *Heaven's Door: Immigration Policy and the American Economy* (1999), the Harvard economist George J. Borjas attributes this growing poverty to recent, huge increases in immigrant numbers, and a higher proportion of underprepared workers, in conjunction with fundamental changes in American business and industry. He is particularly concerned about how these circumstances further aggravate the nation's already excessive income disparities.

In human affairs generally, and certainly in politics, people's beliefs— their reading of the "facts"—is critical. Fully 49 percent of Americans believed immigration was having a negative effect upon the country and 70 percent held that government must limit immigration (*Wall Street Journal*, 5 September 1997). A continuing strong economy has reduced these numbers somewhat, yet in 1998 even the Sierra Club, certainly an inclusive organization, presented its more than half a million members with an option to support immigration reduction as one way to help control U.S. population growth, limit consumption, and slow degradation of the environment.

When the measure was defeated 6 to 4, proponents vowed to bring it back for reconsideration.

Indeed, conflicting goals and curious alliances abound whenever immigration policy is under consideration. For example, the Conservative Right, known for its emphasis on the sanctity of families, is nonetheless skeptical of generous immigration policies aimed at family reunification. They contend that these pay insufficient attention to the potential productivity and self-sufficiency of newcomers. Similarly, many Conservative Republicans who tend to oppose large-scale immigration as eroding American cultural traditions and identity, are at the same time most sympathetic to "Big Business's" clamor for additional immigrant workers.

Democrats, too, have divided impulses, though less extremely so. Immigration- and immigrant-friendly by tradition, they nonetheless worry on behalf of their labor and union constituencies that immigrant competition may disadvantage American job holders and lead to a deterioration of working conditions. They also worry about costs of immigrant services, including education and health care. Centrists and moderates of both parties are concerned about whether a top priority for family reunification can or should be maintained.

The drawn out, ongoing debate in the late 1990s over increasing the number of visas for temporary workers with technical and professional skills dramatically illustrates the strange forces at work in a decision-making process fraught with controversy and ultimately random in its conclusions. In 1998, after much wrangling, the Republican Conservative-led House, with support from some Democrats, passed a bill authorizing a large increase in the number of H-1B visas, good for six years of temporary employment in the U.S. Originally capped at 65,000 by the *Immigration Act of 1990*, the revised House ceilings were set at 115,000 for 1999 and 2000, with a gradual decrease back to the original cap by the year 2002. Although the Senate did not act on the bill, a three-year increase to 115,000 was ultimately included in the *1999 Omnibus Appropriations Act*, along with some funding to provide additional training and education for Americans.

Proponents argued that absent such increases, the United States would lose its world leadership in information technology, citing among other documentation a 1998 work force study by the Information Technology Association of America and the Virginia Polytechnic Institute that declared more than 340,000 high-tech jobs unfilled. Opponents, like Robert Lerman, director of the Human Resources and Policy Center at the Urban Institute, questioned the evidence for such claims and warned of dangerous precedents and policies based on short-term considerations (Lerman 1998).

As we shall see in Chapter 19, the story is far from ended. By June 1999 the new fiscal year 1999 cap had already been reached. Almost at once the high-tech industry began to clamor for further increases. However, nothing was resolved that year. There was division in Republican ranks, and Democrats were reluctant to provide support.

All of this to make a point: Citizens must ask themselves how well such a decision-making process is likely to serve the nation.

PROPOSALS FOR IMMIGRATION REFORM: POLICY AND PRACTICE

The U.S. Commission for Immigration Reform delivered four reports to Congress; the last of these, *Becoming an American: Immigration and Immigrant Policy* (1997), reiterated and expanded the body's earlier conclusions. This powerful document, representing years of research and debate by qualified, thoughtful people, deserves renewed attention now.

Several convictions inform the commission's work: the overarching goal of immigration is to strengthen the nation economically and otherwise; its achievement depends on appropriate policies effectively implemented, which must take anticipated impacts on native American workers into account; illegal immigration harms the nation and must be stopped; the federal government must lead in matters of immigration; sound immigrant policies aiming at the Americanization of future citizens are essential to the success of the entire enterprise. We will return to this last point in our consideration of immigrant policies in Chapter 20.

Based on these values, the commission urged significant reform of our legal immigration systems, while also recommending that Congress lower overall ceilings and redefine priorities for the admission of lawful permanent residents. Priorities were to shift from the extended to the nuclear family and, within an overall reduction of skills-based admissions, from the unskilled to the skilled. Once that had been accomplished, Congress was to authorize ceilings for specified time periods, perhaps three to five years, to assure that numbers would be adequate to support national priorities. The commission anticipated that the reordering would, in and of itself, reduce annual immigrant admissions to roughly 550,000, about where they had been in the 1980s.

In a much broader context, the commission, mindful of the interaction between immigration and foreign policies, urged the federal government (1) to cooperate with other countries to address the factors that might be impelling their citizens to emigrate; (2) to give priority in economic and foreign policy considerations to reducing the causes leading to unauthorized migration over the long term: and (3) to respond generously to migration emergencies.

The commission also urged Congress to undertake a radical restructuring of the whole immigration system, noting that the INS was hopelessly overextended and overloaded, while also crippled because different government agencies were responsible for components of the same functions. To achieve coherence and consistency in all immigrant/immigration matters, INS functions should be redistributed among existing and newly created government departments, each with clearly delineated tasks, as follows:

- immigration enforcement to be relocated in a Bureau for Immigration Enforcement at the Department of Justice;

- applications for various kinds of status to be dealt with in the Department of State, under the jurisdiction of an undersecretary for citizenship, immigration, and refugee admissions;

- enforcement of immigration-related employment standards to be located in the Department of Labor;

- appeals of administrative decisions to be handled in an independent Agency for Immigration Review.

Within this new structure, the State Department would be responsible for formulating and evaluating immigration policy, while also monitoring the possible consequences of foreign policy decisions in the immigration context.

Whether or not one agrees with specific conclusions arrived at by the commission, their work is exemplary in the breadth of its vision; its clear-eyed focus on national perspectives and policies; its concern for human values, and its avoidance of the pitfalls of partisan bias.[1]

Congress, however, took no significant action to reform the U.S. immigration system following the commission's final report. Although many members favored dismantling the INS and redistributing its responsibilities, the Clinton administration vigorously resisted such "fragmentation," insisting that INS functions be kept under one roof within the Department of Justice and continue under a single director. All that was needed to improve the agency's accountability and performance, the White House disingenuously maintained, was to disentangle its law enforcement responsibilities from its role in benefit administration, with distinct structures and chains of command established for each of the two branches.

It is this more modest restructuring that the service itself has been trying to effect, so far with little success. The INS is still the most widely criticized federal agency after the IRS. On 4 October 1999, for example, the American Civil Liberties Union (ACLU) released statistics showing that illegal immigration in the Southwest had apparently increased from 1.2 million to 1.5 million in one year, despite more than 8,000 border agents with a budget of $952 million and multiple "gatekeeper" operations. Naturalization backlogs were said to be worse than ever, and every day brought some new allegation of INS brutality, inefficiency, or fraud. Diane Lindquist, among others, reported that the agency was being charged with granting up to 20,000 visas above the year's authorized cap (Lindquist, *San Diego Tribune*, 9 October 1999). The scandal provided new ammunition to those angrily pursuing INS reform.

Meanwhile, with all sides agreeing that some sort of INS reform is essential, Congress is still without clear direction. Proposals intended to jump start and inform broadly based, serious conversations about the purposes of immigration in the United States, such as the Carnegie Endowment's fine *Reorganizing the Immigration Function Toward a New Framework for Accountability* (Papademetriou, Aleinikoff, and Meyers 1998), continue to appear, but nobody seems to be paying much attention.[2]

By late 1999, the issue had once again landed on the "back burner," according to Jena Heath (*Austin American-Statesman*, 19 November 1999). Possibilities for a compromise solution seemed dim, as Congress, intent on establishing two separate immigration bureaus, accused the White House, in familiar rhetoric, of wishing to create a "Super-INS." By Election 2000, both party platforms called again for "urgent" INS reform. Bemused spectators should ask how well any of these proposals might contribute to more coherent and farsighted policy development, or even coordinated implementation, in the future.

Chapter 19

Bottom Lines:
Economic and Labor Issues

Given the prominent role of economic considerations in the history of U.S. policy development, it's no wonder that financial and labor issues figure prominently in discussions of immigration, immigrants, and the government's responsibilities with respect to both. Naturally, Americans want to know what immigration "costs" them as individuals and families. Does it fatten their pocketbooks, or drain away their hard-earned dollars? And, of course, policymakers at all levels are asking more or less the same bottom-line questions.

For all kinds of reasons, getting answers in these contexts turns out to be extraordinarily complicated. Counting immigrants, as we saw earlier, is a tricky business in any case. So is classifying them by such categories as ethnicity and race. The "facts" that analysts present and the conclusions they draw really can't help being shaped by their goals and assumptions, no matter how honest they mean to be. And assumptions, in particular, are hard to detect by a casual reader. In this realm, as in most human endeavors, we see what we expect to see. Research conducted by opponents of extensive immigration will tend to emphasize its costs; conducted by those with a generally expansionist philosophy, research highlights benefits. As Jodi Wilgoren noted: "There is little consensus—one recent study asserted that immigrants pump an extra $10 billion into the economy each year, but another said they are a $12 billion drag on the nation"[1] (Wilgoren, *Los Angeles Times*, 1998).

What do we mean when we refer to the "costs" of immigration? When we try to assess a cost-benefit ratio? At the simplest level, not simple at all, we're talking primarily in financial terms, asking whether and to what extent the gains to the economy generated by immigrants exceed the dollars laid out in all kinds of services to them. How much do immigrants cost in taxpayer dollars? How much do they pay in taxes? How do these figures compare? (These questions, now being asked about both legal immigrants and naturalized citizens, threaten to make them into a separate class of residents, who alone are asked to justify themselves in a cost-benefit analysis.)

Equally urgent, however, perhaps more urgent in the minds of most Americans, are questions related directly to immigrants' impact on the labor market, on jobs. What effects do they have on employment? Do they "cost"American jobs? Depress wages? If so, do these consequences apply across-the-board or selectively?

As the questions suggest, there are many variables in such calculations. For example, most research agrees that fiscal cost-benefit ratios at the national level tend to show benefits exceeding costs: "Contrary to the public's perception, when all levels of government are considered together, immigrants generate significantly more in taxes paid than they cost in services received," concludes a study conducted by the Urban Institute, a leading source of sustained scholarship in this area (Fix and Passel 1994). But when the locus of measurement shifts to states, regions, and localities, the positive effects begin to decline progressively.

Whereas immigrant households are a tax asset for the federal government, costs and benefits appear to be more or less in balance in states overall, though particular states with high numbers of recent immigrants may be trouble spots. At the regional and local level, especially in major, immigrant-intense urban centers, such as Los Angeles, Chicago, and New York, immigrant services are typically a major fiscal drain. There is general agreement that the largest negative impact is on local governments, which provide about half of the public services to immigrants, while the federal government harvests more than two-thirds of every immigrant tax dollar.

Another variable, even more elusive, is the effect of passing time on such calculations. Were fiscal cost-benefit ratios more advantageous to Americans in the past than they are now? Almost everyone believes they were. Is there a measurable trend? If so, can it be extended into the future? As assessed in a 1997 study by the National Academy of Sciences, immigration is a fiscal burden on the average American household in the short run but continues to produce significant gains over longer periods, as it always has.

Although many other studies come to similar conclusions, there are skeptical voices as well. They emphasize the educational and ethnic differences between current and past immigrants to argue that present realities forbid such positive expectations. Focusing on a growing disjunction between the educational and skills backgrounds of recent immigrants and the apparent needs, current and projected, of ever more sophisticated American (and global) business, they predict increasingly negative cost-benefit ratios; absent revised immigration policies, poorer immigrants will generate fewer taxes and require more services. The large number of Hispanics with low educational levels, and the documented lack of achievement in school by many Hispanic pupils, figure prominently in these presentations.[2]

When the primary focus of cost assessment shifts to the labor market, much has been made of the difference between the impact of high-skill and low-skill immigrant workers on their American counterparts, both native and foreign-born. In very broad terms, it has been widely assumed that whereas our expanding economy provides ample room for all well-prepared workers, so that additional newcomers in this group do not increase competition or depress wages, those with few skills—legal immigrants admitted under the family reunification rubric, temporary workers and illegals—do so. However, these assumptions may turn out to be rather simpler than reality.

Until quite recently, pressure for admission of more low-skill workers—usually on a temporary basis—was typically generated regionally, most persistently in states where agriculture is a large part of the economic pie, like California, Florida and Washington. Claiming that they could not find sufficient American or legal immigrant workers for harvesting and other tasks, growers lamented, as they still do, that without additional foreign-born help their enterprises would fail or at least have to undergo radical and costly transformations. They scarcely pause in lobbying Congress to approve expanded guest-worker programs.[3]

The view from a national rather than regional perspective was rather different. In 1997, for instance, the National Academy of Sciences (NAS) reported a huge 44 percent overall decline in real wages for high school dropouts between 1980 and 1995 as a consequence of immigrant competition for entry-level jobs. Later that year, the U.S. Commission on Immigration Reform, the study's sponsor, came out firmly against guest-worker programs, asserting that they expand rural poverty and are incompatible with democratic values everywhere in the world. In 1998, the General Accounting Office challenged regional employer claims by documenting high unemployment levels and falling wages in the agricultural sector nationally.[4]

Throughout, the Americans most at risk from competition by low-skill, low-wage immigrant workers have been African-Americans, still disproportionately represented among the underprivileged, despite the continuing growth of a Black professional and middle class, and the entrepreneurial wealth of some. In *Heaven's Door: Immigration Policy and The American Economy* the economist Borjas writes of an immigration deficit in the black population, a per person reduction of annual income by $100 to $400. Indeed, these Americans have been especially vulnerable to competition from new immigrant workers since the late nineteenth century, when Frederick Douglas wrote: "Every hour sees the black man elbowed out of employment by some newly arrived immigrant whose hunger and whose color are thought to give him a better title to the place" (Jacobson 1998, 409). Virtually the same point was made by William Julius Wilson, among others, in the 1990s (Wilson 1999). Little wonder that a mid-'90s survey of American attitudes identified African-Americans as the citizen group most entrenched in opposition to immigration (Mitchell 1996).[5]

As we've seen, much of the thinking about cost-benefit ratios generally depends on assumptions about the future. These, of course, are best guesses only. No one can really know whether Rep. Lamar Smith (R-Tex) is correct in his unequivocal assertion in 1999 that over 90 percent of future U.S. jobs will require sophisticated workers, or whether it's the National Immigration Forum that has it right in predicting, that same year, that fully half of all future jobs will require at most a high school diploma. Predictions are a tricky business, and buzzwords come and go with astonishing speed.

Indeed, as 1999 drew to a close, the media were suddenly reporting evidence of widespread worker shortages at the low end of the employment scale, shortages putting pressure on many of the support systems essential to keep ordinary life running more or less smoothly. Within just a few months, that shortage appeared so acute in some enterprises, including hotels, restaurants and nursing, that some employers and chambers of commerce had joined together to form an "Essential Workers Immigration Coalition" to lobby for new legislation (Greewax, *The Atlanta Journal and Constitution*, 12 March 2000).

As to high-skill workers, we noted in Chapter 18 how years of debate about expanding H-1B visas failed to generate a principled, long-term approach to dealing with alleged labor shortages in this sector. Nor did they achieve clarity about the effect of such admissions on American workers.[6] While virtually all parties tended increasingly to agree that our "new" technology-based economy would surely continue to require many more well-qualified workers, there was considerable disagreement about the extent to which Americans rather than immigrants could presently or potentially meet these needs. As recently as 1998, the government's own General Accounting Office (GAO) questioned the alleged shortage of Americans with appropriate educational backgrounds, suggesting, rather, that the industry needed to look beyond pools in a few narrowly defined employment classifications for the help they sought (21 April, 1998).

But even assuming that the GAO's thinking in this matter was overly optimistic, some contended that strengthening our educational system, especially in the "hard" disciplines—math, science, and technology—coupled with improved access for all Americans, could relatively quickly solve industry's problems. Liberals, usually Democrats and labor unions, generally held this view. They tried to hold down increases in H-1B visas and insisted that these be accompanied by expanded funding for training and education to enhance American workers' competitiveness. Conservatives opposed to expansionist immigration on principle and/or motivated by concerns for their own and their party's popularity in coming elections frequently advanced similar views.

By early 2000, however, the cry for skilled immigrant workers and concern about an overall labor shortage had achieved unprecedented intensity. The media were on the case, almost at feeding frenzy, with daily stories about the nation's critical labor shortage and the various responses to a "crisis" focused especially on those with advanced skills, but now also understood to include less privileged cohorts: janitors as well as computer engineers. In this charged context, the extraordinary complexity of the questions surrounding U.S. immigration policy became as evident to some observers as the failure to address them coherently. Demetrios G. Papademetriou, co-director of the International Migration Policy program at the Carnegie Endowment for International Peace, responded to renewed H-1B debates by emphasizing that "we are again showing how not to have the right conversations about foreign-born high-tech workers . . ." (*The Washington Post*, 21 March 2000).

In the process, new alliances favoring one or another version of immigration expansion came into being. "Big Business", of course, continued to predict the disastrous consequences for the national economy of too few qualified workers and to push hard for many more H1-B visas. Now, however, much smaller enterprises, such as representatives of the U.S. tourist industry, joined in the chorus. Addressing the Senate Banking Committee in spring 2000, Federal Reserve chairman Alan Greenspan endorsed expanded immigration as an antidote to the dread threat of inflation that could so easily follow excessive competition for a shrinking pool of workers. Even some labor unions, concerned about their shrinking membership pools, advanced expansionist proposals, as, predictably, did traditional immigrant advocacy groups. In a stunning move, the AFL-CIO, though opposing increases in the number of new legal immigrants, in February 2000 declared support for amnesty and possible future citizenship for the estimated 5 to 6 million workers and their families here illegally or with temporary legal status.

For Congress, particularly for the Republican majority, the situation was trickier than ever. Generally sympathetic to business claims, as usual, they were seriously alarmed at the possibility, even probability, of a backlash from American workers intent on protecting their interests. Thus, Congressional debates, mostly concerned with the H-1B question, were largely about numbers: how high to set visa ceilings and for how long. Proposals to raise employer-paid visa application fees and to allocate these funds to educational improvement were the only concession to more general issues of the nation's well-being in the long run. The *American Competitiveness in the Twenty-first Century Act of 2000* (S. 2045) introduced by Republican senators Orrin Hatch (R-Utah) and Spencer Abraham (R-MI) proposed almost doubling ceilings for three years, with additional generous exemptions from the new caps for universities, research facilities and recent graduate degree recipients from American universities. (One cynic estimated that a third of MIT's graduate school would be eligible for the exemption!) In the House, a modest increase of only 45,000 additional visas for one year only (HR 3814) was proposed by Rep. Lamar Smith (R-TX). The congressman seemed to believe that this bulge could be corrected by dramatic re-reductions in the subsequent two years.

But Democrats, including presidential candidate Al Gore, were also pulled in two directions: their traditional commitment to support American workers and fear that without additional immigrant labor the soaring economy might, indeed, falter. In this context, Senators Kennedy (D-MA) and Feinstein (D-CA) favored an extended cap below that of the Hatch bill, a sliding scale for application fees that would charge the largest corporations $3000 per application, and, most importantly, the use of these funds for what a *Boston Globe* editorial lauded as a "crucial new education and training initiative." Of particular interest because of its long-range perspective is Kennedy's emphasis on support for elementary education "to help close the digital divide for lower-income and minority students," a move aiding the disadvantaged, while assuring the availability of more qualified American workers in the future (*The Boston Globe*, 19 March 2000). According to White House spokesman Jack Siewert, the White House, too, favored a reasonable increase in the number of H-1B visas as part of a balanced approach that protects and prepares the U.S. work force.

In the midst of these chaotic discussions, new perspectives on the labor shortage, with enormous potential implications for the development of U.S. immigration and foreign policy, burst into the foreground. With very little warning, at least for Americans generally, the underlying problem was now widely perceived as a *systemic* shortage, already serious and expected to intensify as the population continues to age. Furthermore, the problem was not peculiar to the United States: all developed nations appeared to be similarly afflicted, not just by aging populations but, for many, by overall population decreases. All were suddenly aware that significantly increased immigrant numbers might be the only possible compensation for a shortage of young indigenous workers. In shortest supply, inevitably, were those at the upper end of the scale.

Replacement Migration: Is it a Solution to the Declining and Aging Population?, a United Nations report examining the demographics of eight countries including the United States, found a severe population crunch that might make radically expanded immigration a necessity in many countries. The report predicted that such huge influxes were likely to cause significant social upheavals. As Papademetriou summed up the situation, the world was face-to-face with a new dimension of global competition. Henceforth nations would battle to keep for themselves the talent the United States had for years been siphoning off for our particular economic benefit (*The Washington Post*, 21 March 2000)

Not surprisingly, such dramatic scenarios redoubled the vigor of firmly entrenched anti-expansionists. Known bodies like the Center for Immigration Studies and the Federation of American Immigration Reform continued to question the extent of the shortages and, rightly, criticized most of the measures being advanced as short-sighted. Over and over they and like-minded others pointed with alarm to America's changing demographics, the progressive swamping of U.S. traditional cultures and values, and the negative effects on American workers of expansionist measures. Lacking positive proposals for how to fuel continued prosperity without more immigrant labor, an occasional voice even questioned the wisdom and necessity of limitless economic growth.

A different kind of question arising whenever the costs of immigration are under discussion is "Who pays?" The question is important, not only for its practical ramifications, but also because it, too, ultimately goes to the broader issues whose significance we have observed throughout: What distribution of responsibilities between and among levels of government best serves the nation?

The American public usually encounters "Who pays?" in relation to specific situations that make the news. In the Southwest, for example, as everyone knows, the INS is waging a massive campaign to apprehend and expel illegal border crossers. Because many of the apprehended men, women and children are ill or injured, the Border Patrol sends them to hospital—humane treatment which, however, generates huge costs! Thus, in November 1998, a single California county faced charges of $750,000 for eleven months of hospital care, with additional expenses of $150,000 for autopsies and funerals (Lelyveld, *The Philadelphia Inquirer*, 11 November 1998). Because it does not take these undocumented arrivals into custody (usually it just despatches them back across the border), the Patrol is not responsible for such expenditures. But who is? The county where people happen to be apprehended? The state? A different federal agency?

Obviously, there is fertile ground here for resentment and angry confrontation. As we noted earlier, the federal government benefits disproportionately from immigrant taxes in any case, while local governments bear most of the cost of services to this population. By assigning additional immigrant-related fiscal responsibilities to the states, the devolutionary legislation of 1996 aggravated this discrepancey. Subsequently, the *1999 Omnibus Appropriations Act*, though increasing the total amount for Block Grants to the states, for the third year in a row significantly reduced funding for social service grants. The biggest losers were four of the states with the largest immigrant populations—California, Texas, New York, and Florida. Fearing that they will have to raise residents' taxes, some states are suing the government to recover costs.

As he urged Congress to pass legislation (S.1709) reimbursing the seventeen states with the worst illegal immigration problems for some portion of their huge expenses for medical care and the processing of aliens accused of crimes, Senator John McCain (R-AZ) stated memorably: "These costs are a federal responsibility and should not be shirked by those in Washington who don't live with the problem of illegal immigration in their midst" (Associated Press, 7 Oct. 1999). A similar argument was advanced by the city of Chicago in *City of Chicago v. Shalala* (99-898): the federal government "should not be allowed to shirk all responsibility" for those legally admitted under its immigration policies. The federal courts, however, thought otherwise. In refusing to hear Chicago's appeal from previous negative decisions, the Conservative U.S. Supreme Court once again held true to its devolutionary stance.

Our point? In this tug of war about costs, we see again, and with particular clarity, how badly the country needs a Federalist approach to government. The many questions surrounding immigration are *national* issues requiring systematic, cooperative and constructive thought. Our present approaches are failing us.

Given so many urgent, unresolved issues, Americans should look once more at the policy recommendation of the bipartisan U.S. Commission on Immigration Reform, noting especially its challenges to the national government: to assert leadership in immigration-related matters; to protect government's ability to respond flexibly to inevitably changing circumstances; and to make coordinated decisions on the basis of promise for the United States as a whole. These are valuable procedural guidelines, pointing a way out of current partisan conflict with its attendant government paralysis and myopic, divisive decision-making on behalf of this or that momentary partisan objective.

As the context for the economic and labor issues surrounding U.S. immigration policy becomes increasingly complex, there is an even greater need for qualities the Congress has not so far displayed: courage, coherence and breadth of vision. Ideologically conflicted and with one eye firmly fixed on future political prospects and the desire for massive contributions to campaign coffers, the legislative bodies lacked the will to undertake the complete overhaul of our immigration policies they, too, recognized as long overdue. Alone in the Beltway, with no consistent source of policy advice, lacking the structures that might have facilitated communication between and among all levels of immigrant administration and committed to the diminishment of the federal government's authority, Congress, dominated by Conservative Republicans, turned to quick fixes. With nothing fundamental achieved, each side could claim "victory."

If, as is overwhelmingly likely, immigration policy issues will have to be evaluated in global contexts, single-issue, short-term considerations will serve even less well than in the past. In such uncharted territory, the "right" conversations will demand the confident leadership of a strong government committed to consultation and cooperation both within the nation and across national lines. One-sided concern with immediate advantage to any individual component of this interconnected web considered in isolation will be increasingly dangerous, not just unproductive: an incitement to chaos and possibly even violent confrontation.

Chapter 20

Immigrant Policy:
Where Are We Now?
Why Does It Matter?

In recent years, Liberals, usually Democrats, have been more inclined than Conservative Republicans to think about policies that might help legal immigrants to realize their potential as a long-term source of strength for the nation. In such areas as education, health care, and benefit eligibility, Liberals have typically advanced immigrant policies concerned with the actual conditions of immigrant life in the United States. These are policies that support the integration of newcomers into our communities and into American society as a whole. In their efforts, proponents have been joined by moderate Republicans, including governors, and the bipartisan Commission on Immigration Reform.

Conservative Republicans, on the other hand, have tended to hew very close to the bottom lines discussed in Chapter 19. *The Welfare Act* and the *Illegal Immigration and Immigrant Responsibility Act of 1996* are in essence the fruit of thinking largely focused on immediate economic advantage. However, Conservatives' views on immigrant policies also frequently reflect their eagerness to protect American traditions and culture against what they see as too much change, too much foreignness.

IMMIGRANT POLICY AND DEVOLUTION

Since 1996, in an effort to correct excessive reductions of support to legal immigrants, some federal benefits earlier taken away have been restored in piecemeal fashion. Congressional support for such modifications of the earlier legislation became easier to win as Republicans began to worry about immigrant and ethnic voters' resentment of their perceived harshness, especially in politically important states like New York and California. However, these changes in federal provisions have actually benefited immigrants rather less than one might have anticipated. Most working adults are still ineligible for food stamps and most of the immigrants who arrived in the United States after the August 1996 target date continue to be ineligible for major federal assistance programs for at least five years (Zimmermann and Tumlin 1999). Troubled by these gaps, and also aware of the importance of the immigrant/ethnic vote for the coming elections, the White House pushed for additional remedies.

In February 1999, the president's fiscal year 2000 budget requested congressional approval for $1.3 million over five years to restore health and disability benefits and food stamps for legal immigrants, including many admitted after the target date. That April, Sen. Daniel Patrick Moynihan (D-NY) introduced the *Fairness for Legal Immigrants Act* to restore eligibility to legal immigrants for a number of safety net benefits earlier denied to them, including food stamps for all those in the United States prior to the August 96 enactment date, and Supplemental Security Income (SSI) for postenactment date arrivals who subsequently became disabled. As of late 1999, no action had been taken. The bill was referred to the Committee on Finance and stayed there. Undeterred, Cinton returned to Congress in February 2000 to renew his plea for extensive benefit restoration.

As we know, Congress had accompanied the 1996 measures to shrink the federal social safety net available to immigrants by provisions greatly expanding the states' powers to formulate immigrant policies. It gave individual states the right to choose whether to exclude current and future immigrants from means-tested federal benefits, as well as from benefits funded by the state or locally, and thus to decide whom to exclude.[1] It gave them responsibility for deciding how to "police" benefits programs and how much of their own state funding, if any, to use on immigrants' behalf. It left to them decisions to establish residency requirements for benefit eligibility, if they wished to, and to decide whether and to what extent to include sponsors' incomes in determining eligibility. In these provisions we see again the kinds of challenges to the responsibilities and powers of the federal government that Conservative Republicans have generally brought since 1994.

Not surprisingly, states exercised their expanded powers and responsibilities in different ways with varying outcomes. Although the race to the bottom feared by some critics of the 1996 legislation has not so far occurred, some states are considerably more immigrant friendly than others in their policies, their actions, and the messages these send to immigrant constituencies and to watching governments and peoples around the world. Most have responded generously and creatively to the new challenges, using state funds to replace lost benefits such as food stamps and medical care for at least some of their current legal residents .

Yet state programs cannot really compensate for federal benefit restrictions. All in all, the social safety net for immigrants is now much weaker than it was; access for noncitizens is considerably more limited than for citizens, and levels of aid vary greatly from state to state. Most newcomers arriving after August 1996 still remain ineligible for federal assistance for at least five years (Zimmermann and Tumlin 1999).

The five-year "bridge funding" Congress provided in 1996 to help states meet their costs during the transitional period before they assumed full responsibility for most social services to the disadvantaged is also proving to be an unstable resource. There is evidence that the federal government is not honoring all of these commitments. It is too early to see how well devolution will serve when bridge funding runs out completely and when states are left to their own desires and means to meet fundamental needs. Or when a weaker economy causes needs and tensions to mount. Growing awareness that the savings claimed for the welfare reform measures are disproportionately indebted to cutbacks in immigrant support is sobering, indeed.

Some observers forecast that a major economic setback will, after all, trigger a race to the bottom, with states vying to make themselves unattractive to potential foreign-born newcomers. Meanwhile, as the numbers of people "on welfare" have declined in a strong economy and in a political context generally unsympathetic to the needy, states are stockpiling unspent funds, against difficult days to come.

WHY IT MATTERS SO MUCH

The significance of the 1996 legislation extends far beyond a concern for benefit levels, however important.

What does it mean conceptually and practically, for example, when some states establish their own residency requirements for legal immigrants seeking benefits? Does such a measure invalidate traditional constitutional protections? In *Saenz v. Roe* (134 F. 3d 1400 [1998]), the Supreme Court decided that such restrictions on citizens do so; the Court did not, however, clarify the status of legal immigrants in this context, people who, under the Constitution, are citizens of the state in which they reside but not of the United States. Does such immigrant exceptionalism promote intolerable, or at least dangerous, divisiveness among neighbors? Will states reluctant to make this and other discriminations be flooded by large numbers of poor immigrants for whom to provide?

More generally, questions like these illustrate how badly the United States needs coordinated, *Federalist* approaches to government's responsibility for immigrant policy. As matters stand now, the unprecedented powers to devise their own immigrant policies that Republican Conservatives, with the president's support, awarded the states will have far-reaching effects on many aspects of American life now and in the future.

First: In the aggregate, unilateral decisions made by states will, if not reversed by the courts, affect the overall patterns of immigration to the United States. For example, decisions made by some states will significantly reduce the chances for those with little education, little money, and sponsors too poor to guarantee self-sufficiency. In effect, responsibilities recognized since the late nineteenth century as belonging to the federal government acting on behalf of all the people, will be progressively undermined by regional and local interests.

Second: Decisions by individual states create state-to-state inequities with both immediate and long-range consequences. For example, when generous immigrant policies make a particular state or region especially attractive to newcomers, its immigrant population increases, often sharply. There is ample documentation that immigrant welfare recipients are clustered in so-called magnet states offering generous benefits. In a supplement to their study *Patchwork Policies: State Assistance for Immigrants Under Welfare Reform* (August 1999), Wendy Zimmerman and Karen C. Tumlin provide complete correlations of benefit eligibility, per capita spending on immigrants, and size of the immigrant population for each of the fifty states. Troubled California leads the list with the highest benefit levels and the greatest number of foreign-born residents.

As immigrants rush in, native populations may respond to the influx by seeking "escape" to more homogeneous locales, whether driven by hostility to foreigners and dislike of changes in the community or by employment and tax concerns. Analogously, when particular locales are known for their inhospitality, immigrants will try to avoid or leave them, fanning out across the nation to the extent they can do so. For evidence of this development we need look no further than daily newspapers in states as widely scattered as Iowa, Alabama, Montana, and Kentucky. The chain of consequences thus set in motion creates a host of new problems which, as matters now stand, will again be approached randomly by lawmakers desperate for solutions to the immediate difficulties in their areas.

However, the most important consequence of the devolution of power to the states and the resulting lack of coordination in matters affecting immigrants is the extent to which these measures aggravate the nation's ever-increasing fragmentation and divisiveness. The current hodgepodge of state measures is counterproductive in its disorganization, but more than that, it threatens fundamental American values and concepts: our will to shape and reshape ourselves as *one* nation which, ideally, listens to many voices and offers equal opportunities and equal justice to all.

CREATING AMERICANS

How do immigrants become Americans? What must happen for "Americanization" to succeed? What are the roles and responsibilities of various levels of government and of communities in this enterprise? The U.S. Commission on Immigration Reform addressed these questions in "The 'Americanization' of Immigrants," part of its final 1997 report to Congress. The commission's goals for immigrant policies as proposed there are clear: to facilitate the process whereby newcomers become Americans in their sense of themselves and their new home, not just legally, and to help all Americans, foreign and native born, old and new, to understand how essential the idea of a shared civic culture is to our nation.

The commission report presents Americanization as a complex, mutually reinforcing process, demanding accommodations by citizens, newcomers, and government. From immigrants it requires voluntary commitment to certain fundamental American principles and ideas, as well as willingness to set aside conflicting loyalties and to defend the United States in times of peril. They must be open to new ways and make the effort to learn enough English, American history, and civics to function side-by-side with other Americans in our "civic culture." The dignified tone of the revised naturalization oath (affirmation) proposed by the commission highlights the significance of each individual's anticipated commitment:

Solemnly, freely, and without any mental reservation, I, [name] hereby renounce under oath [or upon affirmation] all former political allegiances. My sole political fidelity and allegiance from this day forward is to the United States of America. I pledge to support and respect its Constitution and laws. Where and if lawfully required, I further commit myself to defend them against all enemies, foreign and domestic, either by military or civilian service. This I do solemnly swear [or affirm].

From government at all levels, the successful integration of newcomers into local communities and into the national community requires both vigorous leadership and resources. It requires the development of policies that will cultivate a shared commitment to such precious American ideals as liberty, opportunity, and democracy. Educational policies, for instance, must assure ample opportunities for immigrants to learn about, and really understand, such defining constitutional principles as equal protection and justice under the law; freedom of speech and religion; and representative government.[2]

At least as important to the commission as formal learning is the creation of contexts enabling immigrants to *experience* the "fulfillment in practice" of these principles. Placing great emphasis on the American tradition that immigrants do not differ from native-born Americans in their entitlement to full protection of the Constitution and its laws, the commission report rejects the 1996 congressional legislation. It is not, its authors assert, in the national interest to deny safety net programs to immigrants because they are not citizens.

We have dwelt at length on the commission's work because it is hardly possible to overemphasize the profound differences between its generous and farsighted approaches to immigrant policies and the attitudes and values informing the 1996 legislation. To us, the promise of the former seems as clear as the perils of the latter. In the bipartisan report, a forward-looking, pragmatic idealism on behalf of a united nation, consistent with the best of our traditions; in the '96 legislation, overriding partisan concerns with short-term financial and political advantage. Americans will need to choose—soon—which direction to follow.[3]

Chapter 21

California and Beyond

CALIFORNIA: A CRUCIBLE

Nowhere are the centrifugal forces threatening to tear our nation apart more evident than in California the most populous of the 50 states. Nowhere is our question, Can the Center hold? more urgent or the challenges to coherent government at every level more apparent.

The size of the state's immigrant population, its composition, the characteristics of its economy, and the idiosyncrasies of its political traditions all play a part in a drama being played out at an unprecedented level of intensity. The immigrant-related themes of the drama are not all that different, fundamentally, from elsewhere in the United States, but the moves and countermoves are more vivid, the confrontations sharper. In California everything seems to occur at a heightened decibel level on a more brightly lit stage and to rush more unerringly to extremes. As the aptly named book by William A. V. Clark, *The California Cauldron: Immigration and the Fortunes of Local Communities* (1998) points out, the immigration debate, too, is "most intense and most vociferous" in this one state.[1] Thus, in California we observe, magnified, forces that could, absent wise policies, ultimately break the United States apart into hostile, minimally connected fragments. But given such policies, we can also see clearly the latent promise in her ferment.

At 24.9 percent, California's foreign-born population in 1997 was the highest in the nation, well above the national average of 9.8 percent, and roughly 5 percent above that of New York, the second highest. Its illegal population was also the largest, as was the size of its refugee population, numbering 27,000. Most of California's foreign-born come from Central and South America, about half of these from Mexico, with Asians the next largest contingent. At least eighty languages are spoken, posing major challenges to communication and education, and creating a good deal of cultural disjunction in neighborhoods. Asian newcomers tend to be at the high end of the economic and educational spectrum with rapid upward mobility; by contrast, Latinos are often clustered at the lower end of the spectrum, with economic and educational progress lagging behind, sometimes over several generations.[2]

Many native-born Californians fear the extent of the state's increasing diversity. A report issued by the California Research Bureau in October 1999 predicts that in a population of 34 million, whites will have fallen to 50 percent by the year 2000, with Latinos accounting for almost a third of the total. By the year 2021 Latinos (39 percent) and Asians (14 percent) will together account for more than half the state's people. The primary cause of these demographic changes is the high birthrate among Latinos; international migration, most prominently from Mexico, is the second largest contributing factor (Lopez 1999).

In 1997, about 6 million of California's foreign-born residents were not citizens, one of many disruptive factors in this teeming state (Johnson et al. 1999). Some, because they were illegal, others because they were seasonal workers, still others because they chose not to pursue citizenship even if eligible, or were stymied somewhere along the line by INS backlogs and generally cumbersome processes. Mexicans, California's dominant minority, also constituted the highest proportion of these noncitizens.

Mexicans have been traditionally reluctant about naturalization. Their loyalties to the country of their birth, so close by, have typically been unusually strong and enduring, tending to pull them away from full participation in U.S. civic and political culture. Also, until passage of the *Mexican Nationality Act* in 1998, many risked losing property and other rights in Mexico if they chose to become U.S. citizens. Still, it is troubling that the rate of application for citizenship in this population decreased markedly between 1990 and 1997, while rates for immigrants from Asia, Europe, and the Caribbean were climbing. And no one is quite sure why.

The *Mexican Nationality Act* introduced new factors into the mix. Through it, the Mexican government extended a dual nationality option, not just to Mexican-born American citizens, but also to their American-born children. As a result, two million Mexican-born U.S. residents who are already citizens, along with many others who might yet be naturalized, could, sometime before the year 2003, seek to become Mexican citizens as well (*Migration News*, April 1998). Observers believe many will do so; they would gain better treatment under Mexican inheritance and investment laws, expanded rights to buy and sell land there, and access to schools, universities, and government jobs and services. It is too soon to tell to what extent the new options will pull the Mexican-American community more closely into Mexico's orbit, but its potential for aggravated divisiveness is obvious.

Perhaps the concept of dual nationality, which has the potential to affect other constituencies than Mexicans and other states than California, is a welcome precursor of loosening national ties in an increasingly globalized world, as some suggest. Others, however, predict that it will interfere with immigrants' integration into American society by reinforcing already increasing tendencies among many immigrants to maintain closer emotional, political, and financial ties to their nation of origin. They worry especially about possible consequences for border states in the Southwest, where the population of Hispanics generally, and Mexicans in particular, is large, and where immigration/immigrant issues tend to have immediate consequences for the dollar flow, foreign trade, and foreign relations.[3]

California is a state of enormous wealth and great poverty. The income inequalities we observe throughout the nation appear here in exaggerated form, with immigrants, including low-skill workers, both legal and illegal, disproportionately represented among the poor and very poor. After the difficult early 1990s, the state's economy grew dramatically, along with employment opportunities for skilled and educated workers, including immigrants, but not, by and large, for the less well prepared.

In a recent study, *California's Rising Income Inequality: Causes and Concerns*, the nonpartisan Public Policy Institute of California confirmed that the state's widening income gap was increasing at an even faster rate than the nation's as a result of rapid declines at the lower end of the wage scale (Reed 1999). Overall, poverty in California, largely, though not exclusively, immigrant-related, continues to be a major problem: the state's average poverty rate in the late 90s was among the ten highest in the nation.

Despite strong resentment against immigrants and the burdens they are thought to impose on citizens, California has been generous in its response to the 1996 congressional legislation, using state funds to compensate for many of the federal benefits that were withdrawn. However, as a recent Urban Institute study documents, even eligible legal immigrants have generally been very reluctant to apply for public aid. In Los Angeles County, which has more immigrant households than any other place in the United States, immigrant applications fell by 71 percent over just two years, as applications from citizens held steady. The causes suggested to explain the trend include realistic and unrealistic immigrant fears that any contact at all with officialdom could lead to deportation; confusion on the part of many immigrants, their advocates, and public officials; and unpredictable variations in policies and enforcement among regions and officials (Zimmermann and Fix 1998).

Especially afflicted by accelerating poverty have been California's agricultural workers, who typically have no share in the expanding prosperity of the state's second largest industry. A change in the migration patterns of immigrant workers is one contributing factor. Until quite recently, most tended to move back and forth between the United States and their birth country (most frequently Mexico), but many now choose to remain in California throughout the year. Settling as best they can in poverty-plagued, rapidly expanding *colonias*, they and their families are particularly vulnerable to exploitation by labor contractors and by employers willing to look the other way when profits and legality conflict. Intense competition for work among the native and the foreign-born, as well as among older and newer immigrants, sends wages spiraling downward from their already low levels (Taylor, Martin, and Fix 1997). Growers, however, clamor insistently for more imported labor.

When we turn to the state's preeminent industry, the exploding, upward bound world of information technology, we see obvious differences. On the whole, the skilled workers in this sector command good salaries and are a benefit, not a drain on the economy. But here, too, we see the remorseless push for more immigrant workers, permanent or temporary, to fuel growing prosperity, with little thought given to noneconomic considerations or to long-range consequences.

The arguments used to support California's lobbying for revised immigration policies are predictable. A typical scenario portrays the state trapped between the economy's need for more skilled workers, on the one hand, and the increasingly inadequate qualifications of an ever larger immigrant cohort, on the other. Workers at the bottom of the scale, hit by declining wages and lacking options for upward mobility, are poised to become more and more dependent on the state for human services and education. What had been a modestly favorable immigrant cost-benefit ratio, even through the difficult years in the early part of the decade, is likely to reverse. Worst of all, the excess of costs over benefits will occur just when California's supersuccessful technology industry, starved for qualified workers, may begin to lose ground in the global marketplace (RAND Corporation 1997 and Vernez 1998).

Needless to say, such grim predictions, widely broadcast by the media, inevitably fuel intense anxieties and resentments on all sides.

California's business leaders put immense pressure on a Conservative Republican Congress sympathetic to business and frantic to please those who control the state's politics and wealth. Consequently, Congress finds itself in a rather painful bind, since Republicans, in particular, still need to heal the perception of their hostility to immigrants, created by the 1996 federal legislation and reinforced by the actions of Conservative Republican Governor Pete Wilson before and during his governorship (1991–1999).

In his fascinating book *Paradise Lost: California's Experience. America's Future* (1999), the journalist Peter Schrag shows how California's long tradition of seeking to be a law unto itself, its anti-Federalist history of bypassing elected representative government in favor of government by referenda, is now interacting with widespread unease about immigrants, especially illegal immigrants.[4] The fear of being swamped by illegals, fueled by cultural as well as economic concerns, may have peaked during the economic lows of the early 1990s, but it is very powerful still. Thus, on Independence Day 1998, protesters waving American flags braved armed riot police to celebrate a huge sign greeting visitors at the state's border. The message? "Welcome to California: The Illegal Immigration State. Don't Let This Happen to Your State."

Building on the conjunction of these two forces, frightened resentment of immigrants and the tradition of decisions made by voters' direct action through referenda, the Conservative wing of the Republican Party began in the 1980s to mount costly campaigns promoting various propositions hostile to immigrants and minorities generally, or at least seen as such by those affected. Spurred on by Republican Governor Wilson, a sizable majority of angry voters passed three such (soon widely controversial) propositions between 1994 and 1998: Proposition 187 (1994) withheld most public benefits from illegal immigrants; Proposition 209 (1996) eliminated state-sponsored racial preferences; and Proposition 227 (1998) banned bilingual education in California's schools. Although all have been the focus of bitter debate, we will consider Propositions 187 and 227 as most directly related to our purposes here.

English for the Children (Proposition 227), grew out of protracted, emotion-charged debates about California's bilingual education policy, carried on in a climate of distrust and widespread discontent with California's schools, especially in Los Angeles and in other urban centers. Similar controversies are evident in immigrant-intense areas all over the United States. There are now 300 "foreign" languages spoken in the nation and 3.2 million bilingual students. Of these, more than a million, predominantly Latinos, are enrolled in California's public schools. Everyone sees danger in the fact that, Asians excepted, most of these students are lagging in educational achievements: "One of the central issues in California is how second-generation Latinos will do economically and educationally over time," according to Hans Johnson, a demographer at the Public Policy Institute of California (Johnson, *Los Angeles Times*, 20 October 1999). But because the bilingual education issue is a lightning rod for accumulated discontent and a flash point for many immigrants, it is a highly divisive political controversy, with educational arguments often receding into the background.

No one doubts that good English language skills are essential for the future of immigrants and the economy. But the state's residents are deeply divided about how to reach this goal. Some consider bilingual education the surest path and see a disparagement of immigrant values and traditions in its replacement. Others see greater promise in alternatives, especially "English Immersion" programs. At present, following passage of Proposition 227, California's rules call for a single year of total immersion for Limited English Proficiency (LEP) students, followed by "mainstreaming" into regular classes. The California Board of Education, still controlled by appointees of former governor Wilson, bars school districts from applying for exemptions, a rigid position upheld by a ruling of the First District Court of Appeals in late September 1999.

Meanwhile, also in 1998, the Republican-dominated U.S. House of Representatives approved a controversial bill to surrender all federal responsibility for decision making in this area by converting federal funding for bilingual and immigrant education programs into block grants to the states. The Senate, however, adjourned without acting on the bill. The Clinton administration strongly opposed the measure, which, along the way, would also have set a three-year ceiling on funded bilingual classes. In March 2000 education secretary Richard Riley took a firm stand on the issue, asking public school districts to establish 1000 additional dual-language schools in the next five years. "It is high time we begin to treat language skills as the assets they are," he said. "In some places even the idea of bilingual education is controversial. It shouldn't be" (Associated Press, 16 March 2000).

It is, however, Proposition 187, denying most public benefits to illegal immigrants, which has been most deeply divisive and controversial, ultimately raising fundamental questions about the relationship of federal and state authority in immigration/immigrant matters. Originating out of a "Save Our State" movement in the suburbs of southern California and placed on the ballot by the Republican Party in 1994 after three very bad economic years, Proposition 187 was supported by nearly 60 percent of voters—a direct expression of their frustration, fear and anger. (It inspired Congress to pass its even more extreme measures in the 1996 legislation, limiting most public benefits even for *legal* immigrants.) Needless to say, immigrants generally and their advocates passionately opposed the state's action.

In the event, Proposition 187 perished without ever being enforced. Following an initial court-ordered postponement, U.S. District Court Judge Mariana Pfaelzer in 1997 declared its core provisions unconstitutional in *League of United Latin American Citizens v. Wilson* 997-F. Supp. 1244, 1261 (C.D. Cal. 1997). In an important assertion of federal rights and responsibilities, she ruled that since the Constitution gives sole power to regulate immigration to the federal government, "California is powerless to enact . . . its own legislative scheme to regulate alien access to public benefits." Governor Wilson, maintaining his flamboyant campaign against illegal immigrants, at once appealed the ruling.

His successor, Democrat Gray Davis, turned to mediation as a way out of a very messy political situation. More than a year after Pfaelzer's ruling, Patrick McDonnel would report that the "unpalatable endgame" (McDonnel, *Los Angeles Times*, 30 July 1999) was at last concluded: the governor had dropped the appeal in return for a few minor concessions by immigrant advocates. The underlying controversy, however, continues. There is a deep rift between Davis and Lieutenant Governor Cruz Bustamente. Leery immigrants look ahead to further hostile measures, and the proposition's defeated supporters charge the governor with overriding the popular will. By fall 1999 petitions for yet another state ballot measure were underway. This time the intent was to recall the governor. Although the attempt failed, its backers vowed to keep on trying. A little later, in response to Republicans' immigrant-friendly rhetoric in Election 2000, they joined the chorus and disavowed all earlier such intentions.

Hispanics are now playing a larger role as elected officials of California's state government, but it is not at all clear that their influence will finally have sufficient strength to prevail against the power-by-referendum of the state's nonimmigrant majority. As Schrag shows, California has often used binding referenda in defense of a threatened status quo, a way of keeping entrenched power safe against the claims and incursions of newcomers. Probing the consequences of this tradition, he concludes grimly that this time the wealthy white sponsors of the propositions have all but undone the state's elected government, in effect moving it from Sacramento into a new "Initiative Industrial Complex" (Schrag 1999, 189).[5]

In such erosion of the checks and balances the Founders built into our government to assure broad-based participation and deliberative decision making Schrag sees major dangers for the state's future and also for the nation's:

> each enlargement of the [voter initiative] process reduces that much more the power and accountability of legislatures—and thus the general ability to govern, to shape predictable outcomes . . . it also vastly reduces the chances that [government] will produce great leaders and the visionary statecraft they are sometimes associated with. In the battle over the initiative, the framers would be the first to recognize that it is not that our politics have become too conservative; it is that, perceived in the Burkean sense, they are not nearly conservative enough (272).[6]

CALIFORNIA DREAMING

No wonder that the nation's image of California is of a state "dividing and subdividing along a thousand new fault lines of language and identity. . . ." (Beck 1996). But if California is, from one perspective, a crucible representing in concentrated form the unresolved problems and questions surrounding immigration and immigrants in the nation at large, others see it as giving birth to our multicultural future in many desirable respects. Up to a point, Robert Kaplan, writer, futurist, and contributing editor to *The Atlantic Monthly*, is among these. His book, *An Empire Wilderness: Travels Into America's Future* (1998), reports extensively on his explorations of the emerging "internationalized culture" of the American West and Southwest.[7] His accounts embrace visions of hope as well as despair. Yet lurking throughout is a troubling vision of transformative change likely to affect immigrant centers anywhere in the United States and, ultimately, the nation itself.

In southern California, greater Los Angeles, and Orange County, Kaplan encounters a vibrant, upwardly mobile world that seems to hold great promise for the future. Hostilities growing out of immigrants' traditional loyalties and values are being set aside in favor of shared principles of economic advantage, and he sees a close to perfect match between eager immigrants and an American economy hungry for young, vigorous workers as the U.S. population ages. Foreign-born populations and foreign investment are reshaping and sustaining international trade and business on a huge scale, while at the same time entrepreneurial newcomers are establishing all kinds of small businesses, often, but not solely, catering to the tastes of different ethnic populations. Kaplan notes with some astonishment that this region of California resembles the increasingly multicultural and prosperous Pacific Northwest far more than the generally poorer Southwest.

Predicting that the flow of immigrants into California will be controlled in the future, as it has been, by the labor needs of huge corporations, he anticipates that this will on the whole benefit everyone. Over time, the influx of skilled workers and foreign capital, largely Asian, will also broaden opportunities for the less favored, including many Latinos. He is confident that within one or two generations those who are now disadvantaged will also find their place in an expanding multiethnic middle class generally free of ethnic frictions.[8]

Yet, even in the midst of California's pulsing vitality, there is cause for gravest concern. The more closely one observes, the more evident it is that this version of an internationalized Brave New World lacks the social and civic values always necessary as a foundation for community. Accommodations on behalf of a shared faith in economic progress won't do: "Rather than citizens," Kaplan concludes, "the inhabitants of these prosperous pods are, in truth, resident expatriates, even if they were born in America." (Kaplan 1998, 101). According to Rick Reiff, the Pulitzer Prize-winning editor of the Orange County *Business Journal,* whenever economic advancement and profit are the sole points of reference, "Patriotism will be more purely and transparently economic." (100–101).

Economic patriotism? To us, too, it seems poor stuff. Looking ahead, Kaplan predicts the proliferation of "new localisms" all over the West and Southwest. New units of political decision making and governance will dominate: urban conglomerates, whose points of reference will be the specific economic alliances, needs, resources and purposes of particular locales. The federal government "will literally retreat to the periphery," becoming increasingly irrelevant, its functions restricted primarily to matters of defense and foreign policy (295 and passim).

By a very different route than Schrag's, Kaplan has arrived at startlingly similar conclusions about the undoing of government in "the Golden State." Both conclude that these developments, already a reality in California, prefigure our continent's future. We reluctantly concur in their fears and predict that, absent new policy direction, the experience of California suggests much about the national and global future, as well.

Every day brings additional evidence that neither immigration nor internationalization, both within and beyond our borders, can be stopped. Nor should they be. But it is equally clear that absent thoughtful collaborative government at all levels, chaos threatens to undermine the best of the American Dream. Throughout Part IV we have seen powerful centrifugal forces inherent in immigration and immigrant issues and their exacerbation by the short-term, politically expedient approaches our conflicted, increasingly fragmented government is taking to address them. In this, as in so many other spheres of national life, Americans must insist upon a return to Federalist, representative government and to the possibilities of democratic nation building the Founders envisioned.

Conclusion

If once the people become inattentive to public affairs, you and I and Congress, Judges and Governors, shall all become wolves. It seems to be the law of our general nature, in spite of individual exceptions.

—Thomas Jefferson

In the debate between anti-Federalists and Federalists that shaped the years of American Constitution building, those who knew the nation needed a strong, representative national government to protect the freedoms of individual citizens prevailed. In response to Americans' widespread mistrust of government, especially strong national government, they put their faith not in any one person or group, but in everyone. In the American people.

As we have seen, dissenters from the Federalist system of government established under George Washington, people who favored more decision-making authority at state and local levels, have been part of the American political debate from the very beginning. However, with the election of Ronald Reagan in 1980, those who favor states' rights over the long established responsibilities and prerogatives of federal and *Federalist* government in our nation, Conservative Republicans, gained the ascendancy. Since 1994, their ideologically rigid antigovernmentalism has created a suspicion of national government so pervasive and a confusion about its organization, responsibilities, and purposes so deep, that Americans are in danger of losing Federalist democracy as the Founders envisioned it.

Our idea for this book was born on a rain-swept terrace in Geneva in 1995, only months after Americans had seen with alarm the uncompromising moral zealotry with which House Speaker Newt Gingrich and his followers approached their responsibilities in government. In that location and from that distance, one could see clearly the dangers, now documented, in the excessive political partisanship that generated their abandonment of deliberative decision making and their openly asserted unwillingness to support conciliation and compromise with anyone who opposed them. How and why Americans must contravene these dangers to our secular, representative democracy were our overarching themes in this book.

In addressing four questions about the responsibilities of government and of citizens, posed in the introduction, we have made an effort to represent views from the Right and Left of the political spectrum, as well as from the Center, as occupied by President Clinton and his followers after the 1994 midterm election.

Part I probed the history, rationale, and content of the Constitution, so as to help perpetuate broad understanding of the organization and principles of a government designed to protect the freedoms of all Americans. Early challenges to the precepts of the Constitution demonstrate its strength and resilience. They also reveal how short American history is and how similar were early questions about governing to those we face today. Our aim: To recapture the essential character of American *Federalist* democracy in all of its complexity and capacity to assure wise governance for a nation that has almost always seen itself as indivisible and capable of responding to the challenges that come with *e pluribus unum*, from many, one. Our conclusion: Today, American Federalist democracy as envisioned in the Constitution is again in danger, this time from the Conservative Right. It requires informed defense by all Americans.

In Parts II and III, we explored traditional and current questions about the roles and responsibilities of government in the economy and in maintaining relationships between the United States and other nations. Created in a period that also produced Adam Smith's *Wealth of Nations* in 1776, American Federalist government has always been concerned with protecting Americans' opportunities to succeed materially, as in all the many other ways that their imaginations and talents permit. The challenge was and is to reconcile the interests of the people with those of business; to control excessive disparities in income and wealth; and to invest in social capital by maintaining public institutions and services and, as necessary, a safety net for those least able to help themselves.

The evolving roles and responsibilities of government in the U.S. economy (never "free," as many have thought, but always "mixed" with policies of the government) have been part and parcel of government's changing foreign policy initiatives from the beginning. Except when superseded by national security concerns in war, how to strengthen the economy has been the central question of U.S. foreign policy. Over time, the complexities and vast scale of our economy have transformed the context in which government must grapple with traditional and new political challenges. These challenges, like virtually all other aspects of international relationships, have been exacerbated by the relaxation of tensions since the end of the Cold War in 1989, and since the development of unexpected new ones.

In the 1990s, most foreign policy issues were shaped primarily by the anticipated impact of actions on our own and others' economies. We question the wisdom, in the long run, of this almost exclusive domination by economic goals, which have a way of blocking attention to the subtler dimensions of international "relations." And, most important for our purposes in this study, we are gravely concerned that all questions concerned with government's roles and responsibilities in the interrelated spheres of the economy and foreign relations are being driven off course by Rightist antigovernmentalism and by unprecedented partisan ideology and extremism. Together, these dangerously diminish national government and prevent the collaborative, thoughtful deliberation and principled decision making the nation needs.

As nations grow more interdependent in all aspects of political and social life, as all governments become less autonomous, given globalism and the vast power and wealth of multinational corporations, Americans must come to understand better than many now do what is at stake in the Conservative/Liberal/Centrist American politics of today. We argue that Americans need their national government more, not less, than at any time in our history. The aim of Conservative Republican states' rightists to shrink national government in favor of states, localities, and the private sector jeopardizes U.S. credibility on the world stage, as well as equality of opportunity for all Americans. It virtually assures state-to-state inequities in every sphere of our national life.

In Part IV we turned our attention to the sorry state of U.S. immigration and immigrant policies as a case in point, a dramatic illustration of the failures of current government we had explored in Parts I–III. We chose this policy area as especially suited to our purposes for several reasons. First:

its urgency as a challenge to the nation and its government, not, as too many Americans still assume, just a problem for a handful of states with large foreign-born populations. Second: the divisive power of the centrifugal forces inherent in immigration and immigrant issues, in any case. Third: the conviction that in such a context the effects of government failure would be more clearly visible, communicate a more intense message, than could our earlier, broader policy explorations.

Our conclusions? The short-term, politically expedient approaches an increasingly fragmented government is taking to address immigration and immigrant policies is exacerbating problems, not solving them. National in scope, immigration and immigrant issues will never be amenable to solution by individual states. In this, as in so many other spheres of national life, ideological conflict, extreme partisanship, and rigidity have prevented coordinated, Federalist problem solving.

The costs of this failure are many. There is real danger that the "Center" may *not* hold. The widely recognized chaos around immigration is making it far harder for foreign-born and native-born citizens, as well as for legal immigrants awaiting naturalization, to have a clear sense of what it means to be an American. It is also undermining the world's faith in American democracy.

A final cautionary note: All too frequently the vocabulary of Americans' debates about federalism is misleading. Proposals and rulings seem to support federalism while whittling away at the distribution of powers between state governments and the central government that emerged from the Founders' debates. This phenomenon was evident in 1999, when both houses of Congress produced bills ostensibly supporting Federalism. In *The Federalism Accountability Act* and in the *Federalism Act of 1999*, members of Congress deliberately sought to "make it harder for Congress and the executive branch to adopt laws and rules that pre-empt the states on a wide range of issues, like drugs, the environment, health and worker safety" (Stephen Labaton, "Anti-Federalism Measures Have Bipartisan Support" *New York Times*, 6 September 1999).

In fact, both bills were widely opposed, not only by the Clinton administration but by a broad coalition of businesses, environmental groups, labor organizations, and consumer advocacy groups, all fearing the loss of national standards that would, as the National Chamber of Commerce stated, " lead to a balkanization of rules on everything from auto standards to worker safety." A nonpartisan group focusing on government regulatory practices, the Office of Management and Budget Watch, stated that the legislation would "undermine public health, safety, and environmental protections."

Both measures, proposed after Supreme Court decisions in June 1999 (see chap. 4) were written at the request of such state and local government organizations as the National Governors' Association, the National Conference of State Legislatures, the Council of State Governments, and the National League of Cities. Yet, according to Labaton, several agencies of the federal government countered by warning that the legislation would "have sweeping, devastating effects on the ability of the federal government to do business."

In a press release from the Senate Governmental Affairs Committee on 3 August 1999, Conservative Sen. Fred Thompson (R-TN), sponsor of *The Federalism Accountability Act,* stated: "The Founding Fathers divided power between the federal government and the states to prevent abuses of power and because they knew that government closer to the people works best. This legislation reminds us that even where the federal government has the constitutional authority to act, state governments may be better suited to [do so]."

Thompson's words implied that passage of *The Federalism Accountability Act* would be an action in defense of Federalist government. In fact, the complexity and extensiveness of the *Act's* requirements, to be met by the federal government before its taking any action that could, in any way "preempt" a state's authority, would enmesh government in a tangle of legalisms from which it (and the nation) might never escape. The image that comes to mind is Gulliver, trussed and pinned down by the Lilliputians.

The conflict surrounding this proposed legislation illustrates very specifically the divisive, ideological problems of government we've been concerned with throughout this book. *Will* our Center hold? *Can* it? We believe the answers to these questions can and must be "yes." But only, as Madison and Jefferson told us long ago, if Americans remain vigilant to protect the evolving ideals and strategies of American Federalist democracy so brilliantly envisioned at the start.

Endnotes

INTRODUCTION: DEMOCRACY AMERICAN STYLE

1. Gordon Wood (2000, 67) provides an excellent discussion of extreme political partisanship and of origins of political parties in the 1790s. Wood argues that "our present-day Lilliputian leaders" may even seem relatively harmless when we realize that partisanship, scandal-mongering, and scandals, including sex scandals involving high government officials, were even more prevalent two hundred years ago than now."

CHAPTER 1: WHAT'S AT STAKE?

1. See Cornell (1999) for an account of historic opposition to this reading of the distribution of powers in the Constitution. With attention to current debate about the organization of government, Cornell provides a particularly well-documented study exploring anti-Federalists' objections to a strong central government and to Federalists' strategies for power-sharing among federal, state, and local governments. He describes debate about the federalist intentions of the Framers in the years 1788–1828.

CHAPTER 3: THE UNION CHALLENGED

1. When it came almost a century later, the Civil Rights movement was supported early and later by liberal and moderate Republicans and by northern Democrats. Much has been written about the events that gave rise, first to the *Civil Rights Act* of 1957 under Republican President Dwight Eisenhower, and then to the more comprehensive *Civil Rights Act* of 1964, a part of the Great Society legislation under Democrat Lyndon Johnson. Under Eisenhower Chief Justice appointee Earl Warren (1953–1969), the Supreme Court put citizens' rights on the national agenda as never before. In 1954, it rendered a landmark decision, *Brown v. The Board of Education of Topeka* (347 U.S. 483), finding state-sanctioned segregation of public schools a violation of the equal protection guarantee in the Fourteenth Amendment.

CHAPTER 4: ORGANIZING GOVERNMENT IN THE TWENTIETH CENTURY

1. Since 1995, Linda Greenhouse has provided a thorough record of Rehnquist Court actions in relation to cases dealing with federalism. This is available from the *New York Times* ("States Are Given New Legal Shield by Supreme Court" and "The Justices Decide Who's In Charge," 24 and 27 June 1999). Greenhouse's summaries of the issues in federalism cases scheduled during the session beginning 4 October 1999 ("Justices to Rule on Nation's Most Ardent Debates," *New York Times*, 3 October 1999) are helpful in understanding how the Court was moving into what Greenhouse called its "most contentious issue": the arena of civil rights legislation.

CHAPTER 8: YOUR MONEY: HOW DOES GOVERNMENT SPEND IT?

1. In October 1999, the Commerce Department released a long-awaited report on economic growth looking back to 1959. Using new calculations that assigned greater weight to productivity gains generated by computer software and by improvements in banking, it confirmed optimistic predictions for 1998. It described an economy that produced an estimated $248 billion more than had been estimated in 1998. With rates of productivity gain as a key element of economic projections, the 5.3% rate of increase announced by the U.S. Department of Labor in August 2000 for the second quarter supported expectations of continuing economic growth.

CHAPTER 11: GOVERNMENT AND THE GLOBAL ECONOMY: NEW QUESTIONS

1. See also Nicholas Kristof, Edward Wyatt, and David Sanger. Their four-part article is a probing discussion of unresolved international issues in the global economy (Kristof, Wyatt, and Sanger, "Global Contagion," *New York Times*, 15–18 February 1999).

2. For a good discussion of unresolved issues in currency policy, see Blinder (1999).

CHAPTER 12: WHAT'S AT STAKE?

1. Thomas L. Friedman has described "three schools" in the U.S. foreign policy debate that are clear in our own analysis: Conservatives who are "cold warriors, extreme isolationists, or unilateralists; moderates and realists who offer a sound critique of Clinton

administration policies but would rely more on hardheaded U.S. power"; and Democrats "who understand what is essential in the long term, [to achieve] interdependent global relations, but are inconsistent in their convictions." (Friedman, "The War Over Peace," *New York Times*, 27 October 1999).

CHAPTER 13: THE UNITED STATES AND GLOBALIZATION

1. For a detailed assessment of this agenda and recommendations for perpetuating it, see Cutter, *et al.* Intent upon creating strategies for support to the Clinton administration's global trade agenda, the article elaborates government's essential role in the global economy and shows how multilateral approaches to political and economic issues may be created most effectively by disciplined consideration of individual issues, in appropriate forums.

CHAPTER 14: CURRENT DEBATES

1. We are indebted in this summation of UN development to Brian Urquhart's probing discussions of the UN and foreign policy (Brian Urquhart, "Looking for the Sheriff," *The New York Review of Books*, 16 July 1998, 48–53).

2. McDougall's themes are also well-articulated in an article by Robert Kaplan (Kaplan, "Kissinger, Metternich, and Realism," *The Atlantic Monthly*, June 1999, 77). In addition, his objections to "messianism" also echo Arthur M. Schlesinger Jr. in *The Cycles of American History:* "Ideology is the curse of public affairs because it converts politics into a branch of theology and sacrifices human beings on the alter of dogma. It is out of character for Americans. . . . They would do well to sober up from their ideological binge and return to the cold, gray realism of the Founding Fathers, [who] thought that saving America was enough without trying to save humanity, as well" (Schlesinger 1986, 67).

CHAPTER 17: WHAT'S AT STAKE?

1. Immigrant population counts are best estimates only. Illegals are, by definition, elusive and, as the Census Bureau itself admits, its methods tend, for various reasons, to undercount minorities, including immigrants. On its web site (*www.census.gov/population/www/socdemo/ foreign.html*) the bureau identifies three unrelated sources of data: the Census taken at the beginning of each decade (here the 1990 Census); the annual *Current Population Survey* (1994–1997); and the bureau's "Estimates" and "Projections." In addition to its own tallies, the bureau relies on data generated by the INS. Part IV draws on all of these sources, directly and as presented in the media and in analyses by various organizations that regularly monitor demographic data.

CHAPTER 18: ISSUES IN IMMIGRATION POLICY

1. Revisions proposed in *Heaven's Door* (Borjas 1999) agree with the Reform Comm-mission's thinking in a number of important respects: immigration policies should be de-termined in terms of national goals and should be flexible in the context; there must be a sharp reduction in the total number of immigrants; and the newcomer flow should be redi-rected to admit skilled, rather than unskilled, workers. As the author readily admits, how-ever, national well-being is somewhat narrowly defined in this book to mean financial gains for native-born Americans without any further widening of the U.S. income gap.

2. The Carnegie Plan goes beyond a concern with accountability to emphasize the overriding importance of improved coherence in policy and implementation. It would keep the INS intact, incorporating it into a new structure empowered to integrate widely dis-persed immigration and immigrant functions; set up distinct chains of command, and as-sume policy responsibility. The department would have a higher status than the INS; ultimately it rises to Cabinet level.

CHAPTER 19: BOTTOM LINES: ECONOMIC AND LABOR ISSUES

1. Wilgoren's comments followed the appearance of *A Fiscal Portrait of the Newest Americans* (Moore 1998), a joint publication of the Libertarian Cato Institute and the Na-tional Immigration Forum, an immigrant advocacy group. That report, claiming to syn-thesize the findings of thirty earlier studies, made claims for immigrants' contributions to the economy dismissed as utterly extravagant (and sloppily argued) by such other analysts as Steven Camarota, research director at the Center for Immigration Studies, an organiza-tion favoring immigration restrictions. Among Cato's claims: Although immigrants pay dis-proportionately low taxes, they nevertheless pay between $20,000 and $80,000 more in taxes over their lifetimes than they use in services; all immigrants tend to become net con-tributors to the economy after 10 to 15 years; by the year 2022 generally youthful immi-grant workers will have contributed close to $500 billion to our endangered Social Security system. Among Camarota's counterarguments: Cato failed to distinguish between legal and illegal immigrants; they overstated gains by eliminating contradictory information, for in-stance, the high U.S. cost of educating young immigrants; and their conceptual framework oversimplified the complexity of gains and losses by different players in different locations.

2. Borjas is among those concerned about the educational and skills profile of large numbers of recent, mostly Hispanic, immigrants in relation to industry's changing needs. Favoring a reduction in immigrant totals and, especially, a cutback of the poorly qualified, he nonetheless concludes: "After accounting for the impact of immigration on the produc-tivity of native workers and firms and on the fiscal ledger sheet, immigration probably has a small net economic impact on the United States" (Borjas 1999, 126).

3. The Center for Immigration Studies sees temporary workers, in particular, regard-less of their skill level, disadvantaging the native-born. It fears that employers may prefer temporary workers as easier to manipulate than Americans and more likely to put up with

poor salaries and working conditions. Because such workers are unusually dependent on their employers for the green cards they hold, they do not really compete in the free American labor market and consequently are a threat to very fundamental American values.

4. Although some large agricultural enterprises are, in fact, beginning to adapt their processes to a smaller supply of workers, and Congress has defeated several proposals intended to bring in more temporary farm laborers, grower efforts to do so continue. In the summer of 1999 these efforts (again) took a bizarre twist. As Michael Doyle noted, pressure was put on Congress to devise legislation that would enable many of the roughly six hundred thousand illegal immigrants apparently now working on farms to achieve legal status (Doyle, *Sacramento Bee*, 28 September 1999). *The Agricultural Job Opportunity Benefits and Security Act of 1999* would permit undocumented laborers engaged in farm work for at least six months in the past year to apply for temporary visas that could eventually lead to green cards and citizenship. It is hard not to be cynical about such profit-driven moves that almost reduce American citizenship to a tradable commodity.

5. Competition now appears to be at its fiercest between African-Americans at the bottom of the work and pay scale and similarly placed Hispanics. Joseph Daleiden paints a devastating picture of the impact Hispanic immigrants and their descendants have on native-born Blacks' employment opportunities. Among the allegations: The Hispanic rate of growth outpaces that of Blacks in every major occupation group in the Midwest and some other regions; the African-American job share continues to decline: for instance, manufacturing added 139,000 Hispanics but only 5,000 Blacks between 1983 and 1995; during the 1990–1991 recession, African-Americans lost more than 59,000 jobs, as Hispanics and Asians made large gains (Daleiden, "Speaking Out: Immigration's Impact on African-American Job Opportunities," *Headway*, 1 February 1998, 33–34).

6. Borjas (1999) concludes that legal high-skill immigrant workers do decrease job availability and lower wages for their native-born counterparts, but as part of the overall worker pool, they, too, benefit and will continue to benefit, from the immigrants' contributions to America's prosperity.

CHAPTER 20: IMMIGRANT POLICY:
WHERE ARE WE NOW?
WHY DOES IT MATTER?

1. For example, by "deeming," states can choose to include the income of sponsors in calculating the immigrant's eligibility for benefits.

2. The Elian Gonzales debacle illustrated dramatically what can happen without such understanding of a shared civic culture. Before a watching world, a small group of immigrants led the city of Miami in flamboyant rebellion against legitimate, constitutionally-granted authority. "When 20 elected officials in Miami-Dade County said they would not allow the police to aid federal authorities, it proved that the politicians here would choose their own independent foreign policy over the rule of law, say some experts who have followed the Elian case" (Rich Bragg, "Stand Over Cuba Highlights a Virtual Secession of Miami," *New York Times*, 1 April 2000).

The states rights policies and slogans of Conservatives surely helped prepare the ground for this extraordinary event.

3. In a surprising move, the Republican Platform in Election 2000 claimed to endorse the commission's recommendations. In fact, however, the endorsement was very limited. There were no proposals to reform immigrant policies, no recommendations for additional immigrant support, and only silence with respect to the "Americanization" of newcomers.

CHAPTER 21: CALIFORNIA AND BEYOND

1. In the preface to this very valuable study Clark writes:

> In this book I discuss how the blending [of new arrivals, natives, and earlier immigrants] will occur across the geography of California. What are the geographic outcomes of this fundamental transformation of the state's population? What is happening now, and what can and might happen, in California's cities, towns and neighborhoods as the new migrants take up their lives in a new and different society? I explore the constraints, problems, and implications of the intersection of 5 million newcomers in the past 15 years with the 2.5 million residents already in the state. (Clark 1998, preface)

2. For California, too, population data have been gathered from various sources to make the information as current as possible. The nature of such data is evident when the authors of *State Snapshots of Public Benefits for Immigrants*, the supplement to *Patchwork Policies: State Assistance for Immigrants Under Welfare Reform*, admit that their data had to be adjusted in various ways to improve accuracy and consistency among sources (Zimmermann, Tumlin, and Ost, 1999).

3. A trend to exercise dual nationality options, largely dormant until now, may also be accelerating elsewhere in the United States, as it is in Europe. American law does not prohibit such a choice, though naturalized U.S. citizens must formally renounce allegiances to other governments. Countries permitting dual nationality include France, the United Kingdom, and Ireland, as well as several Latin American nations. Currently an estimated 5 to 10 million U.S. citizens are eligible, with the pool growing by about 500,000 yearly. Some suggest that there might eventually be a kind of reverse immigration and work force drain, as American citizens gain access to residence and employment anywhere in the European Union (EU) by virtue of a parent or grandparent.

4. See especially the compelling "March of the Plebiscites" and "The Next America," in Schrag (1999, 188ff. and 257ff.).

5. The 20 initiatives and referendums on the California Election 2000 ballot were the focus of "a fierce electronic war lasting months" with $150 million to spend. The president of the non-profit California Voter Foundation said, "The ads are designed to scare voters, manipulate voters, do everything but inform voters. I think people are going to wonder whether we have too much democracy in California" (Peter Marks, *New York Times*, 5 March 2000).

6. Edmund Burke, a British statesman and political philosopher (1729–1797) is described as follows in the 1967 *Encyclopedia of Philosophy* (NY: Macmillan and Free Press): "Burke was especially critical of revolutionary movements with noble humanitarian ends because he believed that people are simply not at liberty to destroy the state and its institution in the hope of some contingent improvement" (*Encyclopedia of Philosophy* 1967, 430).

7. A slightly different version of these accounts originally appeared in *The Atlantic Monthly*, July and August 1998.

8. Such optimism is especially startling in light of Kaplan's perceptions of California's neighbors in the Southwest, which he sees as virtually sinking under burdens of poverty, neglect, and mutual hostilities. There a mixed Anglo-Latino society is overburdened with complex, interrelated problems that it cannot, on its own, fix. They affect every aspect of existence, corroding political, social, and economic life and destroying the environment. Only in a kind of governmental regulatory tyranny, Kaplan concludes, is there any hope for real improvement.

References

Abshire, David. 1996. "U.S. Global Policy: Toward an Agile Strategy." *The Washington Monthly* 19 (Spring): 41–61.

Agricultural Job Opportunity, Benefits and Security Act of 1999. S1814. 106th Cong., 1st sess., October 1999.

Albright, Madeleine K. 1998. "The Testing of American Foreign Policy." *Foreign Affairs* 77 (November/December): 50–64.

American Competitiveness in the Twenty-first Century Act of 2000. S2045. 106th Cong., 2d sess., February 2000.

Anton, Thomas J. 1989. *American Federalism and Public Policy: How the System Works.* New York: Random House.

Balanced Budget Act of 1997. U.S. Public Law 105-33. 105th Cong., 1st sess., 1 August 1997.

Beck, Roy. 1996. *The Case Against Immigration.* New York: Norton.

Becker, Carl. 1942. *The Declaration of Independence: A Study in the History of Political Ideas.* New York: Random.

Bernstein, Jared et al. 1999. "Tax Cut No Cure for Middle Class Economic Woes." *Living Standards and Labor Markets.* Washington, D.C.: Economic Policy Institute.

Blinder, Alan S. 1999. "Eight Steps to a New Financial Order." *Foreign Affairs* 78 (September/October): 50–63.

Bok, Derek. 1996. *The State of the Nation.* Cambridge: Harvard University Press.

Borjas, George J. 1998. Immigration and Welfare Magnets. National Bureau of Economic Research. Working Paper No. 6813.

———. 1999. *Heaven's Door: Immigration Policy and the American Economy.* Princeton: Princeton University Press.

Bowen, Catherine Drinker. 1966. *Miracle at Philadelphia: The Story of the Constitutional Convention.* Boston: Little, Brown.

Brinkley, Alan, Nelson W. Polsby, and Kathleen M. Sullivan. 1997. *New Federalist Papers: Essays in Defense of the Constitution.* New York: Norton.

Burtless, Gary et al. 1998. *Globaphobia.* Washington, D.C.: Brookings Institution, Twentieth Century Fund, and Progressive Policy Institute.

Camarota, Stephen. 1998. "Review of Cato Institute Report." Washington, D.C.: Center for Immigration Studies.

———. 1999. *Importing Poverty: Immigration's Impact on the Size and Growth of Poor Populations in the U.S.* Washington, D.C.: Center for Immigration Studies.

Cassidy, John. 1997. "The Budget Boondoggle." *The New Yorker* 73 (11 August): 23.

———. 1998. "The Triumphalist." *The New Yorker* 74 (4 July): 58.

Chase, Robert, Emily Hill, and Paul Kennedy, eds. 1999. *The Pivotal States: A New Framework for U.S. Policy in the Developing World.* New York: Norton.

Clark, William A.V. 1998. *The California Cauldron: Immigration and the Fortunes of Local Communities.* New York: Guilford Press.

Cornell, Saul. 1999. *The Other Founders: Anti-Federalism & the Dissenting Tradition in America (1788–1828).* Chapel Hill: University of North Carolina Press.

Croly, Herbert. 1909. *The Promise of American Life.* New York: Macmillan.

Cutter, W. Bowman, Joan Spero, and Laura D'Andera Tyson. 2000. "New World, New Deal." *Foreign Affairs* 79 (March/April): 80–98.

Dionne, E. J. Jr. 1996. *They Only Look Dead: Why Progressives Will Dominate the Next Political Era.* New York: Simon & Schuster.

Donahue, John D. 1997. *Disunited States: What's at Stake as Washington Fades and the States Take the Lead.* New York: Harper-Collins.

Drew, Elizabeth. 1999. *The Corruption of American Politics: What Went Wrong and Why.* Secaucus, N.J.: Birch Lane Press.

Fix, Michael, and Jeffrey S. Passel. 1994. *Immigration and Immigrants: Setting the Record Straight.* Washington, D.C.: Urban Institute Press.

———. 1999. *Trends in Noncitizens' and Citizens' Use of Public Benefits Following Welfare Reform, 1994–1997.* Washington, D.C.: Urban Institute Press.

Fix, Michael, and Karen C. Tumlin. 1999. *Welfare Reform and the Devolution of Immigrant Policy.* Washington, D.C.: Urban Institute Press.

Fort, Denise D. 1995. "The Unfunded Mandates Reform Act of 1995: Where Will the New Federalism Take Environmental Policy?" *Natural Resources Journal* 35 (Summer): 727–730.

Friedman, Thomas L. 1999. *The Lexus and the Olive Tree.* New York: Farrar.

Fukuyama, Francis. 1992. *The End of History and the Last Man.* New York: Free Press.

Garten, Jeffrey E. 1997. "Business and Foreign Policy." *Foreign Affairs* 76 (May/June): 67–79.

Haass, Richard N. 1997. *The Reluctant Sheriff: The United States After the Cold War.* New York: Council on Foreign Relations.

Heilbroner, Robert. "The (Political) Economy of Capitalism." Epilogue to *Making Capitalism Work* by Leonard Silk and Mark Silk. 1996. New York: New York University Press.

————, and Lester Thurow. 1994. *Economics Explained.* New York: Simon & Schuster.

Hofstadter, Richard. 1958. *The American Political Tradition.* New York: Vintage Books.

————. 1960. *Great Issues in American History.* Vol. 1. New York: Vintage Books.

Hollinger, David A. 1995. *Postethnic America: Beyond Multiculturalism.* New York: Basic.

Huntington, Samuel P. 1996. *The Clash of Civilizations and the Re-Making of World Order.* New York: Simon & Schuster.

————. 1999. "The Lonely Superpower." *Foreign Affairs 78* (March/April): 35–49.

Illegal Immigration Reform and Immigrant Responsibility Act. 1996. U.S. Public Law 104-208, 104th Cong., 2d sess., 30 September 1996.

Immigration Act of 1990. U.S. Public Law 101-649, 101st Cong., 2d sess., 1990.

Immigration Reform and Control Act of 1986. U.S. Public Law 99-603, 99th Cong., 2d sess., 1986.

Jacobson, David, ed. 1998. *The Immigration Reader: America in a Multidisciplinary Perspective.* Malden, MA: Blackwell.

Johnson, Hans et al. 1999. *Taking the Oath: An Analysis of Naturalization in California and the U.S.* San Francisco: Public Policy Institute of California.

Judis, John B. 2000. "Are We All Progressives Now?" *The American Prospect* 12 (May): 43–38.

Kaplan, Robert. 1996. *The Ends of the Earth: A Journey at the Dawn of the Twenty-first Century.* New York: Random House.

————. 1998. *An Empire Wilderness: Travels Into America's Future.* New York: Vintage Books.

————. 1999. "Kissinger, Metternich, and Realism." *The Atlantic Monthly* (June): 73–82.

Kennan, George. 1996. *At Century's Ending.* New York: Norton.

Konig, David T., ed. 1995. *Devising Liberty: Preserving and Creating Freedom in the New American Republic.* Stanford: Stanford University Press.

Kurtz, Stephen G., and James H. Hutson, eds. 1973. *Essays on the American Revolution.* Chapel Hill: University of North Carolina Press.

Kuttner, Robert. 1997. *Everything for Sale: The Virtues and Limits of Markets.* New York: Knopf.

Larkin, Daniel et al. 1998. "Business Situation," in *November 1998 Survey of Current Business.* Washington, D.C.: U.S. Department of Commerce.

Lerman, Robert. 1998. *The Labor Market for Information-Technology Workers.* Testimony before the Subcommittee on Immigration, Committee on the Judiciary, U.S. Senate, 2 February 1998. Washington, D.C.: Urban Institute Press.

Lincoln, Abraham. 1953. *The Collected Works of Abraham Lincoln.* Vol. 4. ed, Roy Basler. New Brunswick: Rutgers University Press.

Lind, Michael, ed. 1997. *Hamilton's Republic: Readings in the American Democratic Nationalist Tradition.* New York: Free Press.

Lopez, Elias. 1999. *Major Demographcs Shifts Occurring in California.* Sacramento: California Research Bureau, v. 6, n.5.

Lowi, Theodore J. 1996. *The End of the Republican Era.* Norman: University of Oklahoma Press.

McDougall, Walter A. 1997. *Promised Land, Crusader State.* New York: Houghton.

Madison, James, Alexander Hamilton, and John Jay. 1788. *The Federalist,* ed., Jacob E. Cooke. Hanover, NH: Wesleyan University Press.

Malone, Dumas. 1970. *Jefferson the President: First Term, 1801–1805.* Vol. 4 of *Jefferson and His Time.* Boston: Little, Brown.

———. 1974. *Jefferson the President: Second Term, 1805–1809.* Vol. 5 of *Jefferson and His Time.* Boston: Little, Brown.

———. 1981. *The Sage of Monticello.* Vol. 6 of *Jefferson and His Time.* Boston: Little, Brown.

Massey, Douglas S. 1998. "March of Folly: U.S. Immigration Policy After NAFTA." *The American Prospect* 9 (March/April): 22–34.

———. 1999. "International Migration at the Dawn of the Twenty-first Century: The Role of the State." *Population and Development Review* 25 (2): 303–322.

Mitchell, Susan. 1996. *The Official Guide to American Attitudes.* Ithaca: New Strategist Publications.

Moore, Stephen. 1998. *A Fiscal Portrait of the Newest Americans.* Washington, D.C.: Cato Institute and National Immigration Forum.

Morris, Richard B. 1986. *Witnesses at the Creation: Hamilton, Madison, Jay, and the Constitution.* New York: New American Library.

Nathan, Richard P. 1995. "American Federalism: A Great Experiment." *Spectrum: The Journal of State Government* 68 (Summer): 47–50.

National Academy of Sciences. 1997. *The New Americans: Economic, Demographic and Fiscal Effects of Immigration.* Washington, D.C.: National Academy Press.

National Commission on Civic Renewal. 1998. *Report of the National Commission on Civic Renewal.* New York: Pew Charitable Trusts.

National Immigration Forum. 1999. *Backgrounder.* www NIF Homepage.

Omnibus Appropriations Act of 1999. U.S. Public Law 105-277, 105th Cong., 2d sess., 21 October 1998.

Papademetriou, Demetrios G., T. Alexander Aleinikoff, and Deborah Waller Meyers. 1998. *Reorganizing the Immigration Function Toward a New Framework for Accountability.* Washington, D.C.: Carnegie Endowment for International Peace.

Perry, William, and Ashton Carter. 1999. *Preventive Defense: A New Security Strategy for America.* Washington, D.C.: Brookings Institution Press.

Personal Responsibility and Work Opportunity and Reconciliation Act of 1996. U.S. Public Law 104-193, 104th Cong., 2d sess., 22 August 1996.

Peterson, Paul E. 1995. *The Price of Federalism.* New York: Twentieth Century Fund.

Pollard, Kelvin M., and William P. O'Hare. 1999. *America's Racial and Ethnic Minorities.* Washington, D.C.: Population Reference Bureau.

Rakove, Jack. 1996. *Original Meanings: Politics and Ideas in the Making of the Constitution.* New York: Knopf.

RAND Corporation. 1997. *New Immigrants, New Needs: The California Experience.* Santa Monica: Rand Corporation Press.

Reed, Deborah. 1999. *California's Rising Income Inequality: Causes and Concerns.* San Francisco: Public Policy Institute of California.

Replacement Migration: Is It a Solution to Declining and Aging Populations? 21 March 2000. New York: UN, Dept. of Economics and Social Affairs, Population Div.

Schlesinger, Arthur M. Jr. 1986. *The Cycles of American History.* Boston: Houghton.

Schrag, Peter. 1999. *Paradise Lost: California's Experience, America's Future.* Berkeley: University of California Press.

Silk, Leonard, and Mark Silk. 1996. *Making Capitalism Work.* New York: New York University Press.

Skocpol, Theda. 1995. *Social Policy in the United States.* Princeton: Princeton University Press.

Smith, Adam. *The Wealth of Nations.* 1776. Reprint. New York: Random House, 1937.

Suro, Robert. 1998. *Strangers Among Us: Latinos' Lives in a Changing America.* New York: Knopf.

Taylor, Edward J., Philip L. Martin, and Michael Fix. 1997. *Poverty Amid Prosperity: Immigration and the Changing Face of Rural California.* Washington, D.C.: Urban Institute Press.

Tocqueville, Alexis de. [1834] 1945. *Democracy in America.* Reprint. New York: Knopf.

Unfunded Mandates Reform Act of 1995. U.S. Public Law 104-4, 104th Cong., 1st sess., 22 March 1995.

Urquhart, Brian. 1998. "Looking for the Sheriff." *The New York Review of Books* 45 (16 July): 48–53.

———. 1999. "Mission Impossible." *The New York Review of Books* 46 (18 November): 26–29.

U.S. Census Bureau. 1999. U.S. Census.

———. Current Population Surveys.

U.S. Commission on Immigration Reform. 1997. Legal Report to Congress. *Becoming an American: Immigration and Immigrant Policy.* Washington, D.C.: U.S. Government Printing Office.

———. 1994. *U.S. Immigration Policy: Restoring Credibility.*

———. 1995. *Legal Immigration: Setting Priorities.*

———. 1997. *U.S. Refugee Policy: Taking Leadership.*

Van Doren, Carl. 1948. *The Great Rehearsal: The Making and Ratification of the Constitution of the United States.* New York: Viking.

Vernez, George. April 1998. Testimony before Immigration Subcommittee, House Judiciary Committee.

Walt, Stephen M. 2000. "Two Cheers for Clinton's Foreign Policy." *Foreign Affairs* 79 (March/April): 63–79.

Wills, Garry. 1978. *Inventing America: Jefferson's Declaration of Independence.* New York: Doubleday.

———. 1999. *A Necessary Evil: A History of American Distrust of Government.* New York: Simon & Schuster.

White House Council of Economic Advisors. 1999. *Economic Report of the President.*

Wilson, William Julius. 1999. *The Bridge Over the Racial Divide.* Berkeley: University of California Press.

Wood, Gordon S. 1992. *The Radicalism of the American Revolution.* New York: Knopf.

———. 2000. "An Affair of Honor." *The New York Review of Books* 47 (13 April): 67–72.

Yeats, William Butler. [1921] 1961. "The Second Coming." *Modern Poetry* Vol. VII. eds. Maynard Mack, Leonard Dean, and William Frost. Englewood Cliffs, N.J.: Prentice-Hall.

Yergin, Daniel, and Joseph Stanislaw. 1998. *The Commanding Heights: The Battle Between Government and the MarketPlace that Is Remaking the Modern World.* New York: Simon & Schuster.

Zimmerman, Wendy, and Karen C. Tumlin. 1999. *Patchwork Policies: State Assistance for Immigrants Under Welfare Reform.* Washington, D.C.: Urban Institute Press.

———, and Jason Ost. 1999. *State Snapshots of Public Benefits for Immigrants.* Washington, D.C.: Urban Institute Press.

Zimmerman, Wendy, and Michael Fix. 1998. *Declining Immigrant Applications for Medi-Cal and Welfare Benefits in Los Angeles County.* Washington, D.C.: Urban Institute Press.

Zogby Polls. 30 March 2000. *Culture Poll. American Values Polls II.* Utica, NY: Zogby International.

Index

241